"十二五"职业教育国家规划教材
经全国职业教育教材审定委员会审定

 浙江省高职高专"十一五"规划重点建设教材

 21世纪职业教育教材·旅游系列

饭店英语服务实训

（第二版）

主　编　柯淑萍
副主编　王　君
参　编　柳文娟　余　超

内 容 简 介

本书以岗位实训和服务流程为主线，内容全面，富有时代感，具有鲜明的特色：①以岗位服务为模块，具体服务为技能，服务流程为主线的编写模式；②创建以实训模块为中心的教学模式，以职业技能为中心的互动式教学；③实现岗位实训和就业"零距离"；④培养用英语进行个性化服务和创新工作的能力。

本书可以作为高等职业院校酒店管理等专业的教材，也可作为高星级酒店的培训教材或酒店从业人员自学用书。

图书在版编目(CIP)数据

饭店英语服务实训/柯淑萍主编．—2版．—北京：北京大学出版社，2016.6
（全国职业教育规划教材·旅游管理系列）
ISBN 978-7-301-26678-6

Ⅰ．①饭… Ⅱ．①柯… Ⅲ．①饭店—英语—高等职业教育—教材 Ⅳ．①H31

中国版本图书馆CIP数据核字（2015）第315067号

书　　　　名	饭店英语服务实训（第二版） FANDIAN YINGYU FUWU SHIXUN
著作责任者	柯淑萍　主编
策 划 编 辑	李 玥
责 任 编 辑	李 玥
标 准 书 号	ISBN 978-7-301-26678-6
出 版 发 行	北京大学出版社
地　　　　址	北京市海淀区成府路205号　100871
网　　　　址	http://www.pup.cn　　新浪微博：@北京大学出版社
电 子 信 箱	zyjy@pup.cn
电　　　　话	邮购部 62752015　发行部 62750672　编辑部 62765126
印 　刷 　者	北京虎彩文化传播有限公司
经 　销 　者	新华书店
	787毫米×1092毫米　16开本　18.75印张　320千字 2010年9月第1版 2016年6月第2版　2021年8月第4次印刷　总第8次印刷
定　　　　价	42.00元（含光盘）

未经许可，不得以任何方式复制或抄袭本书之部分或全部内容。
版权所有，侵权必究
举报电话：010-62752024　电子信箱：fd@pup.pku.edu.cn
图书如有印装质量问题，请与出版部联系，电话：010-62756370

前　言

旅游业和酒店业是充满诱惑力的黄金产业，是我国经济发展的支柱产业。据世界旅游组织（UNWTO）《2015年全球旅游报告》，中国元素继续成为关注焦点，国际游客到访量持续增长。预测到2020年，中国将成为世界最大的旅游目的地。入境旅游人数的剧增必然导致国际化旅游人才和酒店人才需求量的增长。面对广阔的市场前景，如何培养出相应的人才以满足巨大的需求，是人们关注的热点问题。酒店管理与服务专业旨在培养具有较强的外语沟通能力，又熟知酒店服务流程并具备专业技能的酒店管理人员和服务人员。"饭店英语"是高等职业院校酒店管理专业一门重要的专业必修课，对英语口语及听力有较高的要求，对专业技能的训练也十分注重。编者根据市场需求修订了《饭店英语服务实训》一书，以岗位实训和服务流程为主线，内容全面，富有时代感，每个实训模块提供了大量的单词和语音训练，经典对话全部模拟真实的饭店情景，具有很强的操作性。本实训教材在编写模式上进行了精心设计，具有一定的创新。

（1）以岗位服务为模块，以具体服务为技能，以服务流程为主线，提高学生饭店岗位英语实用服务技能。

（2）Section A 主要包含 Word Stock（语料库）和 Pronunciation（语音训练）两块。语料库是对该技能训练模块的一次整理，把跟该训练模块相关的词汇全部罗列出来，扩大学生的词汇量和知识点；而语音训练中出现的句型都是灵活的，在不同的场合有不同的应对，而且强调发音的准确性与流利性。

（3）Section B 主要包含 Service Performance（服务演练）、Position Practice（岗位实训）、Listening Practice（听力实训）和 Important（特别关注）四块。服务演练是针对具体技能实训的经典对话，岗位实训则包容了某个技能实训可能出现的各种实训内容，要求学生能够灵活应变，操作性强。听力实训是在学生熟悉实训内容的基础上进一步的岗位演练，特别关注是对该模块可能遗漏的一些要点进行补充。

（4）设计了 Case and Development（案例与创新）。案例要求学生根据该岗位实训的内容进行一次新的演练。"创新"中设计的 Topic 都找不到现成的答案或者有多种答案，要求学生对这些话题进行深入的思考并在自己的岗位上有所创新。

本书由柯淑萍负责模块一至模块四及附录的编写工作，王君负责模块五至模块九的编写工作，余超负责本书的课件制作工作，柳文娟参与本书的资料收集以及课后习题的解答工作。本书附有光盘，可以作为高等职业院校酒店管理等专业的教材，也可作为高星级酒店的培训教材或酒店从业人员自学之用。

由于时间仓促，编者水平有限，本书中的缺点和错误在所难免，欢迎各位专家、同人及读者批评指正。

编　者
2016年4月

目　　录

实训模块一　饭店业须知 Hospitality Industry ABCs ……………………… (1)
　　技能实训 1　饭店类型 Hotel Types ……………………………………… (2)
　　技能实训 2　服务是什么 What Is Service? ……………………………… (10)
　　技能实训 3　客人类型 Different Guests ………………………………… (14)

实训模块二　前厅服务 Front Office ………………………………………… (17)
　　技能实训 4　客房预订服务 Room Reservation …………………………… (18)
　　技能实训 5　入住登记服务 Check In ……………………………………… (27)
　　技能实训 6　礼宾服务 The Concierge …………………………………… (34)
　　技能实训 7　总机服务 Operator …………………………………………… (42)
　　技能实训 8　外币兑换服务 Foreign Currency Exchange ………………… (48)
　　技能实训 9　结账退宿服务 Check Out …………………………………… (54)
　　技能实训 10　商务中心服务 Business Center …………………………… (61)

实训模块三　客房服务 Housekeeping ……………………………………… (67)
　　技能实训 11　打扫房间 Cleaning the Room ……………………………… (68)
　　技能实训 12　洗衣服务 Laundry Service ………………………………… (75)
　　技能实训 13　客房送餐服务 Room Service ……………………………… (83)
　　技能实训 14　维修服务 Maintenance Service …………………………… (89)

实训模块四　餐饮服务 Food and Beverage ………………………………… (95)
　　技能实训 15　餐台预订 Reservations …………………………………… (96)
　　技能实训 16　餐厅迎客服务 Receiving Diners ………………………… (103)
　　技能实训 17　中餐厅服务 At a Chinese Restaurant …………………… (109)
　　技能实训 18　西餐厅服务 At a Western Restaurant …………………… (117)
　　技能实训 19　早餐服务 Breakfast Service ……………………………… (125)
　　技能实训 20　酒吧服务 At the Bar ……………………………………… (131)

  技能实训 21 就餐礼仪 Table Manners ·················· (140)

实训模块五 康乐中心 Recreation Center ·················· (147)

  技能实训 22 健身服务 Gym Service ······················ (148)

  技能实训 23 美容美发服务 Beauty Parlor Service ·········· (155)

  技能实训 24 桑拿服务 Sauna Service ···················· (161)

  技能实训 25 娱乐服务 Entertainment Service ·············· (167)

实训模块六 购物服务 Shopping Service ·················· (175)

  技能实训 26 旅游纪念品 Souvenir ······················ (176)

  技能实训 27 当地特产 Local Specialty ·················· (183)

实训模块七 会展服务 Convention and Exhibition ·········· (189)

  技能实训 28 会议服务 Convention Service ················ (190)

  技能实训 29 展览服务 Exhibition Service ················ (197)

实训模块八 其他服务 Other Services ···················· (203)

  技能实训 30 失物招领服务 Lost and Found ·············· (204)

  技能实训 31 寄存服务 Deposit Service ·················· (211)

  技能实训 32 介绍旅游信息 Tourist Information ············ (217)

  技能实训 33 托婴服务 Baby-Sitting Service ·············· (223)

实训模块九 投诉 Complaints ·························· (229)

  技能实训 34 处理投诉 Dealing with Complaints ············ (230)

  技能实训 35 刁钻客人 Difficult Guests ·················· (237)

附录一 饭店日常英语 100 句 ································ (243)

附录二 饭店常用词汇 ······································ (249)

附录三 饭店常用告示语 ···································· (257)

附录四 中餐特色菜肴 ······································ (261)

附录五 技能实训听力文本 ·································· (265)

参考文献 ·· (293)

实训模块一
饭店业须知
Hospitality Industry ABCs

Introduction: Hospitality industry is part of a larger enterprise known as the travel and tourism industry. The travel and tourism are both vast group of businesses with one thing in common: providing necessary or desired products and services to the traveler. It is one of the largest industries in the world. Hospitality frequently refers to the hospitality industry jobs for hotels, restaurants, casinos, resorts, clubs and any other service position that deals with tourists.

服务业是旅行业、旅游业的组成部分。旅行业和旅游业都是大行业，两者有一个共同点：就是给旅游者提供必要或心仪的产品和服务。服务业是全世界最大的行业之一。"Hospitality"一词通常指与酒店、餐馆、赌场、旅游景点、俱乐部还有其他跟游客相关的服务性工作。

技能实训 1　饭店类型 Hotel Types

Section A

Basic Knowledge for Position 岗位基础知识

Ⅰ. Word Stock 语料库

Commercial hotel	商务酒店
Resort hotel	度假酒店
Convention hotel	会议酒店
Conference center	会议中心
Motel	汽车旅馆
Residential hotel	长住酒店
Suite hotel	套房酒店
Airport hotel	机场酒店
Economy hotel/ budget hotel	经济型酒店
Guesthouse	宾馆
Shangri-la Hotel	香格里拉饭店
Hyatt Regency Hotel	凯悦酒店
Hilton Hotel	希尔顿酒店
Marriott Hotel	万豪酒店
Sofitel Westlake Hotel	索菲特西湖大酒店
Xihu State Guest Hotel	西湖国宾馆
Radisson Plaza Hotel	雷迪森广场酒店
Zhejiang Narada Grand Hotel	浙江世贸君澜大饭店
Merchant Marco Hotel	马可波罗假日酒店
Hangzhou Sunny Hotel	杭州香溢大酒店
Ramada Plaza Haihua	海华广场酒店
Holiday Wuyang	五洋宾馆
Lake View Hotel	望湖宾馆
Zhejiang International	浙江国际
Super 8 Hotel	速8酒店
Express by Family Inn	如家快捷酒店

Jinjiang Inn	锦江之星
Hanting Express	汉庭快捷酒店
Motel 168	莫泰168
Pod Inn	布丁酒店

 Ⅱ. Pronunciation 语音训练

1. A hotel is a home away from home.
   酒店是家外之家。
2. A hotel is an establishment that provides paid lodging, usually on a short-term basis.
   酒店是一个暂时的付费才能住宿的地方。
3. Reputation first, customer foremost.
   信誉第一，顾客至上。
4. New concepts in hotel design have been developed to meet the needs of guests.
   为了满足客人的需要，在酒店设计上已经融入新的理念。
5. In a hotel, we can meet and serve people from all walks of life.
   在酒店我们会遇见各个领域的人并给他们提供服务。
6. Hospitality is a service industry, deciding to work in that means to give a much more and better service.
   Hospitality是一种服务业，你一旦选择了它就意味着要提供更多更好的服务。

Section B

Position Practice 岗位实训

 Hotel ratings according to functions 酒店根据功能划分

1. Commercial Hotel（商务酒店）

All hotels are commercial. Commercial hotels provide services for business guests as well as those just passing through and need a place just for the night. They are usually located in business and downtown areas. The commercial hotel category contains the largest number of hotels.

所有的酒店都是商务型的。商务酒店给商务客人及临时需要住宿的客人提供服务。它们一般位于商务中心或市中心。商务酒店占了酒店的大多数。

2. Guesthouse（宾馆）

A guesthouse typically appears on large properties and estates, and it may be close to the main house or set apart, depending on the taste of the designer. The features of a guesthouse vary widely. In some cases, the structure is designed very simply, with a bedroom and a bathroom and perhaps a lounging area. In other instances, a guesthouse is like an entirely separate house, complete with a kitchen and other amenities. Typically, the guesthouse is designed to blend in with the rest of the property, creating a uniform look and feel.

宾馆通常以大型建筑物及房屋的形式出现，根据设计师的品位不同，它们可能靠近主楼或者与主楼分开。宾馆的特点有很大的不同，在某些情况下，结构设计非常简单，一间卧室和一间浴室，或者还有可供休息的地方。在其他情况下，宾馆就像一个完全独立的房子，有厨房及其他设施。通常，宾馆的设计融入其他房子，给人统一的观感。

3. Motel (汽车旅馆)

The word motel, combination of motor and hotel or motorists' hotel, referred initially to a type of hotel in Columbia, a single building of connected rooms whose doors faced a parking lot. Later long distance road journeys becoming more and more common and the need for inexpensive, easily accessible overnight accommodation sited close to the main routes led to the growth of the motel concept.

汽车旅馆是汽车和旅馆的组合,最早指的是哥伦比亚的一种酒店形式,一幢建筑物拥有一些房间面临停车场。之后长途旅行变得越来越普遍,人们对价格便宜交通便捷的住宿需求引发了汽车旅馆理念的诞生。

4. Residential Hotel (长住酒店)

It is a hotel where individuals can rent apartments, and choose services offered by the hotel. The layout of a residential guest unit may closely resemble that of a suite hotel. People who do not wish to keep house themselves can rent accommodations on a seasonal basis or even permanently in these hotels.

个人可以承租长住酒店的公寓,选择酒店提供的服务。长住酒店的布局与套房酒店很相似。那些不愿意自己打理房子的人可以季节性地承租酒店房间或长期住在酒店里。

5. Airport Hotel (机场酒店)

Airport hotels are popular because they always located near the major travel centers. More than other hotel types, airport hotels vary in size and service level. Typical markets for these hotels include business guests, airline passengers with overnight layovers or canceled flights and airline personnel. Hotel-owned limousines are used to transport guests to and from the airport.

机场酒店很受欢迎因为它们通常位于旅游中心。与其他类型的酒店相比,机场酒店在

规模和服务水平上有很大的不同。机场酒店的客人包括商务客人，因航班延误或航班取消的乘客和空乘人员。酒店的大巴从机场接送乘客。

6. Resort Hotel（度假酒店）

Unlike other types of hotels, resort hotels are the planned destination of their guests. Guests often vacation at a resort hotel. Resort hotels typically provide scenery and activities unavailable at most other hotels. Resort hotel guests normally stay longer than guests at most other types of hotels.

跟其他类型的酒店不同的是度假酒店就是客人的目的地。客人就在度假酒店度假，度假酒店提供的景观和活动是其他大部分酒店无法提供的，度假酒店的客人通常比其他类型的酒店客人逗留的时间更长。

7. Conference Center（会议中心）

Conference centers are specifically designed to handle group meetings. Because meetings are their focal point, conference centers typically place great emphasis on providing all the services and equipment necessary to ensure a meeting's success.

会议中心的顾客群是团队会议，因为会议是它们的焦点，会议中心特别强调会议必需的设施和服务以保证会议的成功。

8. Suite Hotel（套房酒店）

Suite hotels are the fastest-growing part of the lodging industry. Suite hotel accommodations feature guest room with separate bedroom and living room or parlor areas. Some guest suites include a compact kitchen with refrigerator and bar. In exchange for more complete living quarters, suite hotels generally offer less public space and fewer guest services than other hotel types in order to remain price competitive.

套房酒店在酒店行业中增长很快。套房酒店的明显特征是卧室和起居室或休息室分开。有的套房酒店还拥有一个带冰箱和吧台的厨房。为了保持价格上的竞争力，套房酒店因为有了完整的起居室，会提供相对较少的公共区域及服务给客人。

9. Economy Hotel/Budget Hotel（经济型酒店）

Economy hotel is the representation of a new value, instead of the misunderstanding as the cheap hotel equals to the economy hotel. It represents several basic factors as the function, price, standard and service. It is a living place where provides standard services and requires bearable prices for the common people.

经济型酒店是一种新理念的代表,它并不等于便宜的酒店。它包含几个基本的要素,如功能,价格,水准和服务,可为普通人群提供价格合理、服务标准化的居住地点。

Hotel ratings according to stars 酒店根据星级划分

The star classification system is a common one for rating hotels. Higher star ratings indicate more luxury. Food services, entertainment, view, room variations such as size and additional amenities, spas and fitness centers, ease of access and location may be considered in establishing a standard.

星级划分系统是酒店比较常见的划分系统。越是高星级的酒店代表越奢侈。饮食服务,娱乐,景观,房间规模,附加设施,健身中心,交通及酒店的位置等因素在评星的时候都会考虑到。

1-Star hotel provides a limited range of amenities and services, but adheres to a high standard of facility-wide cleanliness.

一星级酒店提供有限的服务和设施,但拥有高星级酒店一样的清洁。

2-Star hotel provides good accommodation and better equipped bedrooms, each with a telephone and attached private bathroom.

二星级酒店提供的住宿条件相对要好点,每个房间都有电话和单独的卫生间。

3-Star hotel has more spacious rooms and adds high-class decorations and furnishings and color TV. It also offers one or more bars or lounges.

三星级酒店空间更大,装修及设施的标准也高,还有一个或多个酒吧间、休息间。

4-Star hotel is much more comfortable and larger, and provides excellent cuisine (table d'hôte and à la carte), room service, and other amenities.

四星级酒店更加舒适豪华,提供极好的膳食服务(零点或套餐),送餐服务及其他设施。

5-Star hotel offers most luxurious premises, widest range of guest services, as well as swimming pool and sport and exercise facilities.

五星级酒店设备十分豪华,服务设施齐全,还有游泳池,运动场所和健身中心。

7-Star hotel is like Burj Al Arab in Dubai. Seven star hotels are largely created as marketing type, as the hotels hope to attract visitors from around the world.

七星级酒店如迪拜的阿拉伯塔主要是作为一种营销的手段,因为酒店旨在吸引全世界的游客。

Section C
Case and Development 案例与创新

Case 案例

You and your partner both have dreams about career in your mind. Discuss with your partner how to make it true. Do not be afraid to set your sights high. Do not be afraid to be laughed by others. Do not be so concerned with what you cannot do now but, rather, with what you want to do now. Remember that it is possible to realize such a dream if you have a little faith and a little luck.

Development 创新

- Discuss as many types of hotels as possible in your city and discuss their differences in functions.
- Do you have any experience of staying in a hotel? What do you think are the most attractive features of a hotel?
- Is hospitality industry a potential industry in the future? And what will the future hotels be like?

技能实训 2　服务是什么 What Is Service?

Section A

Basic Knowledge for Position 岗位基础知识

Ⅰ. Word Stock 语料库

concierge	门房
golden key	金钥匙
tact	老练，得体
courtesy	礼貌，谦恭，彬彬有礼
endurance	忍耐力，耐久力
punctuality	严守时间，正确，规矩
discretion	慎重，谨慎
loyalty	忠诚
honesty	诚实
excellent memory	出色的记忆力
organizing ability	组织能力
language talent	语言才能
flexible	灵活的

Ⅱ. Pronunciation 语音训练

1. I have a real liking for guests and a warm desire to them.
   我发自内心地喜欢客人并想热心帮助他们。
2. Golden management hatches golden service.
   有一流的管理才会有一流的服务。
3. Service is understanding, anticipating and fulfilling needs of others.
   服务是理解、参与、满足他人需要的过程。
4. Good service is a blending of courtesy and efficiency without either familiarity or servility.
   好的服务是礼貌和效率的融合,不过度亲近也不过分谦卑。
5. Due to our excellent services, the guests are willing to return.
   因为我们出色的服务,客人很乐意再度光临。

Section B

Position Practice 岗位实训

 Ten golden keys for service in a hotel 饭店服务的十把金钥匙

1. The customer is king.
   顾客是上帝。
2. Speak to people.
   跟客人交谈。
3. Smile at people.
   微笑。
4. Be sincere, honest and friendly.
   真诚,诚实,友好。
5. Call people by name.
   用名字称呼客人。
6. Be helpful.
   给客人提供帮助。
7. Wear your name badge.
   戴上你的胸牌。

8. Take pride in your appearance.
   对自己的形象有信心。
9. Consider the feelings of others.
   能够体谅别人的感受。
10. Know your job and your hotel.
    了解你的工作和酒店。

What does Service represent 服务代表什么

S——smiles（向每个人微笑）
E——excellence in everything we do（对我们所做的每件事都力求完美）
R——reaching out to every guest with hospitality（热情对待每位客人）
V——viewing every guest as special（把每个客人都当作特别的客人）
I——inviting guests to return（欢迎客人再次光临）
C——creating a warm atmosphere（创造温馨的气氛）
E——eye contact that shows we care（用眼神表示我们的关注）

What is Golden Key / Les Clefs D'or 什么是金钥匙

　　The French words Les Clefs d'Or mean "Golden Keys" in English. Golden Keys are awarded by Union International Des Concierges D'hôtel's. This organization is non-political and non-religious, and definitely not a trade union of any sort but based on friendship between members to assist international travelers and tourists. A concierge who has qualification of wearing a golden key is called "Golden Key". She or he will do anything you asked as long as it is morally, legally and humanly possible. You can actually leave him any types of service that you require and find that all is completed and done to your satisfaction while you are away attending to your business appointment or sightseeing. The Clefs d'Or Concierge is a remarkable man. It took years of hard working and professional training.

　　法语单词 Les Clefs D'or 翻译成英语就是金钥匙。金钥匙由国际金钥匙组织颁发，这是一家非政治、非宗教、非贸易性质的组织，纯粹是出于组织成员中的友谊来帮助国际旅行者和游客。一个有资格佩戴金钥匙标记的门房（Concierge）就被称作"金钥匙"。她/他能为客人提供无微不至的服务，只要是在合理、合法、人性的基础上。您在参加商务活动或旅游观光时可以向他提出任何要求，他一定能够让您满意。金钥匙是一个极为优秀的人，要有多年的努力付出和专业培训才可能做到。

Section C
Case and Development 案例与创新

Case 案例

Work with your partner and give the whole class a presentation about why you choose hotel service and management as your major. The following expressions may be helpful for you.

I enjoy dealing with people because...
I like meeting new people.
People are usually very friendly.
I find it challenging.
Every person you meet is different.
I can experience different culture.

Development 创新

- What does teamwork mean?
- What can you do if you wish most guests to be repeat guests in your hotel?
- What requirements are necessary to be a successful staff member in a hotel?

技能实训 3　客人类型 Different Guests

Section A

Basic Knowledge for Position 岗位基础知识

I. Word Stock 语料库

package tour	包价旅行
tour group	团队
group code	团号
tour leader	领队
walk-in guest	散客
back packer	背包客
pleasure travelers	消遣型游客
business travelers	商务游客
domestic travelers	国内游客
foreign independent travelers (FITs)	国外散客
group inclusive travelers (GITs)	团队全包游客
special interest travelers (SITs)	特种游客
corporate business travelers	团队商务游客
conference participants	参加会议者
independent traveler	旅游散客
repeat guest	回头客
regular guest	老客户

Ⅱ. Pronunciation 语音训练

1. The more information a hotel has about its guests, the better it can meet their needs.
   酒店从客人那里得到的信息越多,就越能够满足客人的需求。
2. The guests don't depend on the hotels but the hotels depend on the guests.
   客人不依赖酒店而酒店依赖客人。
3. Pleasure travelers are people who travel for pleasure.
   消遣型游客出行的目的是为了消遣。
4. Pleasure travelers are generally price sensitive.
   消遣型游客通常对价格比较敏感。
5. Business travelers are people who travel for the main purpose of conducting business.
   商务客人出行的主要目的是为了商务活动。
6. Business travelers are the largest source of hotels.
   商务客人是酒店最主要的客源。
7. Guests desire comfortable, modern surroundings and leisure facilities to relax.
   客人希望拥有现代舒适的环境和可供放松的娱乐设施。

Section B

Position Practice 岗位实训

Classification of travelers 旅游者的分类

1. Pleasure and business travelers as to the purpose of visit.
   按旅行目的划分,有消遣型旅游者和商务型旅游者。
2. Independent and group travelers as to numbers.
   按人数划分,有散客和团体旅游者。
3. Domestic and foreign travelers as to the origin.
   按客源国划分,有国内旅游者和国外旅游者。
4. Package travelers and non-package travelers as to the price.
   按计价方式划分,有包价旅游者和非包价旅游者。
5. Budget travelers, mass travelers and luxury travelers as to the consumption.
   按消费水平划分,有经济型旅游者、大众型旅游者和豪华型旅游者。

There is only one boss in the hotel 酒店只有一个老板

There is only one boss. The customer!
只有一个老板，那就是顾客！
He can fire everybody in the hotel, from General Manager to down.
他可以解雇酒店中的任何一个人，从总经理到最下面的员工。
Simply by spending his money elsewhere!
只要把他的钱花在其他酒店就可以做到！

★ There is very little difference in people. But that difference makes BIG difference. The little difference is ATTITUDE. The BIG difference is whether it is POSTIVE or NEGATIVE!

人与人之间的差别微乎其微，但这个小差别可以带来大差别。小差别指态度，大差别指态度是积极的还是消极的！

Section C

Case and Development 案例与创新

Case 案例

Imagine that one of you is a foreign guest from Australia. He is a professor teaching Chinese ancient culture in a university. Make a conversation about why he comes to China and what will be interesting to him.

Development 创新

- What are the most important reasons you go for traveling?
- What are the advantages and disadvantages of developing tourism in your region?
- How can you be a responsible traveler?

实训模块二
前厅服务
Front Office

  The Front Office is the control center or nerve center of the hotel and staff at the Front Office must be well trained and motivated in order to achieve business objectives of high yield, high occupancy rates and above all top quality service. In this modular, we'll practice reservation procedure; list the steps in check-in and check-out procedures; explain the methods for processing guest charges and payments; describe the hotel telephone system and duties of concierge.

  前厅是酒店的管理中心或中枢。为了达到高产出、高入住率、高质量的服务目标，酒店必须对其前厅部员工进行目的明确的培训。本实训模块通过技能训练让学生熟悉订房、入住、行李、礼宾、电话、商务服务及退房结账等一系列服务流程。

技能实训 4　客房预订服务 Room Reservation

Section A

Basic Knowledge for Position 岗位基础知识

I. Word Stock 语料库

single room	单人间
double room	大床间（供夫妇合睡的）
twin room	双床间，也就是标准间（standard room）
triple room	三人间，配备三张单人床
quad	四人间
studio room	工作室客房
junior suite	普通套间
business suite	商务套间（一间为起居兼办公室，另一间为卧室）
senior suite	大套间
connecting rooms	组合套间
duplex suite	立体套间，起居室在下，卧室在上
deluxe suite	豪华套房
presidential suite	总统套房
lake-view room	湖景房
mountain-view room	山景房
queen-size bed	大号双人床
king-size bed	特大号双人床
room charge	房价
group rate	团队价
discount rate	折扣价
package rate	包价
complimentary rate	免费
recommend	推荐
room availability	客房预订情况（是否有空房间）
reservation record	预订记录
off/ low season	淡季
peak/ high season	旺季

Ⅱ. Pronunciation 语音训练

1. What type of room would you like?
   您想要怎么样的房间?
2. When would you like your room, sir?
   您什么时候要房间?
3. How many people is the room for, madam?
   夫人,请问房间几个人住?
4. How long do you plan to stay, sir?
   先生,您准备住多久?
5. May I have your name and telephone number, please?
   您可以告诉我您的名字和电话号码吗?
6. Could you just spell your name for me please?
   能否请您拼一下您的名字?
7. I'll just check if we have a room available.
   我查一下看看我们有没有空房。
8. Let me just confirm the details of your reservation, please.
   我来确认一下您的预定。
9. The room rate for a standard room is ﹩300 per night.
   一个标准间一个晚上的房价是 300 美元。
10. I'm afraid we have no suite available, would you mind a double room instead?
    我们恐怕没有空余的套间了。您介意改为双人房吗?
11. This is the peak season. I'm sorry, but could you call us again on weekend? We may have some cancellations.
    现在是旺季,非常抱歉,但请您周末再打电话过来好吗? 可能会有人取消预定。
12. Thank you for calling. We are looking forward to seeing you, madam.
    夫人,谢谢您的来电,我们期待您的光临。

Section B

Service Procedure 服务流程

1. Greetings.
   问候。
2. Reservation request: room type and number of people, arrival date and departure date.

订房信息：房型、人数，抵达日期和离店日期。

3. Check the room availability.

   查询住房情况。

4. Get the information from the guest：name，telephone number.

   获取客人的个人信息，如名字、电话等。

5. Confirm the reservation.

   确认预订。

6. Express your wishes.

   表达你的祝愿。

7. Form the reservation record and hand over to reception.

   形成预订记录并交给前厅。

Ⅰ. Service Performance 服务演练

G=Guest（客人）　　　　R=Reservationist（预订员）

R：Good morning，Radisson Plaza Hotel，Room Reservations. Can I help you?

　　早上好，雷迪森广场酒店客房预订部。需要我为您服务吗？

G：Yes，I'd like to book a room.

　　是的，我想预订一间房。

R：Thank you，sir. For which date and how many people will there be in your party?

　　谢谢您，先生。请问您要哪一天的房？还有你们一行一共有几个人？

G：From May 1st to May 5th，just my son and myself.

　　从5月1号到5月5号，就我和我儿子。

R：From May 1st to May 5th and what kind of room would you like，sir?

　　从5月1号到5月5号，请问您要哪种房型？

G：A suite，please.

　　一间套房吧。

R：Is that a junior suite or a deluxe suite?

　　是普通套房还是豪华套房？

G：What's the difference in price?

　　价格上有什么差别？

R：A junior suite is ＄120 per night and a deluxe one is ＄150 per night. Both include buffet breakfast.

　　普通套房一个晚上120美元，豪华套房一个晚上150美元，两种房型都含自助式早餐。

G：I think I will take a deluxe suite，please.

　　我想我还是订一间豪华套房吧。

R：Hold on please. I'll check our room availability…Thank you for waiting，sir. We do have a deluxe suite at $150 per night, will that be all right?

请别挂断，我查一下是否有空房……谢谢等候，先生。我们能够为您预订一间豪华套房，每晚 150 美元，您看行吗？

G: Ok, I'll take it.

好的，我订下。

R: May I have your name and telephone number, please?

能够告诉我您的名字和电话吗？

G: Sure, my name is Goldfield, Tony Goldfield, and my telephone number is 53638696.

当然，我的名字是 Goldfield，Tony Goldfield，我的电话号码是 53638696。

R: Could you spell it, please?

请问怎么拼？

G: G—O—L—D—F—I—E—L—D.

G—O—L—D—F—I—E—L—D.

R: Thank you, Mr. Goldfield. May I know your arrival time, please?

谢谢，Goldfield 先生，能够告诉我您的抵达时间吗？

G: At about 5 p.m. on May 1st.

大概在 5 月 1 号下午 5 点左右。

R: Fine. How would you like to make payment, sir?

好的。您准备用哪种方式付款？

G: Do you accept MasterCard?

你们接受万事达信用卡吗？

R: Yes. May I know the number?

是的，可以告诉我卡号吗？

G: It's 5336876925658721.

卡号是 5336876925658721。

R: Thank you, Mr. Goldfield. You'd like to have a deluxe suite from May 1st to May 5th for 5 nights. Thank you for calling and we are looking forward to seeing you soon.

谢谢，Goldfield 先生。您预订的是一间从 5 月 1 号到 5 月 5 号的豪华套房，一共 5 个晚上。谢谢您的来电，我们期待您早日光临。

Ⅱ. Position Practice 岗位实训

★ Introduce the room type to the guest. （向客人介绍房型）

We have single room, double room, twin room and deluxe suite, which one do you prefer?

我们有单人房、双人房、标房和豪华套房，您要哪一种？

Single Room (单人客房)

Meant for a single occupancy. The room has a single bed.

Double Room (双人单床客房)

Meant for double occupancy and has one large bed meant for two.

Twin Room (标间)

Meant for double occupancy. The room provides two single beds.

Suite (套房)

Meant for single or more occupancy. It has a sitting room connected to one or more bedrooms.

Triple Room（三人套房）

Provided mostly for families. It has twin beds with an extra cot.

Deluxe Suite（豪华套房）

Deluxe suite bedrooms are targeted to the most sophisticated group of people.

Studio Room（工作室客房）

Meant for single or double occupancy. It has one single bed and a sofa which acts as a sofa during the day and can be pulled out into a bed for the night.

Connecting room（连通客房）

Two or more rooms with private, connecting doors.

Adjoining Room（并联客房）

Two or more rooms side by side with a connecting door between them.

★ Introduce room rate to the guest.（向客人介绍房价）
　The room rate for a junior suite is ＄150 per night, including buffet breakfast.
　一间普通套房每晚房价是150美元，包含自助早餐。

★ Confirm the reservation.（确认预订）
　So that's a twin room for Mr. Johnson from June 5th to 7th at ＄120 per night, am I correct?
　Johnson先生预订一间从6月5号到7号的标间，每晚120美元，对吗？

★ Extend the reservation for the guest.（为客人延长预订）
　We'll extend the reservation for you.
　我们将帮您延长预订。

★ Change the reservation for the guest.（帮客人更改预订）
　You'd like to change your double room for a twin room, is that right?
　您想把大床间改成标间，是吗？

★ Cancel the reservation for the guest.（帮客人取消预订）
　Don't worry, sir. We'll make the cancellation for you.
　不要着急，先生，我们将帮您取消预订。

Ⅲ. Listening Practice 听力实训

★ A. Listen to the conversation and fill in the reservation form.

```
                    Zhejiang Narada Grand Hotel
                         Reservation Form
 Mr/ Mrs/ Miss _____
 First Name _____   Last name _____
 Check in _____   Check out _____
 Room Type _____    Room Rate _____
 Tel Number _____
 Remarks _____
```

★ B. Make confirmation about the details of the reservation.

Miss _____, can I repeat the _____ of your reservation? You are reserving a room for Mr. _____, who will be arriving on flight CX 837 at 8 p.m. on _____ and staying until _____ April. Mr. _____ requires a _____ for _____. The room rate is _____ per night. Your address in Singapore is _____ East Street, and your telephone number is _____, is that right?

Important 特别关注

▲ Never deny a reservation without offering an optional date, room type or hotel.
 婉拒订房时应提供可选择的日期、房型或酒店。
▲ Document reason for denial.
 记录婉拒订房的原因。
▲ All changes must be documented.
 所有的预订变化都应记录在案。
▲ All information must be promptly updated in the front office system.
 所有信息应该在前厅的系统中及时得到更新。

Section C

Case and Development 案例与创新

Case 案例

You are a clerk in room reservation in Marriott Hotel. Mr. Brown wants to book 5 twin rooms and two suites for his company from July 10th to 12th. But it's high season, you can offer only 3 twin rooms, two double rooms and two suites. You answer the phone and confirm the reservation details.

Development 创新

- If there are no rooms available in your hotel, what will you do for the guest?
- If you are a clerk at the Room Reservations, how would you confirm a cancellation?
- What kind of reservation do you think would be popular in the future? Why?

技能实训 5 　 入住登记服务 Check In

Section A

Basic Knowledge for Position 岗位基础知识

Ⅰ. Word Stock 语料库

lobby	大堂吧
black list	黑名单
check in	登记入住
ID card	身份证
passport	护照
service charge	服务费
deposit	押金
arrival list	预期抵店客人名单
departure list	离店客人名单
key card	钥匙牌，房卡
date of departure	离店日期
breakfast coupons	早餐券
reconfirm	重新确认
surname	姓，姓氏
first name	名字
nationality	国籍
signature	签名
corridor	长廊，走廊
elevator	电梯
procedure	过程，步骤，程序
registration	登记，注册
walk-in guest	未经预订直接抵店的客人
occupied room	已住客房
check-out room	走客房
blocked room	保留房

Ⅱ. Pronunciation 语音训练

1. Do you have a reservation?
    您有预订吗？
2. How long will you be staying, please?
    您准备住多久？
3. How would you like to pay, please?
    请问您用什么方式付款？
4. Could you sign your name here, please?
    能在这儿签名吗？
5. May I see your passport?
    可以看一下您的护照吗？
6. Do you have a E-mailed confirmation of your reservation?
    您有预订的邮件确认吗？
7. Could you fill in this registration card?
    您能填一下入住登记表吗？
8. Please don't forget to keep your key card with you.
    请不要忘记随身携带房卡。
9. Your room is on the 16th floor, the room number is 1615.
    您的房间在 16 楼，房号是 1615。
10. If you are ready, I'll ask the bellman to show you to your room.
    如果一切就绪，我叫行李员带您去房间。

Section B

Service Procedure 服务流程

1. Greetings.
    问候。
2. Determine reservation status.
    识别客人是否有预订。
3. Record registration information.
    记录入住登记信息。
4. Assign rooms and charge.
    分配房间及收费。

5. Confim ways of payment.

   确认付款方式。

6. Go through registration procedure.

   完成入住登记手续。

7. Document all the information.

   建立相关资料信息。

Ⅰ. Service Performance 服务演练

G＝ Guest（客人）　　　　R＝Receptionist（接待员）

R：Good evening. Welcome to Holiday Inn. Can I help you?

　　晚上好，欢迎光临假日酒店。需要为您服务吗？

G：Good evening. I'd like to check in please.

　　晚上好，我想登记入住。

R：Have you made a reservation, Miss?

　　小姐，请问您有预订吗？

G：I'm afraid I don't have a reservation. Is there a vacant room here?

　　我没有预订，还有空房吗？

R：Just a moment please... Sorry to have you waiting, Miss. We still have some vacant rooms. What do you want, a single or a double room?

　　请稍等片刻……很抱歉让您久等了，小姐。我们还有一些空房。您是要单人间还是大床间？

G：A single please. How much does it cost?

　　单人间就可以了。单人间房价多少？

R：It's ＄100 per night for a single room.

　　单人间每晚 100 美元。

G：Do you give me some discount?

　　能够打折吗？

R：Yes, we give 5％ discount for one week, 10％ for two weeks and over. How long do you intend to stay?

　　是的，如果住一周我们给您5％的折扣，如果住两周或更长时间我们给您10％的折扣。您准备住多久？

G：For a week.

　　住一周。

R：Then we can give you 5％ discount.

　　这样我们可以给您优惠5％。

G：All right. I'll take the room for a week.

　　好吧，我要一间房住一周。

R：Could you fill out the registration form, please?
请填写一下登记表好吗?

G：Fine.
好的。

R：How will you be paying, Miss?
您准备用哪种方式付款?

G：By Visa Card.
用维萨卡付款。

R：May I take a print of your card?
能够刷一下您的信用卡吗?

G：Sure, here you are.
当然, 给您。

R：Thank you, Miss Julie. Your room number is 1211. A bellboy will show you to your room. Enjoy your stay here, please.
谢谢您, Julie 小姐。您的房号是 1211。行李员会带您去房间。祝您在这儿过得愉快!

Ⅱ. Position Practice 岗位实训

★ Determine guest's reservation status. （判断客人的预订情况）

1. Do you have a reservation with us, sir?
   您有预订吗, 先生?

2. Have you made a reservation, madam?
   您有预订吗, 夫人?

3. May I have your name, please?
   能够告诉我您的名字吗?

★ Guest check in walk-in. （散客入住）

1. Which type of room do you prefer, sir?
   先生, 您要哪种房型?

2. How long do you plan to stay in our hotel, madam?
   夫人, 您准备住多久?

3. Just a moment, please. I'll check the reservation record.
   请稍等, 我查一下预订记录。

4. I'm sorry, sir. There is no single room available, would you like a twin room instead?
   很抱歉, 先生, 已经没有单人房了, 来一间标房怎么样?

★ Guest check in group. （团队入住）

1. Pre-allocate appropriate vacant ready rooms to the group's requirements.

按照团队的要求预先分配好房间。

2. Enter group reservation into group check-in screen.

   在团队入住屏幕中输入团队预订。

3. First check-in member of group, then check-in all pre-allocated rooms.

   先登记团队的人员，然后登记预先分配好的房间号码。

4. Enter into group details screen and print required number of rooming lists, Concierge and Reception have a copy.

   把团队的详细信息输入电脑并复印房号，礼宾部和前厅部各持一份名单。

5. Print all room keys.

   记录所有的房号。

6. Attach a rooming list to each key card.

   每张房卡上都应该有房号。

7. Greet guests in a friendly manner.

   用礼貌的方式问候客人。

8. Give all key cards to the group leader, indicating where rooms are situated.

   所有的房卡都交给领队，并说明房间的位置。

9. Offer assistance with luggage.

   为客人的行李提供帮助。

Ⅲ. Listening Practice 听力实训

★ A. Listen to the conversation and fill in the registration form.

Registration Form

Mr/Mrs/Miss _____

Surname _____   Fist Name _____

Check in _____

Check out _____

Room No. _____   Room Rate _____

From _____   To _____

Nationality _____   Passport No. _____

Home Address _____

Purpose of Stay _____

Payment by Cash/ Credit Card/ Traveler's Check/ Company Check

Guest Signature _____

★ B. Complete the following dialogue.

Guest: Good evening, my name is Mrs. John. I've just arrived from New York. I had a reservation.

Receptionist: Welcome to Marriot Hotel. Mrs. John.

Guest: Thank you.

Receptionist: Just a minute, please. I'll check the reservation record for you. _____. Are you traveling with your family?

Guest: No, I'm here on business.

Receptionist: I see. So _____, do you?

Guest: No, of course. My secretary booked _____.

Receptionist: I see. Well, I'm afraid we have made a mistake about the reservation. I do apologize for it. _____?

Guest: Yes, just one moment. Here it is, "one deluxe single" for five nights. That's until 15th.

Receptionist: Mm. Yes, I see. Well, _____ while I find out if there are any deluxe singles still available?

Guest: Very well, but I hope this won't happen again.

Important 特别关注

▲ Immediately acknowledge an arriving guest, regardless of what you are doing.
无论你正在做什么,一定要立刻接待客人。

▲ Use proper sentences, do not simply nod or raise your head.
使用恰当的问候,而不只是点头或抬头。

▲ Seek assistance rather than let a guest wait.
宁愿寻求帮助也不能让客人等候。

▲ Regardless of what the front office receptionist is doing, he must always acknowledge an arriving guest. When talking on the telephone (a business call), the receptionist must tell the person on the phone to hold the line please, greet the guest using a sentence like: "Good afternoon, I will be with you in just a moment", return to the person on the phone and end the conversation as soon as possible. If the receptionist is unable to end the conversation quickly, he must ask a colleague to attend to either the telephone or to the arriving guest.
无论前厅接待员在做什么,他必须时刻关注到来的客人。如果他正在接听电话(当然是商务电话),他必须告诉听电话的一方稍候,向到来的客人打招呼:"下午好,我马上就好了。"然后转向听电话的一方并尽快结束电话。如果他无法很快结束电话,他必须叫他的同事来接听电话或来接待到来的客人。

Section C
Case and Development 案例与创新

Case 案例

The guest's name is Tony Waller. He would like to have a twin room for tonight but he didn't make a reservation in advance.

You are a receptionist. You check the reservation record and find there is no twin room, you suggest a double room for the guest. Then you ask the guest to fill in the registration form. The room rate is 680 yuan. The room number is 608. The bellboy will show the guest to the room.

Development 创新

• What are the main points the receptionist has to tell group guests? Try to list them in your own words.
• If the guest wants to change the room, what will you do?
• As a hotel receptionist, what personal qualities and skills should you possess?

技能实训 6　礼宾服务 The Concierge

Section A
Basic Knowledge for Position 岗位基础知识

Ⅰ. Word Stock 语料库

concierge	礼宾部
bellman	行李员
door man	门童
head porter	行李领班
luggage tag	行李标签
luggage cart	行李车
luggage rack	行李架
luggage deposit	行李存放处
claim tag	取物牌
cloakroom	寄存处
flight number	航班号
pick-up service/limousine service	接机服务
automobile	小汽车
shuttle bus	穿梭巴士
group baggage record	团队行李登记
rooming list	分房单
parking	停车场
health club	健身俱乐部
recreation center	娱乐中心
beauty parlor	美容室
Chinese restaurant	中餐厅
western restaurant	西餐厅

Ⅱ. Pronunciation 语音训练

1. May I help you with your luggage, sir?
   先生，我来帮您提行李好吗？

2. May I take them for you?
   我来帮您提行李好吗？

3. Is this all your luggage?
   这是您所有的行李吗？

4. Is this everything, sir?
   这是全部东西吗，先生？

5. You may leave your luggage in the concierge.
   您可以把行李放在礼宾部。

6. Would you like to check your luggage here?
   您要寄存行李吗？

7. Don't worry, your luggage will be sent up at once.
   别担心，您的行李很快就会被送上去的。

8. Your entire luggage is here, seven pieces in all.
   您所有的行李都在这儿，总共7件。

9. How many pieces of luggage do you have?
   您有几件行李？

10. Is there anything valuable or breakable in it?
    请问里面有贵重或易碎物品吗？

11. I'll show you to the front desk. This way, please.
    我带您到前台，请这边走。

12. I'll show you to your room. May I have your room number, please?
    我带您去房间，请告诉我房号好吗？

13. After you, sir. May I put your suitcases here?
    您先请。我能把行李放在这儿吗？

14. Here we are, sir. Room 1615.
    先生，我们到了，1615房间。

15. May I have your room card?
    能够用一下您的房卡吗？

16. Where shall I put your luggage?
    我把您的行李放在哪儿？

17. Is there anything else I can do for you?
    还有什么需要我效劳的吗？

18. Thank you, sir. You are so kind.
    谢谢您，先生，您真好。

19. Watch your steps, madam.
    女士，小心。

20. Would you like me to call a taxi for you? / Would you want a taxi?
    您需要我为你叫一辆出租车吗？/ 需要出租车吗？
21. About 30 minutes by taxi from here to airport.
    从这里到机场大概需要30分钟。
22. I'm sorry to have kept you waiting.
    对不起让您久等了。

Section B

Service Procedure 服务流程

1. Greetings.
   问候。
2. Help luggage out of the taxi.
   帮助客人从出租车上拿出行李。
3. Confirm pieces of luggage.
   确认行李数量。
4. Show the guest to the front desk.
   带客人到前厅。
5. Wait for the guest while checking in.
   等候客人登记入住。
6. Show the guest to his room.
   带客人去房间。
7. Open the door.
   开门。
8. Extend your wishes to the guest.
   向客人表达祝愿。

Ⅰ. Service Performance 服务演练

G=Guest（客人）　　　B=Bellman（行李员）

B：Welcome to West Lake State Hotel.
   欢迎光临西湖国宾馆。
G：Thank you.
   谢谢。
B：May I help you with your luggage?

我来帮您提行李好吗?

G：Thank you.

谢谢。

B：How many pieces of luggage do you have?

您有几件行李?

G：Seven pieces in all.

总共7件。

B：But here just five pieces.

但是这里只有5件。

G：Oh, two pieces are still in the taxi.

哦,还有两件仍在出租车里。

B：I'll carry them for you.

我来帮您拿吧。

G：Thank you.

谢谢。

B：Just a moment, please. I will bring a luggage cart. Now I'll show you to the front desk. This way, please.

请稍等,我去拿一辆行李车。现在我带您去前厅,请这边走。

G：Thank you.

谢谢。

B：I'll show you to your room when you finish checking in.

您办完入住登记后,我带您去房间。

G：OK.

好的。

（After a while.）（过了一会儿。）

B：Now I'll show you to your room. May I have your room number, please?

现在我带您去房间,请告诉我房号好吗?

G：My room number is 1216.

我的房号是1216。

B：This way, please.

请这边走。

G：Thank you.

谢谢。

B：Here we are. Room 1216. May I have your key card, please?

我们到了,1216房间,我可以用一下您的房卡吗?

G：Sure. Here you are.

当然,给您。

B: After you, sir. May I put your suitcases here?
先生，您先请。我能把行李放在这儿吗？

G: Sure. Just put them anywhere.
可以，放在哪里都行。

B: Shall I open the window for you?
需要打开窗户吗？

G: Yes, thank you.
打开吧，谢谢。

B: Is there anything I can do for you?
还有什么需要我为您服务的吗？

G: No, thank you.
没有了，谢谢。

B: You're welcome. I hope you will enjoy your stay with us.
不用客气。祝您入住愉快！

Ⅱ. Position Practice 岗位实训

★ Confirm the pieces of luggage. （确认行李件数）

1. How many pieces of luggage do you have?
您有几件行李？

2. Your entire luggage is here, five pieces in all. Let me take them to the trunk.
您所有的行李都在这儿，一共 5 件。让我把他们放到后备厢吧。

★ Confirm luggage for group guests. （确认团队客人的行李）

Focus on the number of luggage, damaged or undamaged, and the luggage tags.
关注行李的件数、行李是否损坏、行李的标签。

★ Call a taxi for the guest. （为客人叫出租车）

1. Would you like me to call a taxi for you?
需要一辆的士吗？

2. Where to? Sir.
先生，到哪里呢？

3. Sorry to have kept you waiting, sir.
先生，不好意思让您久等了。

★ Arrange the city tour for the guest. （为客人安排城市观光）

1. May I suggest that you go and visit the West Lake tomorrow? It's a must for tourists in Hangzhou.
我建议你们明天去逛西湖，对来杭州的游客来说西湖是个必去的地方。

2. You can visit the Oriental Pearl TV Tower. People say it's the symbol of our city.
你们可以去看看明珠塔，大家都说它是这个城市的象征。

3. The Palace Museum is one of the most famous tourist attractions in Beijing. It is the largest and most well reserved imperial residence in China today.

故宫是北京最有名的景点之一，是当今中国最大也是保护的最好的皇宫。

★ At the cloakroom. （行李寄存）

1. Excuse me, where can the bag be deposited?

   对不起，哪里能寄存行李？

2. I want to check my luggage.

   我想要寄存我的行李。

3. You can check luggage here.

   您可以把行李寄存在这里。

4. Certainly, sir. Please go through the formalities.

   当然可以，先生。请您办一下寄存手续。

5. Keep the luggage check card, and for drawing, please show the second half of this card.

   请保存好行李寄存卡，当您来取回行李时，请出示这张卡的下半联。

Ⅲ. Listening Practice 听力实训

★ A. Listen to the conversation and fill in the baggage form.

Holiday Inn

Baggage Tag Name _____

Room No. _____

Pieces of Baggage _____

Collecting Time _____

Remarks _____

Handled by _____

★ B. Complete the following Dialogue.

Guest：Hi, I was told to see you about _____.

Concierge：It's my pleasure. _____.

Guest：Concierge? Could you explain that to me?

Concierge：We help direct hotel visitors to _____.

Guest：Very good. So where shall I begin my sightseeing?

Concierge：I would suggest the Forbidden City first.

Guest：Gee, I've already seen the Forbidden City. _____?

Concierge：Let me see. What do you like to do _____?

Guest：Well, I really like climbing mountains.

Concierge: Well, _____ ! Have you ever visited the Great Wall?
Guest: No, but I've been meaning to.
Concierge: Well, the Great Wall _____ . It will really impress you.
Guest: _____ . I'll do that.
Concierge: Enjoy your visit!

Important 特别关注

▲ Always address guest by his name.
  总是用名字来称呼客人。
▲ Every time you see a guest, smile and offer a friendly comment.
  每次遇见客人都面带微笑,进行友好的寒暄。
▲ Answer the guests' questions and requests quickly and efficiently.
  迅速回答客人的问题,高效处理客人的要求。
▲ Anticipate the guests' needs and deal with guests' problems.
  预测客人的需求并处理客人的问题。
▲ Let the guest enter the room first.
  让客人先进房间。
▲ Show necessary items but do not over-stay.
  给客人介绍必要的设施但不能待太久。
▲ Bid proper farewell.
  恰当地道别。

Section C

Case and Development 案例与创新

Case 案例

Make a dialogue with your partner. You are a concierge. You receive a call from a registered guest named Mr. Thompson. His room number is 1619, he wants to check out and go out for an important appointment in 30 minutes. He has no time to deal with his luggage. He calls you for help. You tell him you will send a bellman immediately to get his luggage. You also ask your guest to put his name tag on the cases. Mr. Thompson asks if it is possible to leave his luggage in the hotel until 3 p.m. You tell him everything will be OK.

Development 创新

• What kind of topic should be avoided when you have a friendly talk with the guests?

• When handling the luggage for group guests, what are the most important points you should always remember?

• How can you anticipate the guest's need and offer your best service to him?

技能实训 7　总机服务 Operator

Section A
Basic Knowledge for Position 岗位基础知识

Ⅰ. Word Stock 语料库

operator	话务员
dial	拨电话
inside call/outside call	内线/外线电话
local call	市内电话
long distance call	长途电话
DDD call：Domestic Direct Dial call	国内长途直拨
IDD call：International Direct Dial call	国际长途直拨
area code	区号
country code	国家代码
collect call	对方付费电话
paid call	自己付费电话
station-to-station call	叫号电话
person-to-person call	叫人电话
coin call	投币电话
emergency call	急救电话
wrong number	打错电话
morning call/wake-up call	叫早电话/叫醒电话
put sb through	给某人接通电话
minimum charge	最低收费
extension	分机
directory book/telephone book	电话簿
house phone	内部电话
hold on/hold the line	别挂断

Ⅱ. Pronunciation 语音训练

1. Hello. This is Radisson Plaza Hotel. May I help you?
   您好，雷迪森酒店，可以为您做什么？

2. Hello. This is Room Reservation. Can I help you?
   您好，这是客房预订，可以为您做什么？
3. Who is that? / Who is that speaking?
   请问您是哪位？
4. This is Helen. / This is Helen speaking.
   我是海伦。
5. Lily, you are wanted. / Lily, you are wanted on the phone.
   Lily，你的电话。
6. I'm afraid you have got the wrong number.
   恐怕您打错电话了。
7. Could you put me through to the Front Office?
   可以帮我接通前厅吗？
8. The line is busy now, would you call back later?
   电话占线，您要不要过一会儿再打过来？
9. He is not in the room at the moment, would you like to leave a message?
   他现在不在房间里，您要不要留口信？
10. You are through, sir. Please go ahead.
    先生，接通了，请讲。
11. Would you like to try the extension?
    您要不要试试分机？
12. For inside call, you can dial the room number directly.
    内部电话，您直接拨打房号就可以了。
13. For local call, dial 9 first, then the number you want.
    本地电话，先拨9，再拨您要拨打的电话号码。
14. For DDD call, dial 9 first, the area code, and last the number you want.
    国内长途直拨，先拨9，再拨区号，最后拨您要拨打的电话号码。
15. Local calls made from hotel rooms are free of charge.
    在酒店房间内打市内电话免费。

Section B

Service Procedure 服务流程

1. Greet in saying Good Morning / Afternoon, and identify your department and your hotel.
   问候客人并自报你所在的部门或酒店。

2. Ask whether the guest needs your help.
   询问客人是否需要帮助。
3. Offer assistance and take notes.
   提供帮助并做好记录。
4. Always confirm each point of information you are given.
   要确认所有细节。
5. When transferring a call, inform the guest that you are doing so.
   当你要转接电话时,要告知客人要这么做。
6. Bid farewell to the guest.
   道别。
7. Wait for the caller to hang up first.
   等来电者先挂机。

Ⅰ. Service Performance 服务演练

G=Guest(客人)　　　　O=Operator(话务员)

O：Good evening. Holiday Inn. What can I do for you?
   晚上好,假日酒店。能够为您做些什么?

G：Good evening. I'd like to know how to make a call.
   晚上好。我想知道如何拨打电话。

O：For room to room calls, dial room number directly please. For local calls, first dial 9, then the number you want.
   拨打房间对房间的电话,直接拨房号就可以了。拨打本地电话,先拨9,再拨您要拨打的电话。

G：Thank you. I'd like to make an international call to New York. What can I do then?
   谢谢。我想打国际长途电话到纽约,我该怎么办?

O：You may call directly from your room. Dial 9 first, then the country code, area code and last the number you want.
   先生,您可以直接从房间拨打。先拨9,再拨国家代码和区号,最后拨打您要拨打的电话。

G：I see. Thanks a lot. By the way, what time is it in New York now?
   我明白了,多谢。顺便问一声,纽约现在几点?

O：There is a time difference of 13 hours. It's 9 o'clock in the morning.
   时差是13个小时。纽约现在是上午9点。

G：I'd like to make a call now. You are so helpful.
   我现在就想打一个电话,您给了我很大的帮助。

O: You're welcome, sir. I'm always at your service.
不客气，先生，我很乐意为您效劳。

II. Position Practice 岗位实训

★ Transfer a call.（转接电话）

1. I'd like to transfer your call to the Front Office.
   我把您的电话转到前厅。
2. I'm sorry the number's engaged. Would you care to hold on please?
   很抱歉电话占线，您在意稍等一会儿吗？
3. The line is free now. I'll put you through.
   电话不占线了，我给您接过去。
4. Well, it's ringing, go ahead, please.
   好了，通了，请讲话。

★ Make sure about payment.（确认付款方式）

1. Could I know how you will be paying for this call? Is it a collect call or a paid call?
   请问您用何种方式付这个电话费？是对方付费还是您自己付费？
2. This is the Hotel Operator. I have a collect call from Mr. Smith in London. Will you accept the charges?
   这里是酒店总机，史密斯先生从伦敦打来电话，是由接听人付费的，您愿意付款吗？

★ Take a message.（记录口信）

1. I'm afraid there's no reply from Room 1618.
   恐怕1618房没有人接听。
2. Would you like to leave a message?
   您要留言吗？
3. I'll put you through to the Message Desk.
   我帮您接通留言台。

★ Wake-up call.（叫醒服务）

1. What time would you like your morning call?
   您要几点叫早？
2. May I have your name and room number please?
   请告诉我您的名字和房号好吗？

III. Listening Practice 听力实训

★ A. Listen to the conversation and take the caller's message.

Blue Beach Hotel

To: _____
From: _____
Message: _____

★ B. Complete the following dialogue.

Operator: White Swan Hotel. Can I help you?
Caller: Yes, my flight is 6:00 a.m. tomorrow morning. _____.
Operator: Sure, _____?
Caller: How long will it take to go to the airport?
Operator: About 30 minutes.
Caller: Then 4:30 a.m. will be OK.
Operator: Yes, and _____?
Caller: Certainly. Mr. Spink, room 1215.
Operator: Thank you sir, _____.
Caller: Thank you very much, have a good night.
Operator: Have a good night.

Important 特别关注

▲ Make sure to be prepared for all calls and have a positive attitude.
确保用积极的态度接听所有来电。

▲ Picking up the phone within three rings.
电话铃响三声之内接电话。

▲ Protecting guest's private information.
保护客人的个人信息。

▲ Don't slam the receiver.
放置话筒时要轻。

▲ Use no jargon.
不使用行话、黑话。

▲ Be friendly, not in a hurried manner when ending a call.
结束电话时要友好,不能仓促。

▲ Wait for the caller to hand up first.
等来电者先挂机。

Section C

Case and Development 案例与创新

Case 案例

Guest: You are a new check-in guest at this hotel, and you want to make a collect call to Paris. But you don't know how to do it. You are calling the operator to ask for help.

Operator: You answer the phone and tell the guest how to make an international call from his room. You also tell the guest that the hotel will collect 8 yuan for a collect call.

Development 创新

• What information should an operator learn if someone calls and asks him to pass a message to a registered guest in the hotel?

• Should the operator check with the caller after he learns all the information?

• What kind of rules shall you bear in mind when doing your job as an operator?

技能实训 8　外币兑换服务
Foreign Currency Exchange

Section A

Basic Knowledge for Position 岗位基础知识

Ⅰ. Word Stock 语料库

cashier	收银员
exchange	兑换
one-way change	单向兑换
full change	全向兑换
today's exchange rate	今天的汇率
exchange memo	兑换水单
currency	货币
foreign currency	外币
foreign exchange counter	外币柜台
receipt	收据
USD (United States Dollar)	美元
EUR (European Dollar)	欧元
GBP (Great Britain Pound)	英镑
JPY (Japanese Yen)	日元
MYR (Malaysian Ringgit)	马币
double check	双核对
Bank of China	中国银行

Ⅱ. Pronunciation 语音训练

1. I'd like to change some Euro into Chinese Yuan.
   我想把一些欧元换成人民币。
2. Where can I change money?
   我在哪里可以兑换外币?
3. What's today's exchange rate?
   今天的汇率是多少?

4. How much would you like to change?

   您要兑换多少？

5. Do you accept traveler's checks?

   你这里接受旅行支票吗？

6. I'd like to cash this traveler's check.

   请将这些旅行支票换成现金。

7. I'd like some small change.

   请将大钞换成零钱。

8. May I see your passport, please?

   能看一下您的护照吗？

9. Would you please fill in this memo?

   能填一下这张兑换水单吗？

10. The exchange rate of US dollar to RMB is 1∶6.1.

    美元兑人民币的汇率是1∶6.1。

11. The total is 4000 RMB, please have a check.

    总数是4000人民币，请核对。

12. Please keep the memo well and you may need it.

    保管好兑水单，也许您会用得上。

13. You can go to the Bank of China or the Airport Exchange Office if you want to change it back into dollars by showing the memo.

    如果您要把它换回美元，您可以去中国银行或机场的外币兑换处。

Section B

Service Procedure 服务流程

1. Greetings.

   问候。

2. What kind of foreign currency the guest would like to exchange.

   询问需要兑换的外币。

3. Introduce today's exchange rate.

   介绍当天的汇率。

4. How much he would like to exchange and receive the money.

   兑换多少钱并接收。

5. See guest's passport.

   查看客人的护照。

6. Fill in the exchange memo.
   填写外汇兑换水单。

7. Tell the guest about the amount he could have.
   告诉客人所兑换的金额。

8. Give the money and ask the guest to have a check.
   把兑换的钱给客人并叫他核对。

9. Give the receipt and ask him to keep it well.
   给客人收据并叫他妥善保管。

Ⅰ. Service Performance 服务演练

G= Guest（客人）　　C=Cashier of foreign exchange counter（外币兑换柜台收银员）

C：Good afternoon, sir. Is there anything I can do for you?
　　先生，下午好。有什么可以为您效劳的吗？

G：I'd like to change some US dollars into Chinese RMB.
　　我想把一些美元换成人民币。

C：According to today's exchange's rate, every 100 US dollars comes to 610 RMB. How much would you like to change, sir?
　　根据今天的汇率，每100美元换610人民币。先生，您要换多少？

G：Well, I'll change 300 dollars. Here you are.
　　我想换300美元。给您。

C：Would you please fill in this memo and show me your passport?
　　您能不能填一下兑水单并出示您的护照？

G：Here you are. Is that all right?
　　给您，您看行吗？

C：That's all right. Thanks. What would you want for your money?
　　行，谢谢。您要什么面值的货币？

G：Any kind will be OK. But I'd like some ten-yuan and fifty-yuan notes.
　　都行，最好有一些10元、50元的零钞。

C：Here is 1830 Yuan. Please have a check. And here's your memo. Please keep it well. You can go to the Bank of China or the Airport Exchange Office if you want to change it back into dollars by showing the memo.
　　这是1830元，请核对一下。这是您的兑换水单，请妥善保管。如果您要把它换回美元，您可以去中国银行或机场的外币兑换处。

G：Thank you very much.
　　非常感谢。

C：My pleasure.
　　乐意为您效劳。

Ⅱ. Position Practice 岗位实训

★ English names and symbols of some common currencies.（常见的货币符号及英文名称）

1. CNY（Chinese Yuan）人民币
2. HKD（HongKong Dollar）港元
3. USD（United States Dollar）美元
4. EUR（European Dollar）欧元
5. CAD（Canadian Dollar）加拿大元
6. NZD（New Zealand Dollar）新西兰元
7. SGD（Singapore Dollar）新加坡元
8. AUD（Australian Dollar）澳大利亚元
9. GBP（Great Britain Pound）英镑
10. JPY（Japanese Yen）日元
11. KRW（South Korean Won）韩国元
12. THB（Thai Baht）泰铢
13. CHF（Swiss Franc）瑞士法郎

★ Some popular international credit card.（几种国际通用的信用卡）

1. Visa Card 维萨卡
2. Master Card 万事达卡
3. En Route（ER）在途中
4. Euro Card（EC）欧洲卡
5. American Express Card 美国运通卡
6. International Diner's Club 国际大来俱乐部卡
7. JBC 卡（日本银行发行）
8. Federal Card 联邦卡
9. International Great Wall 长城卡

Ⅲ. Listening Practice 听力实训

★ A. Fill the information in the following exchange memo.

Valentine's Island Resort

Purchased from: _____   Date: _____
Room: _____   Passport No.: _____
Currency Amount: _____   Exchange Rate: _____
RMB Equivalent: _____
Guest Signature: _____
Authorized Signature & Stamp: _____.

★ B. Complete the following dialogue.
Guest: I'd like to change some Euros, please.
Cashier: _____?
Guest: Yes, Here's my room card.
Cashier: _____?
Guest: EUR 500, please. _____?
Cashier: It's 8 yuan 30 to the Euro... So that's a _____.
Guest: Thank you.
Cashier: _____.

Important 特别关注

▲ Since currency exchange rates vary from place to place and day to day, where and how you exchange currency can make a difference in your wallet.
既然汇率每个地方每一天都不一样,你在哪儿或怎么兑换外币会带来一些差异。

▲ Do keep in mind that credit card companies may ask an additional fee for overseas usage. If you're not sure, check with your company before you leave home.
记住:有些信用卡公司对在海外使用的信用卡要收取额外的费用。如果你不确信,在离开家之前去跟发卡公司核对一下。

▲ Some countries' currency and exchange rate are more changeable than others because of their inflationary and unstable economies.
因为通货膨胀和经济不稳定的原因,有些国家的货币或汇率比其他国家要多变。

Section C

Case and Development 案例与创新

Case 案例

Guest: You want to exchange some Euro for RMB. You go through the necessary formalities on request. You find there is something wrong with the amount of the RMB the cashier gives you.

Cashier: You make clear what kind of currency the guest has got and tell him the exchange rate. You accept the foreign currency and ask the guest to go through the formalities. You correct the mistake and apologize.

Development 创新

- Why do most hotels not accept personal checks?
- Why is it much safer to buy traveler's checks than carry a lot of cash?
- What are advantages and disadvantages of using credit cards in our daily life?

技能实训 9　结账退宿服务 Check Out

Section A

Basic Knowledge for Position 岗位基础知识

Ⅰ. Word Stock 语料库

cashier	收银员
cash	现金
credit card	信用卡
traveler's check	旅行支票
change	零钱
exchange receipt	兑换收据
personal check	私人支票
pay in cash	用现金付款
pay by credit card	用信用卡付款
pay with a traveler's check	用旅行支票付款
sign the bill	签单
transfer	转账
invoice	发票
refunds	退款
Long Card	龙卡
Peony Card	牡丹卡
Great Wall Card	长城卡
Kinscard	金穗卡

Ⅱ. Pronunciation 语音训练

1. May I have your room card, please?
   请把房卡交给我好吗?

2. Just a moment, please. The cashier will have your bill ready in a moment.
   请稍等，收银员马上会准备好您的账单。

3. Thank you for waiting, sir. Here is your bill. Would you like to check it?
   先生，让您久等了，这是您的账单，要核对一下吗?

4. Excuse me, sir, did you use the mini bar this morning?
   先生，请问上午您消费过小冰箱里的东西吗？

5. That's a total of 2000 yuan.
   总共 2000 元。

6. How will you be paying, madam?
   女士，您用哪种方式付款？

7. What kind of credit card have you got?
   您持有哪种信用卡？

8. I'm sorry, but we don't accept personal checks according to the hotel policy.
   对不起，根据酒店的规定，我们不收个人支票。

9. Would you like to settle the difference in cash?
   您愿意用现金支付差额吗？

10. I'm terribly sorry for the inconvenience.
    给您带来不便真的十分抱歉。

11. I neglected that detail when I drew up your bill.
    我在开账单时忽略了那个细节。

12. I'll correct your bill, would you mind waiting for a minute?
    我们将把账单改正过来，您介意稍等片刻吗？

13. Here is the money you overpaid.
    这是您多付的钱。

14. May I have your signature, please?
    请您签个名好吗？

15. Here is your card and receipt.
    这是您的卡和收据。

16. I'll call the bellman to take your baggage down.
    我会叫服务员把您的行李拿下来。

Section B

Service Procedure 服务流程

1. Greetings.
   问候。

2. Confirm the departure.
   确认离店。

3. Ask about the name and the room number.
   询问客人的名字和房号。

4. Ask the guest to give you the key card.

要求客人交回房卡。

5. Confirm the way of the payment.

确认付款方式。

6. Tell the guest to have a check about the total.

要求客人核查账单总数。

7. Bid farewell to the guest.

道别。

Ⅰ. Service Performance 服务演练

G＝Guest（客人）　　　C＝Cashier（收银员）

C：Good morning, madam. May I help you?

上午好，女士。有什么可以帮您的吗？

G：Yes, I want to check out now.

是的，我要结账。

C：May I have your room number and room card, please?

告诉我您的房号并交回房卡，好吗？

G：Room 1234, and here is the room card.

1234 房间，这是房卡。

C：Did you use mini bar this morning?

今天上午您使用过小冰箱吗？

C：Yes, I had some drinks.

是的，我喝过饮料。

G：Just a moment please, the cashier will have your bill ready in a moment.

请稍等，收银员一会儿就会把您的账算好。

（After a while.）（过了一会儿。）

C：I am sorry to keep you waiting. The total bill is 1200 yuan, madam.

很抱歉让您久等了，总数是 1200 元，女士。

G：Would you mind letting me check the bill?

您在意我核对一下账单吗？

C：Not at all, please.

当然不，请吧。

G：I'm sorry, I think you made some mistakes. I don't think the figure should go that high. I did not understand what that charge is for.

请原谅，我认为您弄错了。我认为总数没有那么高，我不明白那个项目是干什么的。

C：Let me see. That is the charge of your calls, madam.
　　让我看一下，这是您打电话的费用，夫人。

G：Yes, I remember now. That's ok. Do you take credit cards?
　　哦，我想起来了，这就对了。你们接受信用卡吗？

C：Yes. We certainly accept credit card and what kind of card have you got?
　　是的，我们接受信用卡，您手中持有哪种信用卡？

G：I have Master Card, here you are.
　　我持有万事达卡，给你。

C：Thank you. Would you please sign your name here?
　　谢谢。请在这儿签名好吗？

G：Certainly.
　　好的。

C：Thank you, madam. Here is your receipt. We are looking forward to seeing you again, good-bye.
　　谢谢，女士。这是收据。我们希望再次为您提供服务，再见。

Ⅱ. **Position Practice 岗位实训**

★ The guest pays in cash. （客人用现金付款）
　　Here is your change and receipt. Please have a check.
　　这是找您的钱和收据，请核对。

★ The guest pay by credit card. （客人用信用卡付款）
　　1. May I take a print of your card?
　　　 能够刷一下您的卡吗？
　　2. Would you please sign your name here?
　　　 请您在这里签名好吗？
　　3. I'm afraid it is not enough to cover the amount.
　　　 恐怕卡里的金额不够。

★ Exchange foreign currency. （兑换外币）
　　1. The exchange rate of US dollar to RMB is 1∶6.4, that will be RMB 2010.
　　　 今天的汇率是1美元兑6.4元人民币，这样可以兑人民币2010元。
　　2. I'm afraid that we only offer one way change.
　　　 恐怕我们只能提供单方的兑换。
　　3. Would you like it in small or large bills?
　　　 您是要零钞还是大钞？

★ Deal with miscalculation. （处理误算）
　　1. There has been a mistake.
　　　 这里有错误。

2. I'll check it with the department concerned.
   我会跟有关部门核对。
3. I'm awfully sorry for the mistake. I assure you it won't happen again.
   对该错误我真的十分抱歉。我向您保证这样的错误不会再发生。
4. I do apologize for the mistake.
   我为发生这样的错误真诚向您道歉。

★ Bid farewell to the guest.（向客人道别）
1. I hope you enjoyed your stay with us.
   我希望您过得愉快！
2. We look forward to serving you again.
   我希望再次为您服务。

Ⅲ. Listening Practice 听力实训

★ A. Listen to the conversation and fill in the hotel bill with the information you hear.

Name		No. of Persons	
Nationality		Date	
Room Number		Rate	
1	Room Number		
2	Meals		
3		72.00	
4	City Tour		
5	Bar		
6		60.00	
7	Room Service		
8		1950.00	
9	Total		

★ B. Complete the following dialogue.

Cashier: Good morning, madam. How may I help you?

Guest: I'd like to check out now.

Cashier: _____?

Guest: Klinda Fox in Room 2306, _____.

Cashier: _____?

Guest: Yes, I had a bottle of beer.

Cashier: One moment please. Let me prepare the bill for you.

......

Cashier: _____. Your bill totals 2800 yuan, _____. Please have a check.

Guest: That's ok.

Cashier: You have paid 1000 yuan deposit, haven't you?

Guest: Yes, here's the deposit receipt.

Cashier: Then _____?

Guest: In cash, here is the money.

Cashier: Thank you, here is the receipt. _____.

Guest: Thank you, goodbye.

Cashier: Goodbye, have a nice day.

Important 特别关注

▲ Check if the guest's credit card is in the black list. If it's in the black list or the amount is not enough to cover the expenses, inform the guest to make the payment in another way.
检查客人的信用卡是否在黑名单中,发现在黑名单上或者信用卡账户上余额不足的客人,应及时通知客人改以其他方式付款。

▲ The guests are required to produce the traveler's check with his own signature and his own valid identification certificate, and countersign it on the counter. If both signatures are in conformity, cash can be withdrawn at once.
客人需出具本人签发的旅行支票及本人有效身份证件并在收银柜台当场复签,双签核对相符后即可办理兑付现金。

Section C

Case and Development 案例与创新

Case 案例

Guest: You want to check out. You noticed a mistake on the bill. You are a nonsmoker, but you are charged a pack of cigarettes. You want to know if they'll take a traveler's cheque. And that's all you have got.

Cashier: The guest wants the bill, so you tell him you'll be along in a moment. Apologize for the mistake.

Development 创新

- Do you know how many ways in which the guests usually pay their hotel bills?
- What can you do when you notice the guest is in the black list?
- Why can a cashier's work be dangerous sometimes?

技能实训 10　商务中心服务 Business Center

Section A
Basic Knowledge for Position 岗位基础知识

Ⅰ. Word Stock 语料库

business center	商务中心
typing	打字
copying	复印
copier	复印机
document	文件
original	原件
fax	传真
express	快件
EMS（Express Mail Service）	特快专递
registered letter	挂号信
enlarge	放大
reduce	缩小
folder	文件夹
air mail	航空邮件
addressee	收信人
ordinary mail	平邮
postage	邮费
zip code/postal code	邮编

Ⅱ. Pronunciation 语音训练

1. I'd like to copy my ID card/ my passport.
   我想复印我的身份证/我的护照。
2. I'd like to send a parcel. How much is the postage?
   我要寄一个包裹，邮费是多少钱？
3. How many copies would you like?
   您要复印多少份？

4. Would you like me to make a little darker or a little lighter?
   您要我把颜色调深一点还是淡一点?

5. Shall I copy these on both sides to the paper?
   我进行双面复印好吗?

6. Your original is not very clear. I can't guarantee the copy will be good.
   您的原件不太清晰,我不能保证复印件的效果很好。

7. I'm sorry. The machine is out of order.
   很抱歉,机器出了故障。

8. I'll call you as soon as the machine is fixed.
   机器一修好我就给您打电话。

9. Sending a fax to New York is 10 yuan per minute, including service charge.
   发传真到纽约每分钟10元,包括服务费。

10. Mr. Brown, this is Business Center. We have received a fax for you.
    布朗先生,这里是商务中心。我们收到给您的一份传真。

Section B

Service Procedure 服务流程

1. Greetings.
   问候。

2. Ask for the requirements of the guest.
   询问客人的服务需求。

3. Confirm the requirements and meet the guest's demand efficiently.
   确认需求并有效满足客人的需要。

4. Explain the service charge and make sure of the way of payment.
   说明资费标准并弄清付款方式。

5. Confirm the guest's name and the room number.
   确认客人姓名及房号。

6. Bid farewell to the guest.
   道别。

Ⅰ. Service Performance 服务演练

G= Guest（客人）　　　C=Clerk of Business Center（商务中心职员）

C：Good afternoon, madam. What can I do for you?
　　下午好，女士。有什么能为您效劳的吗？

G：Yes. I'd like to have these copied.
　　我想复印这些资料。

C：Certainly. How many copies would you like?
　　好的。您想复印多少份?

G：Three copies for each.
　　每张三份。

C：That's all right.
　　行。

（After a while.）（过了一会儿。）

C：Here you are.
　　给您。

G：Thanks. And can you send a fax for me?
　　谢谢。你能帮我发一份传真吗?

C：To where?
　　发往哪里?

G：To Chicago. What's the rate?
　　发往芝加哥，你们如何收费?

C：To Chicago it's 10 yuan per minute, excluding service charge.
　　发往芝加哥每分钟10元，不包括服务费。

G：OK. Please send it right now. It's urgent.
　　好的，现在就发吧，是急件。

C：No problem, madam.
　　没问题，女士。

G：Thank you.
　　谢谢。

C：How would you like to make payment, madam?
　　您想如何付款，女士?

G：Go with my room charge.
　　记入房账吧。

C：Would you please show me your room card?
　　请出示您的房卡好吗?

G：Here you are.
　　给你。

C：Thank you. Could you please sign here?
　　谢谢。请您在这儿签字好吗？

G：Sure.
　　好的。

Ⅱ. Position Practice 岗位实训

★ Type documents for guests.（为客人打印文档）

1. What font and size would you like?
   您要什么字体，几号字？
2. Shall I make the space larger?
   我把行距拉开一些好吗？
3. I'm afraid we only save it on our disks, in case of any virus.
   恐怕我们只能存在我们的磁盘上，以防有病毒。

★ Send a fax for guests.（为客人发传真）

1. The minimum charge is 20 yuan, including service charge.
   最低收费是 20 元，包括服务费。
2. Please write down the country code, the area code and his number.
   请写下国家代码、区号和对方的号码。
3. Shall I make a copy of this, and then send the copy?
   我复印一份，然后将复印件传真过去好吗？

★ Explain machine is out of order to guests.（向客人解释故障）

1. The paper is jammed.
   卡纸了。
2. It is out of ink.
   没墨了。
3. The machine is out of order.
   机器出故障了。
4. A repairman is coming to fix it soon.
   修理工很快就过来。

★ Tickets Service.（票务服务）

1. Which day's tickets would you like?
   您要哪天的票？
2. First class or economy class?
   头等舱还是经济舱？
3. One way or a round trip ticket?
   单程票还是双程票？
4. I'm afraid that flight is fully booked.
   恐怕那个航班的票已经订完了。

Ⅲ. Listening Practice 听力实训

 ★ A. Listen to the conversation and fill the information in the fax sending and receiving form.

Guest Name		Room No.	
Fax No. _____ To Country _____			
Charge _____ Payment by _____			
Signature _____			
Remarks			

★ B. Complete the following dialogue.

Clerk：Good morning，sir. _____?

Guest：Yes. I'd like you to _____ for me.

Clerk：What is it?

Guest：It's a company document.

Clerk：_____?

Guest：What do you offer?

Clerk：There are two ways，_____.

Guest：Overnight delivery. What's the charge?

Clerk：It's 20 yuan for your express mail. _____.

Guest：Here you are.

Clerk：And your telephone number?

Guest：1368871××××.

Clerk：_____?

Guest：Go with room charge please.

Clerk：That's fine. Goodbye.

Guest：Goodbye.

 Important 特别关注

▲ If you must use wireless，first determine who is providing the wireless service.
如果你要使用无线上网，首先要判断是谁提供无线服务。

▲ Don't conduct any banking or confidential business via hotel business center PC.
不要在商务中心的电脑上进行金融或保密交易。

▲ When you return to your home or office，change any passwords to accounts you may have accessed through the business center PC.

当你回到家或办公室，马上改变在商务中心用过的个人电脑上的账户密码。

▲ Keep secret. Do not tell the content of fax to any person who has nothing to do with it.

做好保密工作。不得随意向他人谈及客人的传真件内容。

Section C

Case and Development 案例与创新

Case 案例

Mr. Johnson, a hotel guest in room 1716, comes to the Business Center at 10 a.m. He asks Miss Lin to type some documents for him. Miss Lin tells him the charge will be 7 yuan per page excluding service charge. The guest wants Miss Lin to have the work done and send the documents to his room before 4 p.m..

Development 创新

• What shall you do if the guest tells you he has no time to check what you have typed?

• What shall you do when there is a fax for a guest who has checked out?

• What are the key points of fax services in the business center?

实训模块三
客房服务
Housekeeping

Housekeeping is perhaps the most important front office support department. It is responsible for cleaning the guestrooms and making them look clean, tidy and comfortable. To ensure speedy, efficient rooming of guests in vacant and ready rooms, the housekeeping and front departments must inform each other promptly of any changes in a room's status or availability. Thus it makes possible for guest to feel the heart-felt warmth and live in a comfortable temporary home.

客房部是前厅部最主要的辅助部门，主要负责客房的清洁卫生，使客房看起来清洁、整齐、舒适。为保证空房高效有序的分配，前厅和客房对房态及住房率要及时通报信息，客人才能体会到"家外之家"的温馨与舒适。

技能实训 11　打扫房间 Cleaning the Room

Section A

Basic Knowledge for Position 岗位基础知识

Ⅰ. Word Stock 语料库

room attendant	客房服务员
housekeeper	客房部经理
towel	毛巾
bathing towel	浴巾
tissue	面巾纸
toilet paper	卫生纸
soap	香皂
shampoo	洗发水
shower cap	浴帽
shower	淋浴
bathrobe	浴袍
toothbrush	牙刷
toothpaste	牙膏
hanger	衣架
sheet	床单
pillow	枕头
blanket	毯子
slippers	拖鞋
ashtray	烟灰缸
bed cover	床罩
quilt	被子
shaver	剃须刀
curtain	窗帘
mini jar	电开水壶
rubbish bin	垃圾桶

Ⅱ. Pronunciation 语音训练

1. Housekeeping. May I come in?
   客房服务，可以进来吗？
2. I'm your room attendant, I'm sorry to trouble you, may I do your room now?
   我是客房服务员，很抱歉打扰您，现在可以清理您的房间吗？
3. What time will be convenient for you, sir?
   先生，您什么时候方便？
4. Is there anything else I can do for you?
   还有其他可以为您做的吗？
5. I'm always at your service.
   我很乐意为您效劳。
6. Just a moment please. I'll bring it to your room immediately.
   稍等片刻，我马上拿到您的房间。
7. I will send a repairman to your room at once.
   我马上派一个维修人员到您房间来。

Section B

Service Procedure 服务流程

1. Knock at the door gently three time.
   轻轻地敲门三次。
2. Say："Housekeeping. May I come in?"
   问："客房服务，能进来吗？"
3. Greet the guest when allowed to get into the room.
   当得到许可进入房时向客人问候。
4. Ask the guest whether it is convenient to clean the room now.
   问客人现在能否打扫房间。
5. Clean the room.
   打扫房间。
   Open the window.
   开窗。
   Empty the rubbish bin.
   倒垃圾。

Make the bed.

整理床。

Clean the bathroom.

清洁卫生间。

Replenish the supplies.

补充客房物品。

Vacuum the floor.

吸尘。

Self-check.

检查。

6. Express your good wishes.

表达祝愿。

Ⅰ. Service Performance 服务演练

G＝Guest（客人）　　R＝Room Attendant（客房服务员）

R：(Knocking at the door three times) Housekeeping. May I come in?

（轻轻地敲三下门）客房服务，可以进来吗？

G：Come in please.

请进。

R：Good morning, sir. May I do your room now?

早上好，先生。我现在可以清理您的房间吗？

G：You'd better not. You see, we are having some friends over. We're going to have an appointment in the room.

您最好不要清理。有几个朋友马上要过来，我们将在这儿见面。

R：Certainly, sir. What time will be convenient for you?

当然可以，先生。那您什么时候方便？

G：Would you please come back in two hours?

你能够两个小时以后再过来吗？

R：No problem. I'll make up your room in two hours.

没问题，我两个小时以后过来清理您的房间。

G：That's fine. Well, our friends seem to be a little late. Would you please tidy up the bathroom? I've just taken a bath.

好的，我的朋友看来要晚点到，你能否清理一下卫生间？我刚刚洗过澡。

R：Sure, sir.

好的，先生。

(Finishing cleaning the bathroom.)（清理好卫生间之后。）

R：Is there anything else I can do for you, sir?

还有什么可以为您做的吗？

G：Oh, yes. Where can I borrow a hair-dryer?

哦，我在哪儿可以借到电吹风？

R：I'll send one up right away.

我马上给您拿一个过来。

G：Thank you. You are always friendly and helpful.

谢谢，你总是这么友好，这么乐于助人。

R：You're welcome. I'm always at your service.

不客气，很乐意为您效劳。

Ⅱ. **Position Practice 岗位实训**

★ Room Status.（客房房态）

1. VC（Vacant Clean）空房

2. VD（Vacant Dirty）走客房

3. OD（Occupied Dirty）未做住客

4. OC（Occupied Clean）已做住客

5. OOO（Out Of Order）待修房

6. ECO（Estimated Check Out）预计退房

7. NS（No Smoking）无烟房

8. S/O（Slept Out）外睡房

9. D/L（Double Lock）双锁房

10. DND（Do Not Disturb）请勿打扰

11. MUR（Make Up Room）请即打扫

12. RS（Refuse Service）拒绝服务

13. N/B（No Baggage）无行李

14. L/B（Light Baggage）少行李

15. VIP（Very Important People）重要客人

16. LSG（Long Staying Guest）长住客

17. C/O（Check Out）结账

18. C/I（Check In）入住

★ What kind of rooms will be cleaned first?（房间清扫顺序）

1. If the room occupancy is high, the room attendant will do the rooms in the following procedure: Make Up Room, VIP, Vacant Dirty, Occupied Dirty, Long Staying Guest and Vacant Clean.

开房率高时，客房打扫按下列顺序："请即打扫"房，"VIP"房，退房，住客房，长住房，空房。

2. If the room occupancy is low, the room attendant will do the rooms in the following procedure: Make Up Room, VIP, Occupied Dirty, Long Staying Guest, Vacant Dirty and Vacant Clean.

开房率低时，客房打扫按下列顺序："请即打扫"房，"VIP"房，住客房，长住房，退房，空房。

★ Knocking at the door.（敲门）

1. First check if there is "DND" sign on the door or if it is a double lock room.

首先检查一下房门是否挂着"请勿打扰"牌或上"双锁"。

2. Knock at the doors three times softly and say: " Housekeeping. "

轻轻敲三下门，同时报身份："客房服务。"

3. Wait 10 seconds to see the reactions inside. If there is no answer, please knock at the door once again.

在门外等候10秒钟，倾听房内动静，如无反应，可重复以上程序两遍。

★ Opening the door.（开门）

1. After confirming there is no one in the room, open the door slightly and say: "May I come in?" After that you can enter the room.

在确认房内无动静后，使用钥匙将门轻轻打开，报明自己的身份，询问"可以进来吗"后，方可进入。

2. If the guest is in the room, you can only enter the room with guest's permission and ask if you can do the room after greeting the guest.

如果客人在房内，要经客人同意后方可进入，并向客人问候，询问客人"是否可以打扫房间"。

★ Checking the mini bar.（检查小冰箱）

If you find the guest has assumed some drinks and wine in the mini bar, you should fill in the wine list and send it to the cashier in the front office. You should clean the mini bar as well.

发现已消费的酒水，填写酒水单，在下班时递送前台收银处并将小冰箱清洁干净。

Ⅲ. Listening Practice 听力实训

★ A. Listen to the tape and complete the conversation.

Room attendant: _____?

Guest: Come in, please.

Room attendant: Good morning, sir. _____?

Guest: Not now, I have a bad headache.

Room attendant: _____. Shall I get you a doctor?

Guest: Not necessary. Could you give me some aspirin tablets?

Room attendant: Oh, I'm sorry, _____.

Guest: I see. I just need a good rest.

Room attendant: Let me put out _____. If you remove it, I'll know you want me to clean your room.

Guest: All right.

Room attendant: _____.

★ B. Listen to the tape and tell what a room attendant should do and should not do while making up the guestroom. Write "√" for what a room attendant should do, write "×" for what a room attendant should not do.

1. vacuuming the carpet (   )
2. changing linens (   )
3. offering laundry service (   )
4. replacing the toilet needs and toilet facilities (   )
5. refilling the mini bar (   )
6. putting extra bed for the guest (   )
7. looking after the guest's child on request (   )
8. buying medicine for the guest if he doesn't feel well (   )

Important 特别关注

▲ The room attendant can tidy up the guest's documents, magazines and newspapers a bit but he should always put them in the right order and never read them.
清扫时将客人的文件、杂志、书报稍加整理，但不能弄错位置，更不能翻看。

▲ Never throw away the guest's bottles or paper boxes of cosmetic even if it is used up.
客人自带的化妆品即使用完了，也不得将空瓶或纸盒扔掉。

▲ Never touch the guest's camera, laptop computer, notebook or wallet.
特别留意不要随意触摸客人的照相机、手提式电脑、笔记本、钱包等物品。

Section C

Case and Development 案例与创新

Case 案例

New Room attendant: You have finished cleaning the room when the guest is out.

You have put the letters, documents and books in good order.

You have picked up a pair of sun glasses out of the rubbish bin and put it on the writing desk.

The phone on the night stand rings again and again. You are worried there might be something urgent for the guest. You'd like to answer the phone for the guest.

Housekeeper: You come to check the room. You tell the new room attendant that the things on the desk belong to the guest's privacy.

What is in the rubbish bin is waste forever.

You stop the room attendant from answering the phone and tell why.

Development 创新

• What is the difference in responsibility between the room attendant and the PA cleaner?

• Do you buy some medicine for the guest when he tells you he doesn't feel well, why or why not?

• What shall you do if you find a guest gets drunken and needs some help?

技能实训 12 洗衣服务 Laundry Service

Section A

Basic Knowledge for Position 岗位基础知识

I. Word Stock 语料库

laundry	洗衣店；要洗的衣服
laundry form	洗衣单
laundry bag	洗衣袋
collect your laundry	收取衣服
express service	快洗服务
dry cleaning	干洗
machine wash	机洗
hand wash	手洗
washing	水洗
do not wash	不能水洗
pressing only	干烫
same-day	同一天
valet	洗衣工
shrink	缩水
blouse	女衬衣
bow-tie	领结
evening dress	晚礼服
jacket	夹克衫
skirt	裙子
scarf	围巾
pullover	套头毛衣
sweater	毛衣
jeans	牛仔裤
T-shirt	T恤衫
socks	短袜
trousers	裤子

suit	西装
overcoat	外套
cheongsam	旗袍
pajamas	睡衣
stockings	长袜

Ⅱ. Pronunciation 语音训练

1. I have some laundry to be done.
   我有些衣服要洗。
2. My dress needs dry cleaning.
   我的衣服需要干洗。
3. My trousers need to be mended.
   我的裤子需要修补。
4. Do you have any laundry? Have you got any laundry?
   您有要洗的衣服吗?
5. May I know your name and room number?
   可以告诉我您的名字和房号吗?
6. A valet will be up in a few minutes.
   洗衣工几分钟之后就到。
7. Laundry service. May I come in?
   洗衣服务,可以进来吗?
8. I'm here to collect your laundry.
   我过来取您的衣服。
9. You can find the laundry form in the drawer of the writing desk.
   您可以在写字桌的抽屉里找到洗衣单。
10. You can leave the laundry bag in the bathroom.
    您可以把洗衣袋放在卫生间里。
11. Could you please fill in the laundry form?
    请您填写一下洗衣单好吗?
12. How would you like your laundry to be done? Dry-cleaned, washed by hand or just for press?
    您的衣服要怎么洗? 干洗,手洗,还只是熨一下?
13. The laundry will be sent back to your room by 6 p.m..
    您的衣服下午 6 点之前送回来。
14. We offer express service, but you have to pay 50% extra.
    我们提供快洗服务,但要另收 50% 的洗衣费。

15. What will be done if there is any laundry damaged?
    如果衣服洗坏了怎么办?
16. Will it shrink? Will it run in color?
    会缩水吗? 会褪色吗?
17. I'm sorry to give you so much trouble. May I have your room number please? I'll send your laundry back right away.
    很抱歉给您添了这么多的麻烦。能告诉我您的房号吗? 我马上把您的衣服送过去。

Section B

Service Procedure 服务流程

1. Greetings.
   问候。
2. Ask the guest's name and room number.
   询问客人的名字和房号。
3. Collect the laundry and laundry form.
   收取衣服及洗衣单。
   Ask the guest to fill in the laundry form.
   叫客人填写洗衣单。
   Confirm the ways of cleaning.
   确认洗涤方式。
   Any special requirements.
   看看是否有特殊要求。
4. Send the laundry back.
   送回洗好的衣服。
5. Ask the guest to check the laundry and sign the name and room number.
   叫客人核对并签上名字及房号。
6. Bid farewell to the guest.
   道别。

Ⅰ. Service Performance 服务演练

G＝ Guest（客人）   R＝Room Attendant（客房服务员）

R：Good morning. This is laundry service. What can I do for you?

上午好，这里是洗衣服务，有什么可以帮忙的吗？

G：Could you send someone up for my laundry? Room 908，Mrs. Bell.
能不能派个人过来取衣服？908房间，贝尔太太。

R：Certainly，Mrs. Bell. A valet will be with you in a few minutes.
当然可以，贝尔太太。洗衣工几分钟后就到您的房间。

G：Good. I also have a silk dress that needs to be washed. Will the color run in the wash?
好的。我还有一件丝绸的衣服得洗。洗的时候会褪色吗？

R：We'll dry clean the dress. Then the color won't run.
我们将干洗这件衣服，不会褪色的。

G：That's fine. When can I have my laundry back?
这就好了。什么时候能送回衣服？

R：Usually it takes about 12 hours to have laundry done. But would you like express service?
一般来说要12个小时。您要快洗服务吗？

G：What is the difference in price?
价格上有何区别？

R：We charge 50％ more for express，but it only takes 4 hours.
快洗服务我们另外收取50％的费用，但只需要4个小时。

G：I'll have express then. Where can I leave my laundry?
我选择快洗服务。我把我的衣服放在哪儿？

R：Please just leave it in the laundry bag in the bathroom.
把衣服放在洗衣袋里，然后放在卫生间。

G：I see. Thank you.
我明白了，谢谢。

（In the afternoon.）（下午。）

R：Laundry service. May I come in?
洗衣服务，可以进来吗？

G：Come in, please.
请进。

R：This is your laundry. Please have a check.
这是您的衣服，请核对一下。

G：How efficient you are.
你们的效率真高。

R：That's all right，madam. Would you please sign your name and room number here?
应该的，女士。在这儿签上您的名字和房号好吗？

G：Sure.

好的。

R：Is there anything I can do for you?

还有什么要我做的吗?

D：No, thank you. Bye.

不用了,谢谢,再见。

R：Bye.

再见。

Ⅱ. **Position Practice 岗位实训**

★ Confirm ways of cleaning.（确认洗涤方式）

1. How would you like your laundry to be cleaned, sir?

先生,您的衣服要怎么洗?

2. Would you like your silk shirt to be cleaned by hand?

您这件丝绸衬衫要手洗吗?

3. Is it to be dry cleaned or for pressing only?

这件是要干洗还是只要干烫?

★ Give information about laundry.（提供洗衣信息）

1. It will be ready by 6 p. m. this evening.

今天晚上 6 点前送达。

2. There is no laundry service on Sundays.

周日不提供洗衣服务。

3. Laundry collected before 10 a. m. will be returned by 6 p. m. on the same day.

早上 10 点前收取的衣服同一天的下午 6 点前送达。

4. We have a special four-hour service.

我们有 4 个小时的快洗服务。

5. We will deliver it within 4 hours at a 50% extra charge.

4 个小时内送达的衣服我们多收 50% 的费用。

★ Apologize when you can't meet the guest's need.（无法满足客人的要求时向客人道歉）

1. I'm afraid we could not remove the stain.

恐怕我们无法去掉上面的污渍。

2. I'm sorry we can do simple mending.

我们只能做一些简单的修补。

3. I'm terribly sorry we don't have the special equipment to clean leather.

真的很抱歉我们没有清洗皮料的特制设备。

★ Instructions from the guest.（来自客人的洗衣说明）

1. This sweater will shrink.

毛衣会缩水。

2. This blouse will fade.

上衣会褪色。

3. The color will run.

颜色会扩散。

4. Please use soft soap.

请使用液体皂。

5. Please do not use detergent.

请勿使用漂白剂。

6. Please wash it by itself.

请用清水漂洗。

★ Laundry Symbols on Clothes Labels.（衣服标签上的洗涤标识）

○ dry clean 干洗

⊘ do not dry-clean 不可干洗

Ⓟ compatible with any dry-cleaning methods 可用各种干洗剂干洗

⌂ iron 熨烫

⌂̷ do not iron 不可熨烫

△ bleach 可漂白

▲ do not bleach 不可漂白

⊙ tumble dry with no heat 无温状态下放进滚筒式干衣机内处理

⊠ do not tumble dry 不可放进滚筒式干衣机内处理

✋ handwash only 只能手洗

✗ do not wash 不可水洗

Ⅲ. Listening Practice 听力实训

★ A. Listen to the tape and complete the conversation.

Guest: I have some clothes to be washed. Do you have laundry service here?

Room attendant: Yes, sir. _____.

Guest: How long does it usually take to have laundry done?

Room attendant: Usually it takes one day, but _____

_____.

Guest: What's the difference in price?

Room attendant: _____.

Guest: Where can I leave my laundry?

Room attendant: Just _____. Be sure not to forget to

_____ .

Guest: I see. Just one more thing, what is there is any _____?

Room attendant: In such a case, the hotel will pay for it, but the indemnity should not _____ .

Guest: That's OK. I hope that won't happen.

Room attendant: Don't worry. The valets are experienced in their work.

★ B. Listen to the tape and tell what a laundry attendant should do and should not do while collecting laundry. Write "√" for what a laundry attendant should do, write "×" for what a laundry attendant should not do.

1. Check if there is any damage on the clothes. (　　)
2. Check if there are any items left in the pockets. (　　)
3. Confirm the number of clothes. (　　)
4. Check the laundry list. (　　)
5. Check the washing method carefully, especially special costuming. (　　)
6. If there is any missing button, the laundry attendant should mend it for the guest. (　　)
7. The laundry attendant will pay for the damage of the laundry. (　　)
8. There will be no extra charge for express service in laundry. (　　)

Important 特别关注

▲ If DND sign is put on the door of a hotel room, no one shall bother the guest.
　如果门上挂着"请勿打扰"的牌子，没有人可以打扰客人。

▲ Tell the guest not to forget to fill in the laundry form, otherwise our list must be accepted as correct.
　告诉客人别忘了填写洗衣单，否则以饭店计数为准。

▲ The hotel is not responsible for valuables in pockets or fastened to garment.
　对于袋内或系于服装上的贵重物品，酒店概不负责。

Section C

Case and Development 案例与创新

Case 案例

Guest: You have some laundry to be done. Find out if someone can come to your room to collect your laundry. You want to know when you can get it back. You are checking out at 1:00 tomorrow afternoon and need to have it by then.

Housekeeper: The laundry is closed now. There's a laundry bag in the top dresser drawer. If the guest puts his laundry in the bag and leaves it behind the door, the attendant will pick it up early tomorrow morning. He can get the clothes back tomorrow afternoon around 4:00. It won't be possible before 4:00 unless he asks for express service.

Development 创新

- Who should be responsible for the money left in the guest's pocket when a room maid is collecting the laundry?
- How will the hotel make some compensation for the damage done in the laundry?
- If you can't find the guest's mis-delivered laundry, what should you do?

技能实训 13　客房送餐服务 Room Service

Section A

Basic Knowledge for Position 岗位基础知识

Ⅰ. Word Stock 语料库

steak sandwich	牛排三明治
club sandwich	总会三明治
black coffee	清咖啡
white coffee	奶咖啡
French fries	薯条
fruit salad	水果色拉
green salad	蔬菜色拉
dessert	甜点
hot cupboard	保温柜
lamb curry	咖喱羊肉
snack	小吃
fried noodles	炒面
fresh juice	新鲜果汁
trolley	餐车

Ⅱ. Pronunciation 语音训练

1. You may dial 8, then ask for room service.
   请您先拨 8，然后告诉送餐服务台。

2. Room service is available 24 hours a day.
   客房送餐服务一天 24 小时都提供。

3. Breakfast is served from 7:30 to 10:00 a.m., lunch and dinner served from 11:00 a.m. to 12:00 p.m..
   早餐从上午 7:30 供应到 10 点整，午餐和晚餐是上午 11 点供应到晚上 12 点。

4. There is an extra service charge of 15% for room service.
   客房送餐服务要加收 15% 的服务费。

5. What kind of juice would you like, orange juice or papaya juice?
   您喜欢哪种果汁，是橘子汁还是木瓜汁？

6. How would you like your eggs, soft boiled or hard boiled?
   您点的蛋要怎么做？煮得嫩一点还是老一点？
7. How would you like your steak to be cooked? Rare, medium or well-done?
   您点的牛排要怎么烧？三分熟、五分熟还是全熟？
8. Would you prefer rolls or toast?
   您想要早餐包还是烤面包？
9. May I have your name and room number pleasc?
   告诉我您的名字和房号好吗？
10. Shall I serve the soup, sir?
    先生，要我给您上汤吗？
11. Do you have a pen handy?
    您手边有笔吗？
12. I'm afraid there might be a short delay, madam. It's very busy today.
    对不起，女士，可能要等一会，今天特别忙。
13. Your food should be with you in twenty minutes, sir.
    先生，您的菜20分钟可以送到。
14. Would you care to ring room service when you have finished your meal, sir?
    当您用完餐的时候您介意拨打送餐服务吗？

Section B

Service Procedure 服务流程

1. Greetings.
   问候。
2. What the guest would like to have.
   客人要点什么。
3. The guest's name and room number.
   客人的名字和房号。
4. Make confirmation.
   确认。
5. Tell the guest how long it will take to prepare for the order.
   告诉客人送餐需要多长时间。
6. Deliver the food to the guest's room.
   送餐到客人房间。

7. Speak out the order and give the bill to the guest.

报点餐，把账单给客人。

8. Ask the guest to sign his name and room number.

要求客人签上姓名和房号。

9. Express your wishes.

表达祝愿。

Ⅰ. Service Performance 服务演练

G＝Guest（客人）　　R＝Room Service Waiter（送餐服务员）

R：Good evening. Room service. Can I help you?

晚上好，送餐服务。要我帮您吗？

G：Yes, It's Mr. Wang. Could I order something to eat, please?

是的，我是王先生，我想点些吃的东西，可以吗？

R：Of course, sir. May I have your room number?

当然可以，先生。请告诉我您的房号好吗？

G：My room number is 618.

我的房号是618。

R：What would you like to have, sir?

先生，您要点什么？

G：I'd like to have a plate of lamb curry.

我要一盘咖喱羊肉。

R：Er, I'm afraid that's not on our light snack menu.

呃，不好意思，我们的小吃单上没有这个菜。

G：But it's in the room service menu.

可是客房服务菜单上有啊。

R：Yes, sir, but I'm afraid that menu only applies up till midnight. It's one o'clock, sir.

是有，先生，可是那个菜单上的菜只供应到半夜。现在是1点钟了，先生。

G：Oh, OK. So what can I have, then?

哦，好的，那我能吃到什么呢？

R：We have a lot of toasted sandwiches and light dishes you can choose.

我们有各种烤三明治和小吃供您选择。

G：Could you do me a club sandwich?

你们能给我来个总会三明治吗？

R：Yes, sir. And would you like a drink to go with that, sir?

当然可以，先生。您还要来点佐餐饮料吗？

G：Some black coffee, please.

来壶清咖啡吧。

R：So that's a club sandwich and a pot of black coffee, sir?

那么您点的是一份总会三明治和一壶清咖啡，对吗？

G：Yes, that's right. When will it be ready?

对，没错。请问什么时候送到？

R：You should get it in about 15 minutes.

15分钟左右就能给您送去。

G：Fine. Thanks a lot. Good-bye.

好的，多谢。再见。

R：Good-bye.

再见。

Ⅱ. Position Practice 岗位实训

★ Taking room service orders over the phone.（受理送餐电话预订）

1. Could you send up a club sandwich, please?

   能送一个总会三明治过来吗？

2. Can you bring me up a plate of lamb curry, please?

   能否送一盘咖喱羊肉过来？

3. Could you do me a steak sandwich, please?

   能否给我做一个牛肉三明治？

★ Checking and confirming a room service order.（核对和确认订菜单）

1. Can I just read that back to you, sir? That's a steak sandwich and a beer. Is that correct, sir?

   我把它报给您听一下好吗？一份牛肉三明治和一瓶啤酒，对吗？

2. I'll just read it back to you, sir. That's a fried noodles and an orange juice. Is that right, sir?

   先生，我报给您听一下。一份炒面和一杯橙汁，对吗？

3. So that's a club sandwich and a pot of white coffee, madam?

   您点的是一个总会三明治和一壶奶咖，女士？

★ Apologizing in advance.（先行致歉）

1. I'm terribly sorry, but we only serve local drinks, sir.

   先生，很抱歉，我们只供应当地的饮料。

2. I'm afraid that's not on the menu, Madam.

   恐怕不在菜单上，女士。

3. I'm afraid the room service is not in operation, sir.

   恐怕送餐服务现在暂停，先生。

4. I'm terribly sorry, sir, but there is no electricity at the moment.

很抱歉，现在没电，先生。

★ Send food to rooms. （送餐进房间）

1. Where can I put the tray, sir?

   先生，请问托盘放在哪儿？

2. Shall I serve it now or shall I leave it in the hot cupboard?

   要我现在就端出来还是把它放在保温柜里？

3. Would you please sign the bill, please?

   麻烦您把账单签一下好吗？

4. If you prefer, you can leave the tray outside.

   如果您愿意，可以把托盘放在门外。

Ⅲ. Listening Practice 听力实训

★ A. Listen to the conversation and take room service orders.

Bali Palace Hotel
Room Service Orders

Room Number _____

Guest's Name _____

Order

_____

_____

_____

_____

Taken by _____

★ B. Complete the following dialogue.

Room Service：Room Service.

Guest：Come in please.

Room Service：Thank you, madam. _____?

Guest：Yes, sure.

Room Service：_____?

Guest：Yes, that's right. That looks great.

Room service：_____?

Guest：OK! Do you have a pen handy?

Room Service：Here you are, madam.

Guest：Thanks... OK?

Room Service: Yes, madam. _____? They'll come and collect the tray.

Guest: Thank you. I'll do that.

Room Service: Goodbye, madam. _____.

Guest: Thank you. Goodbye.

Important 特别关注

▲ The guest can get the room service by telephone or by doorknob menu.
客人可以通过电话或者填写门把菜单来获得客房送餐服务。

▲ If there is a minimum charge or service charge, you have to explain it clearly in advance.
如果有最低消费或服务费,跟客人预先说清楚。

▲ Sometimes room service waiters serve cocktail parties or dinner in the guest rooms. They are salesmen as well as waiters.
有时候送餐服务员还会在客人的房间里给客人举办鸡尾酒会或送晚餐。他们既可以是销售人员也可以是服务员。

Section C

Case and Development 案例与创新

Case 案例

Mr. Roberts in Room 605 wants to order two steaks with French fries and a bottle of red wine. The clerk of room service answers the phone and accepts the order. She assures the guest the order will be ready in 20 minutes. The room attendant sends the order to the guest's room and asks him to sign the bill.

Development 创新

• To which department does room service belong?

• Do you think it necessary to tell the guest how long it will take to deliver food to his room?

• What shall you ask the guest to do when he wants to add the cost of room service to the room bill?

技能实训 14　维修服务 Maintenance Service

Section A

Basic Knowledge for Position 岗位基础知识

I. Word Stock 语料库

faucet	水龙头
furniture	家具
washing basin	洗脸盆
mirror	镜子
curtain	窗帘
blanket	毛毯
drawer	抽屉
broad band	宽带
bedside light	床头灯
floor lamp	地灯
table lamp	台灯
mini bar	小冰箱
mini-jar	电开水壶
fax machine	传真机
air-conditioner	空调
central air heating/conditioning	中央空调
cipher code	密码
smoker sensor	烟感器
safety deposit box	保险柜
bedside control panel	床头控制板

II. Pronunciation 语音训练

1. I'm very annoyed. My TV isn't working.
   我很恼火，我的电视机坏了。
2. I'm very annoyed. There are not towels in the bathroom.
   我很恼火，卫生间里没有毛巾。

3. It's just not good enough. There's a large pool of water on the floor.
   房间可真差劲，地板上有一大摊水。
4. There's a terrible smell in my bathroom.
   我的卫生间里有一股难闻的气味。
5. The air-conditioner/heating system isn't working.
   空调、暖气坏了。
6. I'm very sorry. I'll make sure the room attendant cleans your room at once.
   真抱歉，我一定马上让客房服务员打扫您的房间。
7. I'm terribly sorry. I'll send an engineer straight up.
   非常抱歉，我马上派工程师来。
8. Please investigate and carry out repairs as soon as possible.
   请尽快调查并进行修理。
9. I'll have someone fix them for you right away.
   我马上派人给您修理。
10. I'll ask the Maintenance Department to look into it at once.
    我马上叫工程部派人来检查。
11. We do apologize for the inconvenience.
    我们很抱歉给您带来不便。
12. It takes time to repair. I'm afraid you have to change to another room.
    修理需要时间。恐怕您得换个房间了。

Section B

Service Procedure 服务流程

1. Greetings.
   问候。
2. Listen to what the guest says patiently.
   耐心听客人述说。
3. Make apologies to the guest and get the guest's room number.
   向客人道歉并问清房号。
4. Tell the guest what will be done immediately.
   告知客人马上要采取的对策。
5. Inform the Maintenance Department to repair at once.
   马上通知维修部进行修理。

6. Repairman comes to offer service for the guest.

维修人员上门服务。

7. Say sorry and repair.

道歉并进行维修。

8. Tell the guest that the problem has been solved.

告诉客人问题解决了。

9. Express good wishes to the guest.

表达祝愿。

Ⅰ. Service Performance 服务演练

R = Room Attendant（客房服务员）　　G = Guest（客人）　　E = Electrician（电工）

R：Good afternoon, sir. What can I do for you?

先生，下午好，能够为您做什么？

G：I'm afraid there's something wrong with the TV. The picture is wobbly.

恐怕我的电视机出问题了，图像在晃动。

R：I'm sorry, sir. May I have your room number?

先生，很抱歉，请告知您的房号好吗？

G：Yes, Room 815, Mr. White.

好的，815房间，怀特先生。

R：I'll inform the Maintenance Department at once. We can have it repaired. Please wait just a few minutes, Mr. White.

我马上通知维修部。怀特先生，我们能修好的，请稍等几分钟。

(Five minutes later, there is a knock on the door.)（五分钟之后，有人敲门。）

E：Maintenance, may I come in?

维修部，可以进来吗？

G：(Opening the door) Yes, please.

（打开门）请进吧。

E：Hello, Mr. White. The TV set is not working well, is it?

您好，怀特先生。电视机不能正常工作是吗？

G：No, it isn't.

是的，坏了。

E：Let me check it. (He finishes the repairing.) Mr. White, everything is OK now. Is there anything else I can do for you?

让我检查一下。（他修完了之后）怀特先生，现在好了，还有什么需要我做的吗？

G：No, thanks. What efficiency! (Taking out some money.) This is for you.

没有了，效率真高。（拿出一些钱）这是给您的。

E: Oh, no. We won't accept tips, but thank you anyway. We wish you a nice stay with us.
哦，我们不收小费的，但还是谢谢您。祝您在这儿过得愉快！

Ⅱ. Position Practice 岗位实训

★ Four categories of Maintenance. （维修的四种类型）

1. Preventive room maintenance 房间保养.
2. Preventive equipment maintenance 设备保养.
3. Routine repairs based on work-orders 按工作程序的日常维修.
4. Emergencies 紧急事件.

★ Emergency annoucement. （紧急通知）

May I have your attention, please? This is emergency. The hotel is on fire now. Please leave your room immediately and follow the emergency exist. Please leave this building immediately. Thank you for your cooperation.

紧急事故，请注意！酒店发生火灾。请立刻离开房间，从紧急出口撤离。请马上离开酒店。谢谢您的合作。

★ About Emergency Exit. （关于紧急出口）

When a guest has checked in into a hotel and escorted by a bellman to his room, he should first look for information in his room about fire safety and locate nearest fire exit. Find one at each end of the hallway. How many doors away? Does the door open easily? Are the exit signs illuminated? If the lights are out, be helpful and contact the Front Desk to let them know.

当客人在酒店登记入住并由行李员带到房间后，他应该立刻寻找他房间里关于消防安全的信息并确定最近的逃生通道。从走廊的两端各找一个。看看距离房间几扇门？通道的门容易打开吗？紧急出口的标识通亮吗？如果灯光熄灭了，一定要通知前厅部。

★ How to use the safety deposit box in the room. （怎样使用房间内的保险箱）

First open the safe. When "Open" is showed, you must inset the code by inputting six-digit password. Then you can put your valuables inside and close the safe. At that time "Lock" will be showed. Remember your password you set otherwise it will cause you much trouble.

首先打开保险箱。当显示"Open"字样时，您得输入六位阿拉伯数字来设定密码。然后放入贵重物品并关上门，这时会出现"Lock"字样。您千万要记住自己设置的密码，否则就麻烦了。

Ⅲ. Listening Practice 听力实训

★ A. Listen to the tape and complete the conversation.

Repairman：(Knocking at the door) _____?

Guest: Yes, come in please.

Repairman: Good afternoon, sir. _____?

Guest: The air-conditioner doesn't work, it is terribly hot.

Repairman: I'm sorry, sir. Let me have a look. Oh, _____ . I'll change one for you.

Guest: Thank you. By the way, there is something wrong with the faucet. I can't turn off the faucet above the washbasin.

Repairman: _____ .

Guest: How long shall I have to wait?

Repairman: About fifteen minutes.

Guest: OK.

Repairman: Everything is all right, sir. _____ .

Guest: That's OK. Thank you very much.

★ B. Listen to the tape and make out what a room attendant should do and what a repairman should do. Write "RA" for room attendant, write "R" for repairman.

1. Making beds in guestrooms. (   )
2. Changing a burnt-out light bulb in a lamp in the guestroom. (   )
3. Polishing the guest's leather shoes. (   )
4. Sending another pair of slippers to the guestroom. (   )
5. Air conditioners must be cleaned or replaced regularly. (   )
6. Be responsible for electrical and plumbing systems. (   )
7. Guest is ill and sends for a doctor. (   )
8. Mini bar in the guestroom is out of order. (   )

Important 特别关注

▲ Report any problems requiring repair or maintenance as soon as you oberve them.
看到任何需要维修或保养的问题都要及时反映。

▲ Safety means preventing accidents which can harm both, employees and guest.
安全就意味着要防止任何危害员工和客人的事故发生。

▲ Accidents are caused by someone's carelessness; they are unplanned or unforeseen events.
事故是由粗心导致的，它们无法计划，无法预计。

▲ A lack of preventive maintenance and attention to detail lie as the root cause of many emergencies.
缺少保养，忽视细节是导致紧急事件发生的真正原因。

▲ In case of fire or other accidents, keep calm and inform the Reception immediately, then evacuate through fire escape.

如发生火灾或其他意外事件时，请勿惊慌，立即通知前厅，并按安全疏散路线迅速撤离。

▲ The Chief Maintenance Engineer must be willing to respond to emergencies, even if after hours.

维修总工程师必须对紧急事件做出应急反应，哪怕是在下班后。

Section C

Case and Development 案例与创新

Case 案例

You are a guest. You are not satisfied with your room. The air-conditioner is too noisy. You'd like the room attendant to change the room for you.

You're a room attendant. You listen carefully to the guest's complaint and make a note of that. You apologize to him and phone the Reception Desk to see if there is room available. You promise to have the room repaired at once. Repairman will arrive in five minutes.

Development 创新

• What are the duties of the Maintenance Department staff?

• How do you understand the saying about emergencies "your poor planning becoming my crisis"?

• What are the new challenges that the Maintenance Department face nowadays?

实训模块四

餐饮服务
Food and Beverage

The Food and Beverage service is the 2nd major activity of most hotels and in many of them it accounts for a larger proportion of employees than other services. This is because meals in hotels may be supplied to nonresidents as well as to resident guests and the provision of meals is relatively labor intensive.

餐饮服务是大部分酒店的第二主业，比起服务部门，餐饮部需要雇用更多的人手。这是因为酒店的餐饮在招待住店客人的同时，也接待非住店的客人，而且餐饮是相对劳动密集型的部门。

技能实训 15 餐台预订 Reservations

Section A

Basic Knowledge for Position 岗位基础知识

I. Word Stock 语料库

Good Day Restaurant	好时光餐厅
Good Luck Restaurant	好运来餐厅
Happy Hours Restaurant	幸福时光餐厅
Lily Restaurant	百合餐厅
White Swan Restaurant	白天鹅餐厅
Black Rose Restaurant	黑玫瑰餐厅
Chinese Restaurant	中餐厅
Western Restaurant	西餐厅
waiter/waitress	男侍应生/女侍应生
Korean Cooking	韩国菜
Japanese Cooking	日本菜
Tai Cooking	泰国菜
Chinese food/Western food	中餐/西餐
speciality restaurant	风味餐厅
tea house	茶室
coffee shop	咖啡馆
snack bar	小吃吧
cafeteria	自助式餐厅
excluding drinks	不包含酒水
including drinks	包含酒水
minimum consumption	最低消费
recommend	介绍
cuisine	菜谱,菜系
off season	淡季
peak season	旺季
guarantee	保证

Ⅱ. Pronunciation 语音训练

1. What time would you like your table, sir?
   先生，订在什么时间？

2. For how many people?
   有多少人？

3. Would you like a table in the hall or in a private room?
   您是喜欢大厅的餐台还是包间呢？

4. At what time will you arrive here?
   您几点光临？

5. I'm afraid we are fully booked for that time.
   恐怕我们那段时间已经订满了。

6. Would you like to be put on waiting list?
   您愿意排在等候名单中吗？

7. Let me check if we have any vacancy.
   我查一下看看是否有空位。

8. Just a moment please. I'll check the record for you.
   请稍候，我看一下预订记录。

9. May I have your name and telephone number, please?
   请告诉我您的名字和电话号码好吗？

10. So that's a table for 10 on Sunday evening, is that right?
    您订的是周日晚上的 10 个人的位置，是吗？

11. Thank you for calling. We're expecting to serve you soon.
    谢谢来电，我们期待着早点为您服务。

12. The minimum charge for a private room is 200 yuan per person.
    包厢最低消费是每人 200 元。

Section B

Service Procedure 服务流程

1. Greetings.
   问候。

2. Ask the information about table reservation, such as the date and number of people, arrival time, the guest's name and telephone number.
   询问预订信息，诸如就餐日期、人数、抵达时间、客人的名字及联系电话等。

3. Make confirmation about reservation.

   确认预订。

4. Express your expectation to the guest.

   表达对客人的期盼。

Ⅰ. Service Performance 服务演练

C＝Reservation Clerk（预订人员）　　G＝Guest（客人）

C：Good morning, Black Rose Restaurant. Can I help you?

　　早上好，黑玫瑰餐厅。能够为您做什么？

G：Yes, I'd like to book a table for dinner.

　　我想订餐。

C：Certainly. What time would you like your table?

　　好的。请问您什么时候用餐？

G：This Saturday evening.

　　这个周六晚上。

C：How large a group are you expecting?

　　你们一共有多少个人？

G：Six couples.

　　六对夫妇。

C：Just a moment please, sir. I'll check the reservation for you.

　　请稍等，先生。我查一下预订记录。

G：May I have a private room?

　　我能够订一间包厢吗？

C：I'm afraid not, sir. All the private rooms are occupied. Would you like to have a table in the hall?

　　恐怕不行，先生。所有的包厢都订满了。大厅里订一张桌行吗？

G：Ok. Would you do me a favor to book a table a little bit quiet?

　　好吧。你能否帮忙订一个安静点的位置？

C：Sure. I'll book the table by the window for you.

　　当然可以。我把靠窗户的位置给您。

G：Thank you.

　　谢谢。

C：And what time can we expect you, sir?

　　你们什么时候到达餐厅？

G：At about 6 o'clock.

　　大约6点钟。

C：May I have your name and telephone number?

请告诉我您的名字和电话号码好吗？

G：My name is Ron Kollitz, K-O-L-L-I-T-Z, and my telephone number is 13956678×××.

我叫 Ron Kollitz, K-O-L-L-I-T-Z, 我的电话是 13956678×××.

C：Thank you. So that's a table for six couples in the name of Mr. Kollitz on Saturday evening, your phone number is 13956678×××... is that right?

谢谢。Kollitz 先生预订这个周六晚上一桌 12 人的晚餐，您的电话号码是 13956678×××，对吗？

G：Yes, that's right.

没错。

C：Thank you for your calling sir. We're looking forward to serving you soon.

谢谢您的来电，先生。我们期待着早点为您服务。

Ⅱ. Position Practice 岗位实训

★ Four different reservations.（四种不同的预订方式）

1. Face to face reservation.

   面对面预订。

2. Telephone reservation.

   电话预订。

3. Fax reservation.

   传真预订。

4. Internet reservation.

   网上预订。

In whatever way the reservation is made by the guest, you are supposed to confirm the following information about the arrival time, the number of the guests, the name and telephone number of the person who makes the reservation.

无论客人用何种方式预订用餐，你都要确认以下信息：客人抵达餐厅时间，来用餐的人数，预订人的姓名和电话号码。

★ Banquet reservation.（宴会预定）

1. May I know what the banquet is for?

   请问这个宴会是什么类型的？

2. How much would you like to spend for each person?

   请问每个人的标准是多少？

3. How would you like us to set up the banquet?

   您想要我们怎么布置宴会呢？

4. There's a minimum charge 3000 yuan for each table.
   每桌最低消费 3000 元。
5. Is there anything special you'd like to have on the menu?
   您对菜单有什么特殊要求?
6. How would you like to make payment, madam?
   女士,请问您用何种方式付款?
7. We'll fax the banquet menu and details to you tomorrow.
   明天我们把菜单和宴会细节传真给您。

★ Refuse a reservation politely. (婉拒预订)

1. I'm afraid we're fully booked for tonight.
   很抱歉,今天晚上全部预订满了。
2. Would you like to make a reservation at another restaurant in our hotel?
   您是否愿意在我们酒店的另一家餐厅订餐?
3. Shall I transfer your call, Madam?
   能够把您的电话转接过去吗?
4. Would you like to be put on the waiting list?
   您愿意被放在等候名单中吗?

★ Giving information about restaurant. (告知营业信息)

1. We are open round the clock.
   我们 24 个小时营业。
2. We are open until 10:00 p.m., but our last order for dinner is at 9:00 p.m..
   我们一直营业到晚上 10 点,但晚餐点菜的截止时间是 9 点。
3. We serve a great variety of popular Chinese dishes in table d'hote and a la carte.
   我们供应各种各样的中国名菜,有套菜也有点菜。

Ⅲ. Listening Practice 听力实训

★ A. Listen to the tape, decide what each short dialogue is about and mark (√) where appropriate.

	Bar	Cafe	Restaurant	Cafeteria	Banquet Hall
Dialogue 1					
Dialogue 2					
Dialogue 3					
Dialogue 4					
Dialogue 5					

★ B. Complete the following conversation.

Reservationist: Babylon Hotel. Can I help you?
Caller: Yes. Could I make a booking at the Bay view Restaurant?
Reservationist: Certainly, madam. _____?
Caller: It's for me and my husband on Friday the twenty-third.
Reservationist: _____. In what name, please?
Caller: Hudson.
Reservationist: Ms. Hudson. Thank you, madam. _____?
Caller: 7:30.
Reservationist: _____. That's a table for two at 7:30 on Friday the twenty-third _____.
Caller: Yes, that's correct.
Reservationist: Thank you very much, Ms. Hudson.
Caller: Thank you. Goodbye.
Reservationist: Goodbye.

Important 特别关注

▲ If the restaurant has minimum charge, you should make it clear in advance to the person who makes the reservation.
如果餐厅有最低消费限制，要事先跟预订人说清楚。

▲ For a large-scale or an important banquet reservation, a face-to-face talk is suggested.
如果是大规模或重要的宴会预订，就需要面对面的商谈。

Section C

Case and Development 案例与创新

Case 案例

Guest: You would like to book a table for 6 in Maya Restaurant of Hone Xing Hotel on Saturday evening. You want the table in the non-smoking area with the windowseat. And a baby seat is also needed.

Reservation Clerk: You answer the phone on Thursday afternoon. And put down the reservation as required.

Development 创新

• If your restaurant is fully booked for the time the guest reserves, what would you say to him? what kind of suggestions do you usually make?

• Do you repeat the reservation for confirmation, why or why not?

• If it is a banquet reservation, what are the main points you have to make sure?

技能实训 16　餐厅迎客服务 Receiving Diners

Section A

Basic Knowledge for Position 岗位基础知识

Ⅰ. Word Stock 语料库

individual	散客；零星的
diner	就餐者
head waiter, head waitress	领班
supervisor	主管
smoking area	吸烟区
non-smoking area	非吸烟区
arrange	安排
meal voucher	餐券
extra	额外的，另加的
Food and Beverage Manager	餐饮部经理
Catering/Banquet Manager	宴会厅经理
Restaurant Supervisor	餐厅主管

Ⅱ. Pronunciation 语音训练

1. Good evening. Welcome to our restaurant.
   晚上好，欢迎光临我们的餐厅。

2. Do you have a reservation, sir?
   先生，请问您有预订吗？

3. How many, please?
   一共几位？

4. Are there only two of you?
   就你们两位吗？

5. May I have your name and phone number?
   可以告诉我您的名字和电话号码吗？

6. Just a moment please, I'll check the record.
   请稍等，我查一下记录。

7. Yes, a table for two under the name of Bill Smith.
   是的，Bill Smith 订的两个人的餐桌。

8. Would you come with me, please?
   请跟我来。

9. Would you prefer to sit by the window?
   您喜欢靠窗户的位置吗?

10. Yes, we have booked a table for you.
    是的，我们给您预订了一张桌。

11. Will this table be all right for you, madam?
    女士，这张桌子可以吗?

12. I'm afraid that table has been booked.
    恐怕这张桌子已经被预订了。

13. Take your time, please.
    请慢慢来。

14. A waiter will come to take your order.
    服务生会过来给您点单。

15. Would you mind sharing a table?
    您在意拼桌吗?

16. It's rather busy at the moment.
    现在很忙。

17. Sorry, the restaurant is full. Would you try some Western food?
    对不起，本餐厅已满座。您能否改为品尝西餐?

Section B

Service Procedure 服务流程

1. Greetings.
   问候。

2. Ask the guest whether he has a reservation.
   询问客人是否有预订。

3. Check the reservation record if there is a reservation.
   如果有预订查一下预订记录。

4. Arrange a table for a guest without a reservation.
   给没有预订的客人安排餐台。

5. Show the way.
   带路。
6. Ask the guest to take a seat.
   安排入座。
7. Inform the guest the waiter will be with him soon.
   告知客人服务生很快就到。

Ⅰ. Service Performance 服务演练

H＝Hostess（迎宾员）　　G＝Guest（客人）

H：Good evening, ladies and gentlemen. Welcome to our restaurant. Are you the members of the same group?
　　晚上好，女士们先生们，欢迎光临。你们大家是一起的吗？

G：Yes, we are. We have a reservation in your restaurant.
　　是的。我们有预订的。

H：May I know who made the reservation, please?
　　请告诉我是谁预订的好吗？

G：Mr. Thompson.
　　汤普森先生。

H：OK. Let me have a check. Yes, your table is in private room 615. This way, please.
　　好的，我查一下。是的，你们的餐桌在615包厢。请这边走。

G：Thank you.
　　谢谢。

H：Will this table be all right?
　　这张餐桌行吗？

G：I think so.
　　可以。

H：Please take your seats.
　　请就座。

G：Miss, are the drinks included in the minimum charge?
　　小姐，请问酒水含在最低消费中吗？

H：No, I'm afraid you'll have to pay extra for drinks.
　　不含的，恐怕您得另外付酒水。

G：Yes, I will. I'd like to have a look at the menu.
　　好的，我想看看菜单。

H：Just a moment, please. Here is the menu. You can choose what you like from the menu. The waitress will take your order later.
　　请稍等。这是菜单，您可以随便选，服务生过会给您点单。

G：Thanks a lot.

多谢。

H：You're welcome. I hope you will enjoy your meal.

不客气，希望你们在这儿用餐愉快！

Ⅱ. Position Practice 岗位实训

★ Telling the guest there isn't a table. （告诉客人餐厅客满）

1. I'm sorry, there aren't any tables left for... would you please wait in the waiting room?

   很抱歉，现在没有桌位了，您愿意在等候室等吗？

2. I'm sorry, the restaurant is full now.

   很抱歉，餐厅坐满了。

3. We can seat you in 15 minutes.

   我们可以在15分钟之后给您安排座位。

4. Would you care to have a drink in the lounge while you wait? We'll accommodate your party as soon as possible.

   您愿意在休息室喝杯东西等候吗？我们将尽快安排你们入座。

★ Receiving guests with a reservation. （迎接有预订的客人）

1. Do you have a reservation?

   请问您有预订吗？

2. May I have your name, please?

   请问您贵姓？

3. I'm afraid the table you reserved is not ready yet.

   恐怕您预订的餐桌还没有准备好。

4. We're expecting you.

   我们正在恭候您的光临。

★ Arranging the table for the guest. （给客人安排餐桌）

1. Would you mind sharing a table?

   您介意和别人同桌吗？

2. Would you mind sitting separately?

   你们是否介意分开坐？

3. I'm afraid that table is reserved.

   恐怕那张桌子已经有人预订了。

4. Would you prefer smoking area or non-smoking area?

   您想坐在吸烟区还是无烟区？

★ Table d'hote and a la carte. （套餐及零点餐）

1. Table d'hôte means the restaurant menu offers 3 or more courses for one price;

usually consisting of appetizer, two or three choices of main course and dessert. Beverages are not usually included.

套菜指的是餐厅菜单中以设定的价格提供三道或者三道以上的菜肴，通常包括开胃小吃，两到三种可供选择的主食及甜点。酒水一般不包含。

2. A la carte means that a guest orders his items individually according to the menu and each item has its own separate charge on the bill.

零点餐指的是客人根据菜单一道一道点菜，每一道菜价格都是分开的。

Ⅲ. Listening Practice 听力实训

★ A. Listen to the conversation and tell different features of four main cuisines.

Four Main Cuisines	Features
Guangdong Cuisine	
Sichuan Cuisine	
Shandong Cuisine	
Huaiyang Cuisine	

★ B. Complete the following the conversation.

Clerk: Good evening, sir. Welcome to our restaurant.
Diner: Good evening. I'd like a table for five, please.
Clerk: _____?
Diner: No, I'm afraid not.
Clerk: This way, please.
...
Clerk: _____.
Diner: Well, I prefer a table by the window.
Clerk: I'm sorry, but _____.
Diner: Oh, I see. We'll have to make up with this one.
Clerk: _____.
Diner: Can we smoke?
Clerk: Sorry, this is _____.
Diner: OK.
Clerk: Hers is the menu. _____.
Diner: Thank you.

Important 特别关注

▲ To avoid making guests feel embarassed and unpleasant, you should explain it to the guests politely if there are special clothing requirements in some luxury hotels.
有的高档餐厅对客人有着装上的要求,这时要向客人礼貌地说明,以免造成尴尬和不快。

▲ To avoid ignoring communications with other guests, couples are not arranged to seat together having small talks in formal banquets.
西餐正式宴会中,餐位的安排一般是夫妇不坐在一起,以免各自聊家常而忽略与其他宾客间的交际。

Section C

Case and Development 案例与创新

Case 案例

Guest: You come into a crowded restaurant. You haven't made any reservation. You don't like the table the hostess offers you, because it's too close to the toilet. You don't mind sharing the table with other people.

Hostess: You greet the guest and seat him. If he doesn't like the table near the toilet, ask him to share the table with other people.

Development 创新

- What's the job of a hostess? Who also greets and sends off the guest?
- What should be kept in mind when a hostess arranges seats?
- What can you do for the guest if there is an overbooking in your restaurant?

技能实训 17　中餐厅服务 At a Chinese Restaurant

Section A

Basic Knowledge for Position 岗位基础知识

Ⅰ. Word Stock 语料库

Shandong cuisine	鲁菜
Guangdong cuisine	粤菜
Sichuan cuisine	川菜
Hunan cuisine	湘菜
Jiangsu cuisine	苏菜
Zhejiang cuisine	浙菜
Fujiang cuisine	闽菜
Anhui cuisine	徽菜
boil	水煮
steam	蒸
braise	焖
stir	炒
fry	煎
deep fry	炸
smoke	烟熏
roast	烤
stew	煨，炖
bake	烘焙
preserve	腌制
barbecue	烧烤
rice wine	米酒
ginger	生姜
garlic	大蒜
shallot	葱
vinegar	醋
soy sauce	酱油

salt	盐
pepper	胡椒
sugar	糖
SMG	味精
still wine	酿造酒，如 Japanese sake（日本清酒）
distilled wine	蒸馏酒，如 whiskey, brandy, vodka
fortified wine	掺有烈酒的酒，如 sherry（雪利酒）
sparkling wine	有气泡的酒，如 champagne（香槟酒）

Ⅱ. Pronunciation 语音训练

1. Many guests give high comments on Maotai.
   许多宾客对茅台赞赏备至。
2. It never goes to the head.
   （不管喝多少）它也不上头。
3. I suggest that you have a taste of Sichuan dishes.
   我建议你们尝尝四川菜。
4. Try the green crab if you don't mind.
   如果您不介意的话，不妨尝一下这种青蟹。
5. You'll regret if you don't have a taste.
   如果您不尝一下，您准会后悔的。
6. It's delicious and worth a try.
   它鲜美可口，值得一试。
7. I'm sorry to have kept you waiting.
   很抱歉，让您久等了。
8. I'm really sorry, but I seem to have disserved a dish.
   真对不起，我好像上错了一个菜。
9. I do apologize for giving you the wrong soup.
   我上错汤了，真抱歉。
10. Please feel free to contact us if you have any questions.
    如果您有什么问题，请随时和我们联系。
11. How do you like the fish cooked this way?
    您觉得鱼这样烧怎么样？
12. What do you think of Chinese food?
    您认为中国菜怎么样？
13. Do you think the soup is tasty?
    您认为这个汤可口吗？
14. What's your opinion of their service?
    您对他们的服务有什么意见吗？

Section B

Serivce Procedure 服务流程

1. Greetings.
   问候。

2. Offer tea.
   上茶。

3. Take orders and serve dishes.
   点菜上菜。

4. Service during the meals.
   餐间服务。

5. Dessert and fruits.
   上甜品、水果。

6. Settle the bill.
   结账。

7. Bid farewell to the guests.
   送客。

Ⅰ. Service Performance 服务演练

W＝Waitress（服务生）　　G＝Guest（客人）

W：Good evening, sir. Would you like some green tea?
　　晚上好，先生。来点绿茶吗？

G：Yes, please.
　　好的。

W：Are you ready to order now, sir?
　　准备好点菜了吗，先生？

G：Yes. But this is our first visit to China. We love Chinese food, but we know very little about it.
　　是的。但这是我们第一次来中国。我们喜欢中国菜，但对它一无所知。

W：Well, there are eight main cuisines in China, such as Guangdong food, Sichuan food and Zhejiang food...
　　嗯，中国有八大菜系，如粤菜，川菜，浙菜……

G：How is Zhejiang food different from Sichuan food?

浙菜与川菜有何不同?

W: Zhejiang food tends to be fresh and mild while most Sichuan dishes are spicy and hot.
浙菜比较温和、新鲜,而川菜比较麻、比较辣。

G: That sounds great, we'd like to try some Zhejiang food.
听起来不错,我们想尝尝浙江菜。

W: Yes, sure.
好的。

G: Let's have Shelled Shrimps with Longjing Tea Leaves, please.
我们要龙井虾仁。

W: It's one of the famous dishes of Hangzhou. It looks nice both in shape and color, it is very delicious.
这是很有名的杭州菜之一,色香味俱全。

G: And what else do you recommend?
你还推荐什么菜?

W: Beggars Chicken and Dongpo Pork are also typical dishes.
叫花子鸡和东坡肉也是很经典的菜。

G: OK, we'd like to have a try.
好的,我们尝尝。

W: What about vegetables and soup?
来点什么蔬菜和汤?

G: Broccoli and Mushroom Soup please.
来点西兰花和蘑菇汤吧。

W: So you order Shelled Shrimps with Longjing Tea Leaves, Beggars Chicken and Dongpo Pork, Broccoli and Mushroom Soup, is that right?
您点了龙井虾仁、叫花子鸡、东坡肉、西兰花还有蘑菇汤,是吗?

G: Yes, that's right!
是的,没错。

W: Your dishes will be ready in 15 minutes.
您的菜15分钟后上。

G: OK.
好的。

(15 minutes later.)(15分钟之后。)

W: This is Shelled Shrimps with Longjing Tea Leaves, enjoy your meal.
这是您点的龙井虾仁,请慢用。

G: Thank you.
谢谢。

W: That's all for your dishes. If you need anything else, please let us know.

您的菜上齐了，如果还有什么需要请告诉我们。

G：Sure.

没问题。

W：May I take your plate away, please?

能够把您的盘换一下吗？

G：Yes, thank you.

好的，谢谢。

W：Enjoy your meal, please.

请慢用。

G：Waitress, bill, please.

服务生，买单。

W：Yes, the total is 350 yuan. How would you like to make payment, sir?

好的，总数是350元，您要怎么付款？

G：By cash, please.

现金付款吧。

W：OK, this is your receipt. Thank you for your coming and we are looking forward to serving you soon.

好的，这是您的收据，谢谢光临，希望下次再为您服务。

G：Good bye.

再见。

Ⅱ. Position Practice 岗位实训

★ Characteristics of Chinese cuisines. （中国菜系的特征）

Chinese food is divided into four main Chinese cuisines: Shandong Cuisine, Sichuan Cuisine, Guangdong Cuisine and Huaiyang Cuisine. Shandong Cuisine has a heavy taste while Guangdong Cuisine is light and fresh; Sichuan Cuisine is spicy and hot but Huaiyang food is well known for its cutting techniques and original.

中国菜分成四大菜系：鲁菜，川菜，粤菜和淮扬菜。鲁菜口味重而粤菜清淡新鲜，川菜麻辣而淮扬菜则以它的刀工和原味著名。

★ Two types of Chinese wine. （两种传统的中国酒）

Traditional Chinese wines can be generally classified into two types, namely yellow liquors and clear (white) liquors. Chinese yellow liquors are brewed directly from grains such as rice or wheat. Such liquors contain less than 20% alcohol. And white liquors are distilled wine containing more than 30% alcohol in volume. There are a great many varieties of distilled liquors, both unflavored and flavored.

传统的中国酒大致可分为两类，即黄酒和白酒。黄酒直接由大米或小麦酿制而成，酒精度低于20度。白酒则是蒸馏酒，酒精度通常超过30度，白酒有很多品种，有芳香型的蒸馏酒也有不含香味的蒸馏酒。

★ Introduce soft drinks (drinks without alcohol).［向客人介绍软饮料（不含酒精的饮料）］

juice 果汁
black coffee 清咖啡
white coffee 奶咖啡
green tea 绿茶
black tea 红茶
brick tea 砖茶
flower tea 花茶
soda water 苏打水
mineral water 矿泉水
Coca Cola 可口可乐
Pepsi Cola 百事可乐
Sprite 雪碧
Fanda 芬达

★ Introduce different kinds of juice.（向客人介绍不同种类的果汁）

orange juice 橙汁
apple juice 苹果汁
watermelon juice 西瓜汁
lemon juice 柠檬汁
kiwi juice 猕猴桃汁
papaya juice 木瓜汁
coconut juice 椰子汁
cucumber juice 黄瓜汁
tomato juice 番茄汁
corn juice 玉米汁

★ Introduce some famous wines to guests.（向客人介绍著名的几种酒）

Wuliangye（五粮液）：It's rather strong, but never goes to the head.
五粮液度数较高，不过从不上头。
Maotai（茅台）：It's the best Chinese spirit.
茅台是一种很好的中国烈酒。
Swellfun（水井坊）：Swellfun has a history of more than 600 years, full of traditonal culture flavor, purest nature with simplest style.

水井坊拥有600多年的历史，纯正、自然、简约，有极其深厚的文化底蕴。

Fenjiu（汾酒）：Fenjiu Liquor has a history of over 1,500 years. It is sparkling and crystal clear, pure and refreshing, and delicious with a delicate aroma.

汾酒拥有1500多年的历史，晶莹纯净，清新芳香，十分诱人。

Tsingtao（青岛啤酒）：No. 1 beer brand in China, founded in 1903.

青岛啤酒是中国啤酒的第一品牌，创建于1903年。

Budweiser（百威啤酒）：No. 1 beer brand in America, founded in 1876.

百威啤酒是美国啤酒的第一品牌，创建于1876年。

Beck's（贝克啤酒）：No. 1 beer brand in Germany, founded in the 16th century.

贝克啤酒是德国啤酒的第一品牌，创建于16世纪。

Ⅲ. Listening Practice 听力实训

★ A. Listen to the short passage about snacks and fill in the missing words.

Snacks can be _____ in every city and all over the city. Steamed buns, wonton and other _____ can be seen everywhere in China. If you are _____, you can have a beer from a corner beer shop, and _____ you may try a small dish of peanuts. If you are in South, it's worth _____ at least one meal in dim sum restaurant. In North you _____ go to a "small snack" restaurant. This is _____ people meet, from morning until afternoon, to _____ the latest news or even to discuss business. These restaurants are usually large, _____ but always bring happiness to the guests.

★ B. Complete the following conversation.

Hostess: _____, sir and madam?

Man: Yes, please. First, a Beijing Roast Duck.

Woman: I overheard that Steamed Mandarin Fish is very nice.

Hostess: Yes, _____.

Man: What kind of soup can you recommend?

Hostess: I'd like you to try Mushroom Soup, _____.

Woman: OK. And some Green Beans, please.

Hostess: _____?

Man: No, that's all.

Hostess: _____ a Beijing Roast Duck, Steamed Mandarin Fish, Mushroom Soup and Green Beans, is that right?

Woman: Yes, that's right. How long will it take?

Hostess: About 20 minutes. _____, sir and madam?

Man: Yes, a bottle of red wine, Dynasty, please.

Hostess: OK. Just a minute please.

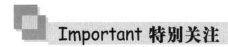

▲ Close watch personal hygiene, wash hands before beginning work, wash again after doing messy work.
密切关注个人卫生，开始工作前或干过脏活后都要洗手。
▲ No jewellery, rings, bracelets or wrists watches.
不佩戴珠宝、戒指、手镯或手表。
▲ Well-groomed, hair either short or tied back. Beards should be well-groomed as well.
衣着整洁，留短发或把头发盘在后面，胡须也要修理干净。
▲ Solid working shoes with non-slippery soles.
穿防滑的牢固的工作鞋。

Section C

Case and Development 案例与创新

Case 案例

Waiter: You receive a couple who come to celebrate their 30th marriage. You congratulate them and make a few suggestions on Chinese food. You take the order and serve the dishes.

Guest: You are Mr. and Mrs. Tylor. Your are spending your holiday in China. Today is your marriage anniversary, you want to have something different.

Development 创新

- Have Chinese eating habits changed a lot, why or why not?
- How can you teach the foreigners to use the chopsticks?
- Can you give foreigners some examples of symbolism in Chinese cuisine?

技能实训 18　西餐厅服务 At a Western Restaurant

Section A

Basic Knowledge for Position 岗位基础知识

Ⅰ. Word Stock 语料库

steak house	牛排馆
a la carte	照单点菜
table d'hôte	套餐
coffee shop	咖啡馆
menu	菜单
French/Italian Cuisine	法国/意大利菜
continental cuisine	欧式西餐
today's special	今日特餐
chef's special	主厨特餐
buffet	自助餐
fast food	快餐
specialty	招牌菜
aperitif	餐前酒
French fries	炸薯条
baked potato	烘马铃薯
mashed potato	土豆泥
pudding	布丁
pastries	点心
pancakes	煎饼
appetizer	开胃小吃/头盘
salad	色拉
dessert	甜点
rare	三分熟
medium	五分熟
well-done	八分熟
caviar	鱼子酱
goose liver	鹅肝

Ⅱ. Pronunciation 语音训练

1. Are you ready to order sir? / May I take your order, sir?
   先生，准备好点菜了吗？
2. What would you like to have, coffee or tea?
   您要喝咖啡还是茶？
3. What about a drink to start with?
   要不要来点开胃酒？
4. Would you care for a drink with your dinner?
   餐间要不要来点酒？
5. What would you like for your main course?
   您主菜点什么？
6. How would you like your steak to be done?
   您的牛排要几成熟？
7. What would you like to go with your steak?
   牛排的配菜要点什么？
8. I'm sorry, we have run out of it. But we have…
   很抱歉，这个菜今天卖完了，但是我们有……
9. Today's special is seafood.
   今天的特色菜是海鲜。
10. It's our chef's recommendation.
    这是我们主厨的拿手菜。
11. Do you prefer à la carte or table d'hôte?
    您喜欢零点餐还是套餐？
12. What would you like for your dessert?
    甜点来点什么？
13. You may sign the bill. The hotel will charge you when you leave.
    您可以签账单。离店时会给您结账。
14. I'm sorry, but I didn't quite catch what you just said.
    对不起，我没有听明白您刚才的话。
15. I beg your pardon? /Pardon?
    对不起，请再说一遍。
16. Sorry, sir, but I don't understand what you mean.
    很抱歉，先生，我没有听懂您的意思。
17. Pardon, madam. I am afraid I didn't follow you.
    对不起，女士，我没有听明白。
18. How would you like the steak/eggs?
    您喜欢怎么样做的牛排/鸡蛋？

19. May I suggest California red wine for the steak?
    我建议您喝加利福尼亚红酒配牛排。
20. We look forward to having with us soon.
    我们期待您的下次光临。

Section B

Serivce Procedure 服务流程

1. Receive diners.
   迎客。
2. Seat the guests.
   安排入座。
3. Offer iced water and menu.
   上冰水及菜单。
4. Take orders.
   点菜。
5. Serve the dishes during the meal.
   上菜。
6. Take the bill.
   结账。
7. Bid farewell to the guests.
   送客。

 Ⅰ. Service Performance 服务演练

W＝Waitress（服务生）　　G1＝Guest1（客人甲）　　G2＝Guest2（客人乙）

W：Good evening. Welcome to our restaurant. Have you made a reservation?
    晚上好，欢迎光临，请问有预订吗？
G1：No, we haven't.
    没有预订。
W：Only two of you?
    是两位吗？
G2：Yes.
    是的。

W: This way, please. How about this table?
　　这边请。这张餐台怎么样?

G1: It's fine.
　　 很好。

W: Are you ready to order now, madam?
　　可以点餐了吗?

G1: For an appetizer, I'll have Smoked Salmon. John, what would you like to have?
　　 来一道开胃菜,熏三文鱼。约翰,你要什么?

G2: I'll have the sole, please.
　　 我要一份比目鱼。

W: And for the main course?
　　请问要什么主菜?

G1: Well, I would like some meat. Two T-bone steak, please.
　　 我想来点肉,两份 T 骨牛排。

W: How would you like your steak done, madam?
　　牛排要几分熟?

G1: One medium-well, the other medium.
　　 一份七分熟,一份五分熟。

W: Would you like some vegetables, sir?
　　先生,需要来点蔬菜吗?

G2: I'll have some fresh peas.
　　 我要新鲜的豌豆。

W: And you, madam, what salad would you like?
　　您呢,女士,要什么样的色拉?

G1: I would like some fruit salad, please.
　　 我要水果色拉。

W: Thank you. What soup would you like, Sir?
　　谢谢,先生,你们要什么汤?

G2: Fish soup, French style.
　　 法式鱼汤。

W: Certainly, sir. Anything for dessert, sir?
　　好的,先生,需要甜点吗?

G2: Strawberry ice cream for both, please.
　　 两份草莓味冰淇淋。

W: And will you have some drinks?

喝点什么吗？

G2：Some red wine, please.

　　红葡萄酒吧。

W：Will there be anything else, madam?

　　还需要别的吗？

G1：No, thanks. Bring me the bill, please.

　　没有了，谢谢。请买单。

W：Here it is, madam. The total is 368 yuan.

　　给您，女士，总共368元。

G1：Is the service charge included?

　　服务费算在内了吗？

W：Yes, madam, 10% service charge. Who would like to pay please?

　　算在内了，女士。10%的服务费，谁买单？

G1：It's me. Here is 390 yuan.

　　我来，这是390元。

W：Thank you. Here is the change, please have a check.

　　谢谢，这是找您的钱，请核对。

G1：Thank you for your good service.

　　谢谢你的服务。

W：We look forward to seeing you again.

　　希望再次为您服务。

Ⅱ. Position Practice 岗位实训

★ Procedure of Western Food. （西餐程序）
　　appetizer 头盘
　　soup 羹汤
　　side orders 副菜
　　main course 主菜
　　salad 色拉
　　dessert 甜食
　　coffee or tea 咖啡或茶

★ Famous Brands of Western Wines. （著名洋酒品牌）
　　REMY MARTIN 人头马
　　MARTELL 马爹利
　　GORDON'S GIN 哥顿金酒

SMIRNOFF 斯米诺夫
MATINI 马天尼
COINTREAU 君度
HENNESSY 轩尼诗
BLACK LABEL 黑方
RED LABEL 红方
BOLS 波尔斯
TEQUILA 龙舌兰
BEEFEATER 必富达
MYERS RUM 美雅士

★ Menu.（菜单）
sunshine salad 胡萝卜色拉
vegetable salad 蔬菜色拉
mixed salad 什锦色拉
fruit salad 水果色拉
smoked salmon 熏三文鱼
braised goose liver in red wine 红酒鹅肝
pan-fried whole sole 煎比目鱼
assorted vegetables 什锦蔬菜
stuffed tomato 酿西红柿
sour mushrooms 酸蘑菇
fried fish with tomato sauce 番茄汁炸鱼
smoked herring 熏鲱鱼
sour cucumbers/pickled cucumbers 酸黄瓜
pickled cabbage/sour and sweet cabbage 泡菜
rump steak 牛腿排
T-bone steak T骨牛排
beef steak curried 咖喱牛排
roast veal 烤小牛肉
sauté pork chop 嫩煎猪排
roast lamb 烤羔羊肉
ham and sausage 火腿香肠
abalone 鲍鱼
shark fin 鱼翅
scallops 干贝
lobster 龙虾

australian fresh shellfish 澳洲鲜贝
fried rice with sea food 海鲜炒饭
fried rice with beef 牛肉炒饭
assorted fried rice 什锦炒饭
Japanese seafood noodle 日式乌冬面
Luosong soup 罗宋汤

Ⅲ. Listening Practice 听力实训

★ A. Listen to the tape, decide what each short dialogue is about and mark "√" where appropriate.

	Starter	Soup	Main Dish	Dessert	Drink
Dialogue 1					
Dialogue 2					
Dialogue 3					
Dialogue 4					
Dialogue 5					

★ B. Complete the following conversation.

Receptionist: Good evening, madam. _____?
Guest: Yes, for two people _____ of Clarkson.
Receptionist: Thank you, madam. This way, please.
…
Waiter: _____, madam?
Guest: Yes, I think so. I will have sole to begin with. Is it good?
Waiter: Oh, Yes, madam. _____.
Guest: Well, I'm going to have meat, T-bone steak, please.
Waiter: _____, madam?
Guest: Well-done please.
Waiter: _____?
Guest: Fresh peas with my sole.
Waiter: _____ something to drink with your meal?
Guest: Half a bottle of _____ will be all right.
Waiter: Certainly, madam.

Important 特别关注

▲ In general, a lady will not take orders directly and a gentleman will do it for her.
一般男士为女士点菜，女士不直接接受点菜。

▲ It is not very normal for one person to order for the whole table. Each person orders separately, except in the most expensive restaurants.
一个人点一桌子人的菜不合适，每个人各点各的菜，除非是在特别昂贵的餐厅。

Section C

Case and Development 案例与创新

Case 案例

Mrs. Brown enters the Western restaurant for dinner. She can not decide between beef and tuna fish, so you recommend a tuna fish, the chef's specialty to her. She asks for wine and you suggest a white Bordeau wine（法国波尔多地区产的红葡萄酒）. She also takes a vanilla ice-cream. She doesn't want anything before dinner. Everything is good.

Development 创新

- If a guest orders something that has already sold out, what should you do?
- What would a waiter do if the dishes the guests orders are not to be served immediately?
- What kind of guest can sign the bill in the restaurant?

技能实训 19　早餐服务 Breakfast Service

Section A

Basic Knowledge for Position 岗位基础知识

Ⅰ. Word Stock 语料库

breakfast knob	早餐牌
American breakfast/full breakfast	美式早餐
continental breakfast/simple breakfast	欧洲大陆式早餐
full English breakfast	全英式早餐
buffet breakfast	自助式早餐
Chinese breakfast	中式早餐
jam	果酱
butter	黄油
cream	奶油
oatmeal	麦片
oatmeal porridge	麦片粥
omelet	炒蛋卷
scrambled egg	炒蛋
boiled egg	煮蛋
fried egg	煎蛋
sunny side up	单面煎蛋
easy over	双面煎蛋
poached egg	荷包蛋
cookie	曲奇饼
toast	土司
roll	面包卷
ham/bacon/sausage	火腿/培根/香肠
rice congee	白米粥
steamed buns	包子
steamed bread	馒头
noodles	面条

soybean milk	豆浆
pickled vegetable	酱菜
sesame balls	芝麻球

Ⅱ. Pronunciation 语音训练

1. Would you like tea or coffee this morning?
   今早您是要茶还是咖啡?
2. How would you like your eggs?
   请问鸡蛋要怎么煮?
3. The price includes bed and continental breakfast.
   这价钱包括床铺和欧洲大陆式早餐。
4. We have continental breakfast and full English breakfast.
   我们有欧洲大陆式早餐和全英式早餐。
5. May I have your meal voucher, please?
   请把餐券给我好吗?
6. Would you please show your room card?
   请出示您的房卡好吗?
7. Sorry to have kept you waiting.
   抱歉让您久等了。
8. What kind of jam would you like?
   您要哪种果酱?
9. Would you like separate bills? Would you like to go Dutch?
   账单分开? 餐费平摊?
10. Buffet breakfast is included in the room charge.
    房价已经包含自助早餐。

Section B

Serivce Procedure 服务流程

1. Greetings.
   问候。
2. Make sure the number of diners and show the way.
   了解就餐人数,将宾客带到适当餐桌。

3. Seat the guest.

    安排客人就座。

4. Make sure of the juice the guest would like to have. If not, offer the guest ice water.

    问清宾客需要何种果汁饮料,如不需要则替宾客倒冰水。

5. Offer the guest menu.

    递呈菜单。

6. Take orders and pay special attention to boiled eggs, fried eggs and kind of meat.

    点单,特别关注煮蛋、煎蛋还有肉类。

7. Serve the breakfast.

    早餐服务。

8. Bid farewell to the guest.

    道别。

 Ⅰ. Service Performance 服务演练

G= Guest（客人）   W=Waitress（服务生）

W：Good morning, sir. Welcome to our restaurant.

    早上好,先生,欢迎光临。

G：Thank you.

    谢谢。

W：How many of you, please, sir?

    先生,请问一共几位?

G：Just two. My wife is coming soon.

    就两位,我妻子很快就到。

W：Yes, sir. This way, please. How do you like this table?

    好的,先生,请这边走。这张桌子可以吗?

G：Fine.

    行。

W：Here's the menu, sir. May I take your order now?

    先生,这是菜单,现在可以点单了吗?

G：Yes, is there a price difference between continental breakfast and American breakfast?

    可以,欧陆式早餐和美式早餐价格上有何区别?

W：Yes, a continental breakfast is 38 yuan per person while an American breakfast is 58 yuan per person.

    欧陆式早餐每位38元,美式早餐每位58元。

G：Well, a full breakfast for both of us.

    那么我们两人都来美式早餐。

W: Certainly, sir. Coffee or tea?
　　好的，先生，咖啡还是茶？

G: Two coffees.
　　两杯咖啡。

W: What kind of juice would you like to have?
　　您要哪种果汁？

G: One tomato juice for me and one pineapple juice for my wife.
　　我要番茄汁，我妻子要菠萝汁。

W: Yes, sir. One tomato juice and one pineapple juice. For bread, would you like soft roll, toast or croissant?
　　好的，一份番茄汁，一份菠萝汁。面包呢，您要早餐包，土司还是羊角包？

G: Both my wife and I would take toast. And two oatmeals.
　　我们两位都要土司，还要两份燕麦粥。

W: Yes, sir, two toast, two oatmeals. How about eggs?
　　好的，先生。两份土司，两份燕麦粥。鸡蛋呢？

G: My wife like a boiled egg, hard boiled and I want fried eggs, sunny side up.
　　我妻子要水煮蛋，煮得老一点，我要煎蛋，单面煎。

W: Served with bacon, ham or sausage?
　　是配培根、火腿还是香肠？

G: With bacon, please.
　　培根吧。

W: Yes, sir. I'll bring them to you right away.
　　好的，先生，很快就可以给您拿来。

Ⅱ. Position Practice 岗位实训

★ Difference of three kinds of western breakfast. （三种西式早餐的不同）

Western breakfast can be divided into American breakfast, continental breakfast and full English breakfast. American breakfast is also called full breakfast. It usually consists of the following: chilled orange, eggs and bacon, ham or sausages, rolls or toast with butter and coffee or tea. Continental breakfast is basically the same as American breakfast except that eggs with bacon, ham or sausages are not served. It is light and simple. A Full English Breakfast may have black pudding, baked beans and fried bread and eggs but may not include meat.

西式早餐可分为美国式、欧陆式及英国式三种。美式早餐也称作丰盛的早餐，通常包含冰果汁，新鲜的蛋和培根、火腿或香肠，黄油土司，咖啡或茶。欧陆式早餐量小简单，一般无蛋无肉，其他与美式早餐差不多。英国式早餐可能会提供黑布丁、烤豌豆、烤面包和鸡蛋，但没有肉。

★ Make sure about how the guest would like his eggs.（确认客人想怎么做鸡蛋）
How do you like your eggs? Fried, poached, boiled or scrambled?
您想怎么做鸡蛋？煎蛋，荷包蛋，煮蛋，还是炒蛋？
★ Make sure about how the guest would like his fried eggs.（确认客人要什么样的煎蛋）
How do you like your fried eggs? Sunny side up or over easy?
您要鸡蛋怎么煎？单面煎还是双面煎？
★ Make sure about how the guest would like his boiled eggs.（确认客人要什么样的煮蛋）
How do you like your boiled eggs? Soft boiled or hard boiled?
您要鸡蛋怎么煮？煮得嫩一点还是老一点？

Ⅲ. Listening Practice 听力实训

★ A. Listen to the short passage and note the difference of American breakfast and continental breakfast.

Difference	Description	Place	Offer
American Breakfast			
Continental Breakfast			

★ B. Complete the following conversation.

Waiter: Good morning, sir.
Guest: Good morning. How are you this morning?
Waiter: I'm fine. Thank you, sir. _____?
Guest: Yes, I did. Thank you.
Waiter: _____?
Guest: Coffee, please. Make it real hot.
Waiter: All right, sir.
Guest: And I'll have some cornflakes, one fried egg and two pieces of toast, please.
Waiter: Cornflakes, one fried egg and two pieces of toast. And _____?
Guest: Oh, over easy, please. Thank you.
Waiter: _____?
Guest: Bacon, please. And make it crisp, please.
Waiter: Just a minute, sir.
Guest: Thank you.
Waiter: _____?
Guest: That's all right, thank you.
Waiter: Would you like some more coffee?

Guest: No. Thank you.

Important 特别关注

▲ More than 70% of the room service is breakfast.
早餐占客房送餐服务的70%以上。

▲ Whole-grain toast with 100% fruit spread and one cup of low-fat milk or yogurt is good for your breakfast.
全麦吐司加100%果汁，一杯低脂牛奶或酸奶作为早餐很不错。

▲ Choose whole fruits instead of juice and include whole grains such as oatmeal, or ready-to-eat cereal. These foods provide fiber, vitamins, and minerals that you need.
选择整个水果而不是果汁，再加全麦，如燕麦片或即食谷类食物，这些食物提供您所需要的纤维、维生素和矿物质。

Section C

Case and Development 案例与创新

Case 案例

Guest: You are from Sydney. You are having breakfast in a restaurant. You'd like to try a typical Chinese breakfast.

Waiter: Ask what the guest would like. Introduce some typical Chinese Dim Sum to the guest.

Development 创新

- What are the differences between a continental breakfast and a full English one?
- If guests are late for breakfast, how can you deal with their complaint?
- How to introduce typical Chinese breakfast to a foreigner?

技能实训 20　酒吧服务 At the Bar

Section A

Basic Knowledge for Position 岗位基础知识

I. Word Stock 语料库

bartender	调酒员
barman	酒吧男招待
barmaid	酒吧女招待
recipe	酒谱
champagne	香槟酒
cocktail	鸡尾酒
apple wine	苹果酒
whiskey	威士忌
brandy	白兰地
vodka	伏特加
rum	朗姆酒
gin	杜松子酒/金酒/琴酒
bitters	苦啤酒
liquor	力娇酒
spirits	烈酒
drought beer	生啤
stilled wine	没有气体的酒
sparkling wine	有气体的酒
distilled wine	蒸馏酒
fortified wine	掺加烈性酒的酒
red wine	红葡萄酒
white wine	白葡萄酒
dry red wine	干红
base	基酒
chaser	辅饮
night cup	睡前的饮料

straight up	纯饮
on the rocks	加冰
proof	美国较常使用的酒精计量单位，是酒精度数的一半
sober up	醒酒
tie me up	续杯
age	陈年
cellar	酒窖
close the bar	收吧

Ⅱ. Pronunciation 语音训练

1. What can I get for you, sir?
   先生，给您来点什么？

2. What would you like to drink?
   您要喝点什么？

3. Straight up or on the rocks?
   纯饮还是加冰？

4. With or without ice?
   加冰还是不加冰？

5. Up or down?
   加冰还是不加冰？

6. Tie me up, please. /Make it two.
   请再来一杯。

7. Do you like to have a drink with us?
   你要不要和我们去喝两杯啊？

8. I'll buy you a drink.
   我请你喝一杯吧。

9. It's on me. /My treat.
   我请客。

10. Draft, please.
    请给我生啤酒。

11. Do you want domestic or imported beer?
    你是要国产的还是进口的啤酒？

12. I am still sober.
    我还很清醒。

13. If you want to puke, just go ahead.

如果你想吐的话，就去吧。

14. Cheers! /Bottoms up. /Let's make a toast.
    干杯!

15. Would you like to have cocktail or whisky on the rocks?
    您要鸡尾酒还是要威士忌加冰?

16. Please bring me a pot of hot coffee.
    请给我一壶热咖啡。

17. Can you act as my interpreter?
    你可以做我的翻译吗?

18. There is a floor show in our lobby bar. Would you like to see it?
    大堂酒吧里有表演，您愿意去看吗?

19. Please feel free to tell us if you have any request.
    请把您的要求告诉我们。

20. Miss Chen is regarded as one of the best barmaid in the bar.
    陈小姐被认为是酒吧里最好的女调酒师。

21. Here is the drink list, sir. Please take your time.
    先生，这是酒单，请慢慢看。

22. I do apologize. Is there anything I can do for you?
    非常抱歉，还有什么可以为您效劳吗?

23. The base of Old Fashioned cocktail is whiskey.
    古典鸡尾酒的基酒是威士忌。

24. Frankly speaking, I don't like this wine.
    老实说，我不喜欢这种酒。

25. It never goes to the head.
    (不管喝多少) 它也不上头。

Section B

Serivce Procedure 服务流程

1. Greetings.
   问候。

2. Seat the guest.
   领座。

3. Take orders for the guest.
   为客人点酒。
4. Prepare the wine for the guest.
   为客人调酒。
5. Serve the wine to the guest.
   为客人送酒服务。
6. Settle the account.
   为客人结账。
7. Bid farewell to the guest.
   道别。

Ⅰ. Service Performance 服务演练

G1＝Guest 1（客人甲）　　G2＝Guest 2（客人乙）　　W＝Waitress（服务生）

W：Anything to drink, gentlemen?
　　喝点什么吗，先生们？
G1：Well, we've been drinking whisky a lot. We'd like to have a change. Can you recommend some famous Chinese liqours?
　　哦，我们经常喝威士忌，今天想换换口味。你能向我们介绍一些中国酒吗？
W：What about Wu Liang Ye, one of the most famous liquors in China? It's made from five kinds of cereal. It's fragrant and it never goes to the head.
　　五粮液怎么样？它是中国的名酒之一，由五谷酿制而成，非常芳香，而且不上头。
G1：All right, we'll have some.
　　好吧，来点五粮液。
W：May I remind you all the Chinese liquors are served by the bottle here?
　　我能提醒您一下这儿的酒都是按瓶卖的吗？
G1：I see. Any other brands of liquor?
　　我明白，还有其他的品牌吗？
W：Yes, Mao Tai, Fen Jiu, Swellfun, etc.
　　茅台，汾酒，水井坊，等等。
G2：I hear Great Wall wine is a famous brand.
　　我听说长城葡萄酒是著名品牌。
W：Yes, it is. Would you like to try one bottle?
　　是的。您是否要来一瓶？
G2：OK, bring me the white wine as well. Make sure it is well chilled.
　　好的，我要白葡萄酒。记住要冰镇的。

W：Yes，sir. A bottle of well-chilled white wine. Have you ever heard about Shaoxing wine? It's a kind of still wine made from rice，somewhat like Japanese sake.

好的，先生。一瓶冰镇白葡萄酒。你们有没有听说过绍兴黄酒？是一种用米酿制的酒，有点像日本清酒。

G1：I believe it is，but you see we've got enough，we'll drink it next time.

我相信是的，但我们今天点的够多了，下次再喝吧。

W：Yes，sir. So you've ordered one bottle of Wu Liang Ye and one bottle of Great Wall white wine. Just a moment，please，gentlemen.

好的，先生，你们点的是一瓶五粮液，一瓶长城白葡萄酒。请稍等，先生们。

Ⅱ. Position Practice 岗位实训

★ Classification of bars.（酒吧的分类）

Lobby Bar 大堂吧

Lobby Lounge 大堂酒廊

Main Bar/Cash Bar 主酒吧（装饰考究、别致，客人可以全面欣赏调酒师的全套操作过程）

Service Bar 服务酒吧（较主酒吧简单，调酒师不需要直接与客人打交道）

Theme Bar 主题酒吧［特点突出，以销售饮料为主，如 Soda Bar（水吧），Oxygen Bar（氧吧），Internet Bar（网吧），Book Bar（书吧等）］

Grand Bar 多功能酒吧（大多设在娱乐场所）

Banquet Bar 宴会酒吧（临时为宴会设立的酒吧，临时性强，供应酒水品种随意性大）

★ Introduce different kinds of drinks to the guest.（向客人介绍不同的饮料）

soft drink 不含酒精的饮料

hard drink 含酒精的饮料

cold drink 冷饮

mineral water 矿泉水

green tea 绿茶

black tea 红茶

black coffee 清咖啡

white coffee 奶咖啡

soda water 苏打水

★ Introduce cocktail decorations to the guest.（向客人介绍鸡尾酒上的缀饰）

cherry 樱桃

lemon 柠檬

clove 丁香

pineapple 菠萝

onion 洋葱

strawberry 草莓

olive 橄榄

cucumber 黄瓜

mint 薄荷

grapefruit 西柚

★ Be familiar with bar tools. （熟悉酒吧用具）

counter 吧台

stool 高脚凳

bottle opener 开瓶刀

corkscrew 酒钻

ice shaver 削冰器

ice maker 制冰机

ice bucket 小冰桶

cocktail shaker 调酒器

pouring measure 量酒器

electric blender 电动搅拌机

straw 吸管

bar spoon 酒吧匙

★ Get to know famous western wines. （了解西洋名酒）

Whiskey：威士忌是一种最具代表性的蒸馏酒，主要分为：苏格兰威士忌（Scotch Whiskey）、爱尔兰威士忌（Irish Whiskey）、加拿大威士忌（Canadian whiskey）和美国威士忌（American Whiskey）。

Gin：金酒也称杜松子酒，可分为荷兰式金酒和英国式金酒两类。荷兰式金酒色泽透明清亮，香味突出，风格独特，适宜于单饮。英国金酒也称为干金酒，酒液无色透明，气味奇异清香，口感醇美爽适。

Sherry：法国的葡萄酒加上白兰地就是雪利酒，经常作为餐前酒（Aperitif）使用。

Vodka：伏特加是俄罗斯最具有代表性的白酒，无色、无香味，具有中性的特点，不需贮存即可出售。由于伏特加无色透明，与金酒一样，可与其他酒类混合调成各种混合饮品和鸡尾酒。

Brandy：白兰地是一种蒸馏酒，以水果为原料，经过发酵、蒸馏、贮藏后酿造而成。法国是世界上首屈一指的白兰地生产国。法国人引以为豪的白兰地叫干邑（Cognac），是世界上同类产品中最受欢迎的一种，有白兰地之王之称。

Champagne：香槟酒是法国出产的名酒，由其原产地 Champagne 而得名。在开瓶后，会爆出巨响，冒出泡沫，经常用于增添喜庆气氛。

Vermouth：苦艾酒主要产地是法国和意大利。一般都当作餐前酒，也经常用来调制鸡尾酒。

Rum：朗姆酒以甘蔗提炼而成，大多数产于热带地区。朗姆酒按颜色也可分为三类，即白朗姆酒（Silver Rum）、金朗姆酒（Golden Rum）和黑朗姆酒（Dark Rum）。

Liquer：利口酒混合白兰地、琴酒、朗姆酒、威士忌等烈酒，再加上香料和糖浆共同调制而成，常作为餐后甜酒。

Cocktail：鸡尾酒是以各种蒸馏酒为基酒，再加上各种饮料及香料调制而成，常用于各种宴会。

★ Identify ages of Brandy.（辨别白兰地的年份）

法国白兰地用字母或星印来表示白兰地酒贮存时间的长短，白兰地需贮藏很长的时间，且时间越长，酒质越好，最佳的陈年时间是 20～40 年。

"V.O" 为 10～12 年陈的白兰地酒；

"V.S.O." 为 12～20 年陈的白兰地酒；

"V.S.O.P." 为 20～30 年陈的白兰地酒；

"X.O" 一般指 40 年陈的白兰地酒；

"X" 一般指 70 年的特陈白兰地酒。

"V" 是 Very 的缩写，是非常的意思；

"S" 是 Superior、Special 的缩写，是特殊的意思；

"O" 是 Old 的缩写，是陈年、陈酿的意思；

"P" 是 Pale 的缩写，有清澈的意思。

白兰地酒用星印来表示贮存时间：一星表示 3 年陈酿；二星表示 4 年陈酿；三星表示 5 年陈酿。

Ⅲ. Listening Practice 听力实训

★ A. Listen to the tape, decide what each short is about and mark "√" where appropriate.

	Liquor	Cocktail	Soft Drink	Wine	Traditional Drink
Dialogue 1					
Dialogue 2					
Dialogue 3					
Dialogue 4					
Dialogue 5					

★ B. A Waiter is introducing some wines to the guest, try to complete the missing information.

1. Bordeau is a _____ from southwest France.
2. Rioja is a full-bodied red wine _____ .
3. Chalish is a very dry white wine _____ .
4. Chianti is _____ from Italy.
5. You may like an Australian Chardonnay, which _____ your lobster.
6. Bourbon whiskey is a type of _____ whiskey-a distilled spirit _____ .
7. Burgundy wine is wine made in the Burgundy region in _____ .
8. Sauternes is a _____ wine.

Important 特别关注

▲ Never move barstools without asking. Barstool positions are often numbered for the bar staff and food runners.
没有得到许可不得移动吧椅,为方便酒吧员工送餐,吧椅通常都有编号。

▲ Introduce yourself and learn your bartender's name. Using a bartender's name makes the interaction more respectful and human. But, never shout the bartender's name down the bar to get his attention.
自我介绍并记住酒吧侍者的名字,用名字称呼酒吧侍者使得沟通更显尊敬和人性化,但是千万不能为了引起他的关注而大嚷他的名字。

▲ Never ask the dreaded, insulting questions, for example, is this your real job? Or, What else do you do?
永远不要问愚蠢的带有侮辱性的问题,比如:这是你真正的工作吗?或者,你还做其他什么工作?

▲ Sharing your personal issues (especially quarrels between couples) with the rest of the bar makes everyone uncomfortable. Remember that you're sharing space with other people. Be aware of your volume.
你个人的问题(尤其是夫妻之间的吵架)拿来跟其他人讨论会让别人不自在。记住你跟别人共享同一个空间,注意控制你的声音。

Section C

Case and Development 案例与创新

Case 案例

Bartender: you greet the guest and ask him for his order. You make a few suggestions on Chinese liquors. You take the order and serve the drink.

Guest: You ask for a typical Chinese drink. You take one of the recommendations. And you ask the business hours of the bar. You accept the advice given by bartender and pay your bill.

Development 创新

- What qualifications should a bartender have?
- What can you do if you notice a guest has drunk too much?
- Make a presentation of mixing cocktail.

技能实训 21　就餐礼仪 Table Manners

Section A

Basic Knowledge for Position 岗位基础知识

Ⅰ. Word Stock 语料库

table manners	餐桌礼仪
custom	习俗
etiquette	礼仪
difference	不同点
similarity	相同点
compare	比较
appropriate	合适的
utensil	餐具
culture	文化
observe	遵守
standard	标准
elegant	优雅的
acceptable	可以接受的
offensive	冒犯的
appetite	胃口
edible	可以食用的
knife and fork	刀叉
napkin	餐巾
table cloth	桌布
tableware	餐具
salad fork	沙拉餐叉
dinner fork	正餐叉
steak knife	牛排刀
butter knife	黄油刀
soup spoon	汤勺
tea spoon	茶匙

Ⅱ. Pronunciation 语音训练

1. What would you like to have, coffee or tea?
   您要喝咖啡还是茶?
2. Would you like to have some wine with your dinner?
   您用餐时要喝点酒吗?
3. It never goes to the head.
   (不管喝多少) 它也不冲脑。
4. Have you decided what to drink?
   您决定了喝什么吗?
5. What kind of food would you like to have?
   您想吃什么菜?
6. I'm sorry, but I didn't quite catch what you just said.
   对不起, 我没有听明白您刚才的话。
7. I beg your pardon? /Pardon?
   对不起, 请再说一遍。
8. It's delicious and worth a try.
   它鲜美可口, 值得一试。
9. I do apologize for giving you the wrong soup.
   我上错了汤, 真抱歉。
10. Let me wish you every success.
    祝您一切顺利。

Section B

Table Manners 就餐礼仪

Seat the guest 入座

　　You should take your seat from the left unless the left is against the wall. Gentleman or host is supposed to sit by the aisle so that ladies or guests can sit against the wall. Napkins by your left hand and glasses by your right hand are for you.
　　要从座位的左侧入座, 除非左侧靠墙。男士或者主人应该坐在靠过道的位置, 让女士或者客人靠墙, 左侧的纸巾和右侧的杯子是自己使用的。

★ Bread before dinner. (餐前小面包)

Bread is taken in the fingers, it is never taken with a fork. Even bread is very small, you should tear it by pieces and have one at a time.

用手指拿着面包,绝对不要用叉子吃面包。即使面包很小,也一定要一小块一小块撕下来塞进嘴里。

★ The soup course. (汤)

Dinner usually begins with soup. The largest spoon at your place is the soup spoon. It will be beside your plate by the right hand. Use your spoon to drink soup and don't take too much soup at a time in case it may spread and it's impolite as well. Never utter noises or blow it when having soup. Remember to keep quiet always!

正餐通常从汤开始,你的位置上最大的那把就是汤匙,放在你餐盘的右手边。汤要用汤匙慢慢舀起来送到嘴巴里,舀的时候不要装太多,那样看起来既没有礼貌,也可以避免中途汤汁滴落。喝汤时切忌吹气或发出呼噜呼噜声。记得吃西餐始终要保持安静。

★ The fish course. (鱼)

If there is a fish course, it will probably follow the soup. There may be a special fork for the fish, or it may be similar to the meat fork. Often it is smaller.

如果正餐中有鱼的话,一般就在汤后面。有可能有专门的鱼叉,也可能跟肉叉合用。鱼叉要小一点。

★ The meat course. (肉)

The majority of meat courses (with the exception of poultry and ham) will call for red wines. As a general rule, simply cooked roasts need better bottles and those with some age. Spicy dishes or those with lots of different flavours would be better with younger wines. When you cut a piece of steak, you should have it right now. Never cut the steak into pieces at one time, cold steak won't be so delicious.

吃绝大部分的肉时(除了家禽和火腿)都会配红酒。一般来说,简单烧烤的肉需要好一点的年份久一点的红酒,而一些有辣味或添加了许多调味品的肉就选用清淡一点的红酒。切一块吃一块。不要一次把肉都切开,牛排冷了就没有鲜味了。

★ The salad course. (色拉)

A salad is eaten with a fork only held in the right hand with points turned up.

吃色拉时只能用叉子,右手持叉,叉子的尖朝上。

★ Dessert and beverage. (甜点和饮料)

If there are some decorations in the dessert that are not edible, the waiter will tell you in advance, or you should eat them up. The last course is coffee or tea. The small tea spoon is to stir sugar and coffee mate, it is not used in drinking coffee. You should hold coffee cup and drink it slowly.

如果甜点上有不可食用的缀饰,服务生会明确告诉你,否则还是要全部吃完。最后是咖啡或茶,调羹是用来搅拌糖和咖啡伴侣的,不是用来舀咖啡喝的。喝的时候用手端起杯子慢慢喝。

I. Position Practice 岗位实训

★ What does 6M represent in a western restaurant? 西餐厅中的6M代表什么?

1. Menu 菜单:In a restaurant, a menu is a printed brochure that shows the list of options for a diner to select.
菜单指餐厅为就餐者提供的列有各种菜肴选择的清单。

2. Music 音乐:Deluxe western restaurants should have a band and play soft music.
豪华高级的西餐厅要有乐队,演奏一些柔和的乐曲。

3. Mood 气氛:Surround the dining area with scented candles, dim the lights, and scatter rose petals on the table. Keep it tasteful, and coordinated.
就餐的地方如果点有香薰蜡烛、灯光暗淡、餐桌上撒有玫瑰花瓣,会显得非常有品位、非常和谐。

4. Meeting 会面:The world is full of romantic places where you can escape and have quality time together, a western restaurant is really a good choice.
世界上有许多浪漫的地方可以让你度过高品质的时光,西餐厅绝对是好选择。

5. Manner 礼仪:Table manners are the rules of etiquette used while eating. Different cultures observe different rules for table manners. Pay attention to what you should do and what you shouldn't do.
餐桌礼仪是用餐的时候要遵循的规则。不同的文化有不同的餐桌礼仪。注意你该做什么不该做什么。

6. Meal 食品:Western-style food is simple but Chinese food is complicated, more delicious and nutritious.
西餐的食物比较简单,而中餐的食物比较复杂,更美味也更注重营养。

★ Using knife and fork. (刀叉的使用)

If you have English and American friends you will notice a few differences in using knife and fork. For the main or meat course, the English keep the fork in the left hand, point curved downward, and bring the food to the mouth by sticking the points onto it. Americans carve the meat in the same position, then lay down the knife and taking the fork in the right hand with the point turned up, push it under a small piece of food and bring it to the mouth.

如果你有美国和英国的朋友的话,你可能会发现他们使用刀、叉的习惯略有不同。在上主菜时,英国人用左手拿叉,叉头朝下,把食物挑到叉上再送入口。而美国人则在切分好肉以后,把刀放下,换用右手拿叉,叉尖朝上插入小块食物下面,铲起食物送入口。

★ Helping yourself and refusing. (自助与拒绝)

If a waiter passes food around, he will pass the dish in at your left hand so that you can conveniently serve yourself with your right hand. Never serve yourself while the dish is on your right, it is then the turn of your neighbor on the right. It is polite to take some of everything that is passed to you. But if there is something you may not like, you may quietly say: "No, thank you."

如果服务生分菜，他会把菜放在你的左手边方便你用右手取菜。如果菜在你的右手边，是你的邻座取菜，而不该你取菜。取一点向你递过来的菜是礼貌的做法。如果真的不喜欢，就轻轻地说一声："不用了，谢谢。"

Ⅱ. Listening Practice 听力实训

★ A. Listen to the following passage about table manners and complete the missing information.

Table manners are the _____ of etiquette used while eating. _____ observe different rules for table manners. Many people _____ when dining simply because they don't know how to follow _____, especially if they have been _____ a nice place. Talking about table manners, unlike the West, where everyone has _____ of food, in China the dishes are placed on the table and everybody _____ . If you are being treated by a Chinese host, be prepared for a ton of food. And sometimes the host will _____ with his or her own chopsticks to guests to show his or her hospitality. This is a sign of _____ . If you feel _____ with this, you can just say a polite "thank you" and _____ there. There are some other rules that are suggested you follow to make your stay in China happier, though you will be forgiven if you _____ what they are.

★ B. Listen to the statements and put a "DO" or a "DON'T" in front of each statement.

1. _____ eat and drink at the same time.
2. _____ chew with your mouth open.
3. _____ put elbows on the table.
4. _____ wipe your mouth with the corners of your napkin.
5. _____ sit up straight while eating.
6. _____ eat and talk at the same time.
7. _____ place your silverware on the table after use.
8. _____ place your napkin on your lap before eating.
9. _____ make loud eating noises.
10. _____ use a napkin to clean your face.
11. _____ excuse yourself if you must leave the table during a meal.

12. _____ stand up to get the salt if it is out of your reach.

 Important 特别关注

▲ Sit up straight on your chair.
坐在椅子上要保持身体笔直。

▲ Don't eat with your hands.
不要用手拿东西吃。

▲ Do not put much food in your mouth at a time.
不要一次塞进嘴巴太多食物。

▲ Drink only when there is no food in your mouth.
只有当你的嘴巴没有食物的时候才喝酒水。

▲ Do not make any noise when you eat.
吃饭的时候不要发出很多噪音。

▲ Do not clean your teeth at the table or anywhere in public, either with your finger or a tooth pick, not even with your tongue.
不要在餐桌或其他公众场合清洁你的牙齿,不管是用手指还是牙签,哪怕是用舌头也不行。

▲ When passing someone an item such as the salt shaker, set it on the table in front of the person, not in his hand.
当传递比如盐罐之类的东西给某人的时候,应放在他的前面,而不是放在他的手里。

▲ Don't put your elbows on the table.
不要把胳膊肘搁在桌子上。

▲ Eat slowly and pace your eating to that of the others at the table.
慢慢吃,与餐桌上其他人保持同步。

▲ When in doubt, do what the natives do. Watch and imitate.
如果有疑问,就按当地人的做法去做。观察并模仿他们。

Section C

Case and Development 案例与创新

Case 案例

Work with your partner and brainstorm a list of table manners. Then compare and contrast your list with the information of others. You are encouraged to talk about dinner table manners in your families and customs practiced in your own homes. Each person can make a "Top Tens at My Table" poster to share with the class.

Development 创新

• Can you identify the similarities and differences between Chinese and American dinner table customs?

• Do you know any special table customs in other countries?

• What table manners do you think everyone should obey? What table manners do you think are not necessary in our culture?

实训模块五

康乐中心
Recreation Center

Recreation Center, as an auxiliary part to a hotel, aims first of all to fulfill an excellent reception service. The service in Recreation Center has all the characteristics of other hotel services, enthusiastic, polite, patient and considerate and the like. But it has many of its own distinguished features as well.

康乐中心的首要功能是作为酒店的配套附属设施,目标是高质量地完成接待任务。康乐中心服务具有酒店服务特点的许多共性。如:热情好客、文明礼貌、耐心周到等。但它仍有许多鲜明的特征。

技能实训 22　健身服务 Gym Service

Section A

Basic Knowledge for Position 岗位基础知识

Ⅰ. Word Stock 语料库

gym/gymnasium	健身房，体操房
fitness center	健身中心
health club	健身俱乐部
get fit	保持体态
lose weight	减肥
gain weight	增重
build muscle	增强肌肉
shape your body	塑身
trainer	健身教练
sneaker	运动鞋
locker	置物柜
membership fee	入会费
ball games	球类运动
basketball	篮球
bowling	保龄球
volleyball	排球
badminton	羽毛球
golf	高尔夫球
tennis	网球
table tennis/ping-pong	乒乓球
basketball court	篮球场
go bowling/rolling	打保龄球
bowling alley	保龄球馆
golf course	高尔夫球场
indoor tennis court	室内网球场

outdoor tennis court	室外网球场
warm-up	热身运动，准备活动
body building/physical culture	健美（身）运动
shape-up exercise	形体训练
bodybuilder/physical culturist	健美运动员
Miss World	世界小姐

Ⅱ. Pronunciation 语音训练

1. We have a well-equipped gym with the latest recreational sports apparatus.
   我们有设备良好的健身房，里面有最新式的娱乐体育器械。

2. It's becoming a trend for modern people to work out in the gym.
   现代人在健身房健身已慢慢成为一种趋势。

3. A calorie-controlled diet will help those who want to lose weight.
   控制热量的饮食对想减肥的人很有帮助。

4. I work out every day in order to increase the muscle in my chest and arms and get rid of the fat around my waist.
   我每天健身，为的就是增加我胸部和手臂的肌肉，并消除腰部的脂肪。

5. We all should warm up before doing some exercises.
   开始做运动前，我们都应该暖身。

6. Every time you work out you should begin and end with a few stretches.
   每次健身的前后，都应该做些伸展的动作。

7. You can use a heart rate monitor to know your heart rate.
   你可以使用心跳显示器得知你的心跳率。

8. Our body can take the time necessary to metabolize fats.
   我们的身体需要足够的时间来把脂肪代谢掉。

9. Bowling is one kind of sports which has a long history and many people are keen on.
   保龄球是一项具有悠久历史的体育项目，深受人们喜欢。

10. Hope you all have a pleasant time. If you need any help, please let me know at once.
    祝你们玩得愉快，有什么需要帮忙的请告诉我。

Section B

Service Procedure 服务流程

1. Greetings.
   问候。
2. Introduce service items and facilities.
   介绍服务项目和设施。
3. Introduce the charge.
   介绍费用。
4. Examine the room card.
   检查房卡。
5. Go through the procedure.
   办手续。
6. Lead the guest to the place.
   带客人到指定位置。
7. Settle the account.
   结账。
8. Bid farewell to the guest.
   道别。

Ⅰ. Service Performance 服务演练

A=Attendant, Liu Fang（服务生）　　　G=Guest, Mr. Brown（客人）

A: Hello! Welcome to the table tennis room. I'm Liu Fang, an attendant here. It's my pleasure to serve you.
　　您好！欢迎光临乒乓球室！我是这里的服务生刘方，能为您服务不胜荣幸！

G: Hello! The room looks nice and bright.
　　你好！这里看起来很宽敞明亮。

A: Yes. You know table tennis is popular not only in China, but many countries in the world. So we want to give our guest first class practice here.
　　是的。您知道乒乓球不仅在中国很普遍，在世界很多国家也是很著名的。所以我们希望能在这里给我们的客人一流的实践。

G: Wonderful! We are sure to enjoy ourselves here.
　　太好了！我们肯定会玩得很开心。

A: Do you like watching table tennis match? Can you name some of the Chinese famous table tennis players?

您喜欢看乒乓球比赛吗？您能说出一些中国著名的球星的名字吗？

G：Yes, I do. Deng Yaping, Wang Nan for Women's, and Liu Guoliang, Ma Lin for Men's, they are famous all over the world.

当然知道。女子的有邓亚萍、王楠；男子的有刘国梁、马琳等，这些人在全世界都是很著名的。

A：Great! How many people are there in your party?

真棒！请问你们一共有几位？

G：There are altogether five of us. Can we have two tables?

我们一共有五位。我们可以用两个乒乓球台吗？

A：Certainly you can. But we charge each table 25 RMB for an hour. Please go through your procedures in the service counter when you leave.

当然可以。但是每台桌子每小时收费25元人民币。请在活动结束后到服务台办理结账手续。

G：OK. That is acceptable. We want two.

好的，这个价格可以接受。我们要两张球桌。

A：Do you have your own table tennis bat and ball? If you don't have, we can provide you free of charge.

你们自己有乒乓球拍和乒乓球吗？如果你们没有，我们可以免费提供。

G：Thank you.

谢谢。

A：Anything you want to drink?

请问你们要喝点什么？

G：Just bottles of mineral water.

来几瓶矿泉水就可以了。

A：OK. Is there anything else I can do for you?

好的。请问还有其他需要吗？

G：Not now. Thank you!

现在没有了。谢谢！

A：Hope you all have a wonderful time. If you need any help, don't hesitate to let me know.

祝你们玩得愉快。有什么需要帮忙的请告诉我。

Ⅱ. **Position Practice 岗位实训**

★ What items are included in gym services?（健身包括哪些项目？）

It mainly includes basketball, volleyball, badminton, tennis, golf, table tennis, bowling, arrow shooting, gymnastics, etc. Different hotels provide different items according to their own conditions.

它主要包括篮球、排球、羽毛球、网球、高尔夫球、乒乓球、保龄球和射箭、体操等健身项目。不同酒店根据自身情况设置不同的项目。

★ World famous tennis competitions.（世界著名网球比赛）

All-England (Wimbledon) Lawn Tennis Championships 全英（温布尔登）草地网球锦标赛

French Open Tennis Championships 法国网球公开赛

US Open Tennis Championships 美国网球公开赛

Australian Open Tennis Championships 澳大利亚网球公开赛

ATP（Association of Tennis Professionals）Tour 国际职业网球联合会巡回赛

WTA（Women's Tennis Association）Tour 女子网球协会巡回赛

★ Introduce the items for gym service.（向客人介绍健身项目）

We have many kinds of items for gym service such as playing basketball, volleyball, table tennis, etc. You can also swim in the swimming pool.

我们有很多项目的康体运动，比如打篮球、排球、乒乓球等。您还可以去游泳池游泳。

★ Introduce the price for each item.（向客人介绍各项目价格）

Can I introduce the rate for each item of sports?

我能向您介绍各运动项目的价格吗？

★ Remind guests of the matters to be attended to when doing sports.（提醒客人注意事项）

You'd better do some warm-up training before the exercises in order to avoid ankle sprain, muscle injury or knee hurt.

运动之前，请先做好热身运动，以免发生脚踝扭伤、肌肉拉伤、膝盖损伤等意外事故。

★ Announce guests of settling account.（告诉客人结账事宜）

Would you please pay the money at the Service Centre after the training?

请您在运动后去服务台结账，可以吗？

★ Remind guests of indemnity for damage.（提醒客人损坏赔偿事宜）

As the hotel policy, if there is any damage for the equipment, you have to make the compensation with full price.

按照酒店规定，如果有器械损坏，您将照原价赔偿。

Ⅲ. Listening Practice 听力实训

★ A. Listen to the following passage about gym service and complete the missing information.

Like other travellers, you hope for a _____ at any hotel. With services like gym facilities, visitors in Radison Plaza Hotel find it to be a _____ for both _____ . The hotel provides a variety of services all designed with _____ in mind. You will also be given _____ on technique and exercise advice during the exercise. Gym service _____ all the guests staying in our hotel. Gym service is included in your _____ . Come to our gym center and _____ energetic!

★ B. Complete the following conversation.

Attendant: Good afternoon, sir. May I help you?

Guest: Yes, please. Life has been easy and _____ .

Attendant: I think the best way to _____ is to do some exercises.

Guest: What activities do you offer?

Attendant: We offer _____, running, cycling, muscle building and chest expanding.

Guest: Do you have a coach here to supervise the exercises?

Attendant: Yes, we have a resident coach here. _____ .

Guest: And your service hour?

Attendant: _____ .

Guest: Good. I'll try cycling first.

Important 特别关注

▲ Remind the guests of changing sport shoes.
   提醒客人要换运动鞋。

▲ Remind the guests of proper training.
   提醒客人适量运动。

▲ Close watch the guests in case of the accident.
   密切关注客人，以免发生意外。

Section C

Case and Development 案例与创新

Case 案例

Suppose you work in the Recreation Department. Now there comes a long-stay guest. Make a conversation between two of you. The attendant should greet the guest and introduce the service to the guest while the guest should ask questions to find out what he wants to know.

Development 创新

- How much do you know about Taichi? Why does Taichi become more and more popular among foreigners?
- What advice can you give the guest to keep fit?
- What kind of life style can be called healthy life style?

技能实训 23 美容美发服务 Beauty Parlor Service

Section A

Basic Knowledge for Position 岗位基础知识

 I. Word Stock 语料库

foaming cleanser	洗面奶
day cream	日霜
night cream	晚霜
eye cream	眼霜
cosmetic	化妆品
lip stick	口红
powder	粉饼
make up	化妆
bridal make up	新娘妆
evening make up	晚妆
day make up	日妆
beauty salon	美容院
beautician	美容师
anti-wrinkle	抗老防皱
essence	精华液
foundation	粉底
freshener	化妆水
mask	面膜
normal	中性皮肤
oily	油性皮肤
remover	去除、卸妆
permanent	烫发
cut/hair cutting	剪发
color/hair coloring	染发
hair design	发型设计
massage	按摩

full service	全套服务
brow pencil	眉笔
cosmetic bag	化装包
fashion	发型
haircutter	理发师

Ⅱ. Pronunciation 语音训练

1. I want my hair dyed.
   我想染发。

2. Your present hair style does not suit you that much.
   您现在的发型不太适合您。

3. Can I have my hair thinned out a bit?
   能把我的头发削薄一点吗?

4. We have separate locker rooms over there. You can use them free of charge.
   我们有单独的带锁的更衣箱,您可以免费使用。

5. So far as I know, it takes a long time to have a good command of it.
   据我所知,要花很长时间才能掌握它。

6. The beard fits your face just perfectly.
   那胡子很配您的脸型。

7. Would you like a facial massage?
   您需要脸部按摩吗?

8. Your personality shines through the right hairstyle.
   您的个性可以通过合适的发型显示出来。

9. Have you taken a look at any of the new styles lately?
   您最近有没有看到什么新的发型?

10. I think you would look cute with short hair.
    我认为您剪短发一定很好看。

11. Do you think that would look good? I'm worried it will make my hair look unnatural.
    你认为那样会好看吗? 我担心那会使我的头发看起来不自然。

Section B

Service Procedure 服务流程

1. Greetings.
   问候。

2. Introduce service items and facilities.

   介绍服务项目和设施。

3. Introduce the charge.

   介绍费用。

4. Lead the guest to the place.

   带客人到指定位置。

5. Settle the account.

   结账。

6. Bid farewell to the guest.

   道别。

Ⅰ. Service Performance 服务演练

H＝ Hairdresser（美发师）　　G＝Guest（客人）

H：It's been a long time, Mrs. Lee.

　　李太太，很久没见了。

G：Yes. I went to Hawaii on a vacation with my husband.

　　是的。我和我丈夫刚从夏威夷度假回来。

H：When did you come back? Did you have a good time?

　　什么时候回来的？玩得好吗？

G：We came back the day before yesterday. I enjoyed myself there very much. The beach was beautiful. The sun was lovely, too. You should go there some day.

　　我们是前天回来的，在那儿玩得很开心。那里的阳光和沙滩都漂亮极了，以后你也应该去玩玩。

H：I will. How would you like your hair to be done today? The same style as usual?

　　我会去的。今天打算做什么发型啊？和平时一样的吗？

G：I have a wedding ceremony to attend tonight, and I'd like to change styles.

　　我今晚要参加一个婚宴，我想改变一下发型。

H：Here are some samples of hair styles. What do you think about this one?

　　这里有一些发型款式。这个怎样？

G：No, I don't like short hair... I like this one. The wave looks beautiful, and fits my age too.

　　不，我不喜欢短发。我喜欢这个，波浪形看起来很漂亮，也适合我的年龄。

H：Very well. You're not in a hurry, are you?

　　好的。你不着急吧？

G：No. You can take your time... Oh, I also want a manicure while I'm having the perm.

　　不急，你慢慢来。哦，烫头发的时候我还想随便修一下指甲。

H：OK. The manicurist will be right here.
好的。美甲师马上就过来。

G：Thank you. How much will this cost?
谢谢。多少钱？

H：It's one hundred and twenty dollars in all.
总共120美元。

Ⅱ. Position Practice 岗位实训

★ Introduce the price for each item. （向客人介绍各项目价格）
That'll cost you 600 yuan, madam.
那个项目要花600元，夫人。

★ How would you like your haircut? （你要剪什么样的发型）
Madam, we have various models: hair bobbed, hair sweptback, Chaplet hair style, shoulder length hair style, hair done in a bun.
太太，我们这里可以做各种各样的发型：短发、后掠式发型、盘头、齐肩发、发髻。

★ Introduce the therapeutic items provided. （向客人介绍保健项目）
The services which we can provide are skin-whitening, wrinkle-proofing, moist-keeping, and so on.
我们有美白、防皱、保湿等项目。

★ Announce guests of settling account. （告诉客人结账事宜）
Would you please pay the money at the Service Centre after the service?
请您在做完后去服务台结账，可以吗？

Ⅲ. Listening Practice 听力实训

★ A. Listen to the following passage about beauty salon and find out the missing information.

There are many different kinds of _____. The different types of salon services provide _____ for the body from head to toe. _____ are the most common. The style of service varies in _____ hairdressing salons. Day Spa salons may also serve guests tea _____ a light lunch. Services at a day spa often _____ massage, facials and skin care treatments. Many different types of salons feature _____. Makeup services are _____ at many kinds of salons. Traditionally, salon cosmetic services _____ women only, but increasingly, men's makeup options are also available.

★ B. Complete the following conversation.

Beautician: Hi. _____?

Customer: Yeah. I'd like to get my hair trimmed a little. Nothing fancy. Just a basic trim.

Beautician: Well, can we interest you _____?

Customer: Um... Nah, nah...

Beautician: We'll shampoo, cut, and style your hair for one unbelievable low price of _____.

Customer: Well, I don't know. I don't have much time, and ...

Beautician: _____!

Customer: Well, okay. I just want to get my hair trimmed. _____. That's all. I mean, that's all.

Beautician: _____. You're in good hands. Okay, here we go.

Customer: Hey, can I see a mirror?

Beautician: Nothing to worry about, sir. Relax. I'm just making some adjustments to the hair trimmer.

Customer: Oh, that really hurt! What are you doing anyway?

Beautician: Relax, sir, relax. _____.

Customer: Yeah, just wait till I get finished with you!

Beautician: Okay, now let's dry your hair, if you're not completely satisfied...

Customer: Satisfied? _____. I want to talk to the manager... now!

Beautician: I'm sorry, but he's on vacation, and he left me in charge, so if you...

Important 特别关注

▲ Talking in the proper terms of cosmetology, body-caring, etc.
使用美容、美体等专业术语。

▲ Pay attention to the complaint in cosmetology and body-caring, etc.
注意解决美容、美体等中的投诉。

▲ Remind the guests of stopping services in case of allergy.
提醒客人如有过敏症状,及时停止。

Section C

Case and Development 案例与创新

Case 案例

A middle-aged lady is an American who teaches English at a University in Beijing. She wants to have a cold wave. You, the hairdresser is serving her.

Development 创新

• How can you politely suggest the guest try a new hair style?
• If a guest's skin is very sensitive, what should be avoided when you do the facial massage?
• Why can a beautiful haircut make a person more elegant?

实训模块五　康乐中心　Recreation Center

技能实训 24　桑拿服务 Sauna Service

Section A

Basic Knowledge for Position 岗位基础知识

Ⅰ. Word Stock 语料库

bathrobe	浴衣
celsius	摄氏的
comfortable	舒适的
Fahrenheit	华氏的
festive	节日的，喜庆的
Finnish sauna	芬兰浴
fortune	财富，运气
inexperienced	没经验的，没经历过的
ingredient	成分，因素
inhabitant	居民，居住者
locker	橱柜，存物柜
lotion	沐浴液
mental	精神的，智力的，脑力的
moisture	潮湿，湿气
relax	放松
sauna proper	桑拿浴室
shower	淋浴
solely	独自地，单独地
stand	忍受
task	任务
temperature	温度

Ⅱ. Pronunciation 语音训练

1. Welcome to our Bathing Center! What can I do for you?
   欢迎光临洗浴中心！请问您需要什么服务项目？
2. Do you have a sauna?
   你们有桑拿浴室吗？

3. Good ideas are born in a good sauna.
   好的桑拿浴可激发好灵感。
4. We have a sauna bath with a massage service there, too.
   在那里还有桑拿浴室并提供按摩服务。
5. After you take a sauna, you will feel relaxed.
   洗过桑拿，您会感觉很放松。
6. Her face glowed when she came out of the sauna.
   当她从桑拿浴中出来时她的脸在发光。
7. I'd like to take a sauna. What is your charge?
   我要洗桑拿。请问收费标准是什么？
8. Please take on your slippers and take a shower first. Let me show you the way to the shower bath room.
   请您换好拖鞋，先去淋浴。让我带您去淋浴间吧。
9. May I know how many kinds of sauna bath you have?
   请问你们这里有几种蒸法？
10. The sauna bath services in our hotel include damp, dry, salt and ice steam bath.
    我们有湿蒸浴、干蒸浴、盐浴和水蒸浴4种。

Section B

Service Procedure 服务流程

1. Greetings.
   问候。
2. Introduce service items and facilities.
   介绍服务项目和设施。
3. Introduce the charge.
   介绍费用。
4. Examine the room card.
   检查房卡。
5. Go through the procedure.
   办手续。
6. Lead the guest to the place.
   带客人到指定位置。
7. Settle the account.

结账。

8. Bid farewell to the guest.
   道别。

Ⅰ. Service Performance 服务演练

C=Recreation Attendant（康乐中心服务生）　　G=Guest（客人）

C：Here are hotel's sauna rooms. Is there anything I can do for you?
这里是我们酒店的桑拿室。有什么需要帮助的吗？

G：I'd like to take sauna. What shall I do first?
我想洗桑拿，我得先做什么？

C：For the guest's health's sake, those who have heart disease or high blood pressure are not allowed to take sauna.
考虑到健康的原因，有心脏病和高血压的人是不允许洗桑拿的。

G：Thank you for telling me this. I'm in good condition.
谢谢你告诉我。我的健康状况良好。

C：First, change your shoes to slippers. Then walk up to the changing room to get prepared for a shower. After the shower, you can enter the bath room proper you choose.
先换拖鞋。然后去更衣室准备冲淋浴。淋浴之后，您就可以走进你选好的桑拿间里。

G：I see. By the way, is there any difference between Finnish sauna and Turkish sauna?
我明白了。顺便问一声芬兰浴与土耳其浴有何不同？

C：In the Finnish sauna room, there's a stove in the sauna, fired with wood, and on top of the stove is a pile of stones, which keep the heat. Throw some water on the stones, and dry steam is given off. In the Turkish bath room, you are supposed to change the temperature on the thermometer.
在芬兰式桑拿间里有一个用木头做燃料的炉子，炉子上有一堆石头，这是为了保持温度的。在石头上浇一些水，这样就会散发出干蒸汽。在土耳其式浴室里是根据温度计调节温度的。

G：Why should you have dry steam?
为什么要用干蒸？

C：That is to step up the blood circulation and produce vigorous perspiration. You'll be sweating bullets. After ten minutes or so it's time to cool off under a shower or go for a quick swim.
这是为了促进血液循环和大量的排汗，会让你汗珠一直往下淌。大约过10分钟左右就可以去冲个澡或游一会泳以便让温度降下来。

G：Sounds crazy to me.
听起来有点疯狂。

C：Actually it's fun. People usually go back into the bath room itself three times.
事实上是很有意思的。通常每个人都要进去蒸三次。

G：What happens then?
洗完以后呢?

C：Then you wash yourself, or rather to be washed. And then you wrap yourself up in your sauna robe. You can have a snack, if you'd like it.
然后冲洗干净。穿上浴袍，您还可以吃点小点心。

G：I see. Thank you for telling me.
知道了。谢谢你给我介绍。

G：My pleasure.
很高兴为您服务。

Ⅱ. Position Practice 岗位实训

★ Introduce the price for each item. （向客人介绍各项目价格）
Can I introduce the rate for each item of sauna?
我能向您介绍各桑拿项目的价格吗?

★ Remind guests of the matters to be attended to when sauna. （提醒客人桑拿注意事项）

1. That is to step up the blood circulation and produce vigorous perspiration. You'll be sweating bullets.
那会加快血液循环，流汗很多。你整个人就会像汗人了。

2. If you feel hungry, just relax yourself by having some soft drinks and cakes at the poolside bar.
如果你感觉饿了，就到池边的酒吧里去喝些饮料，吃点蛋糕，放松一下。

3. We have separate locker rooms over there. You can use them free of charge.
我们有单独的带锁的更衣箱，您可以免费使用。

★ Announce guests of settling account. （告诉客人结账事宜）
Would you please pay the money at the Service Centre after sauna?
请您在洗桑拿后去服务台结账，可以吗?

★ Introduce dry sauna to the guest. （向客人介绍干蒸浴）
Dry Sauna bath, also called Turkish bath, started in Eastern Europe. People sit in round in a wooden room bathing the steam from the mineral stones which are sprinkled by cold water after burnt in red.
干蒸浴又称土耳其浴，该浴法起源于东欧，即浴客们围坐在一个木质结构的浴室里，室内设有矿石炉，经通电烧红后，再浇上冰水，由此产生大量蒸汽供客人沐浴。

实训模块五　康乐中心　Recreation Center

★ Sauna Bath, also named as Steam Bath, is one kind of health care bathing. It has an effect of eliminating tiredness and enhancing quality of body. It is also helpful to treat some diseases.

桑拿浴又称蒸汽浴，是一种健身型沐浴方式，具有消除疲劳、增强体质的功效，并对某些疾病有治疗的作用。

Ⅲ. Listening Practice 听力实训

★ A. Listen to the following passage about sauna and complete the missing information.

Sauna has a long history. In Finland it has at least _____ of history. Sauna is a _____ or hut heated to around _____ degrees centigrade. It is used for bathing as well as for _____ relaxation. While a hot sauna may seem a cruel punishment to _____ bathers, it is actually a very _____. All you need is a _____ and at least half an hour of time. Start with _____, and then enter the sauna for a few minutes, _____ your senses. When you've had enough, take a refreshing shower, _____ for a while and repeat _____. And there is no need to _____, it's entirely safe.

★ B. Complete the following conversation.

Attendant: Good evening, sir. _____ .

Guest: Good evening. What kind of sauna do you have here?

Attendant: Ours is Finnish _____ .

Guest: What's the temperature in the sauna proper?

Attendant: About 212°F. _____ .

Guest: I see.

Attendant: Here's the key to the locker and towel.

Guest: Thank you.

(A few minutes later, the guest rushes out, sweating all over.)

Attendant: _____?

Guest: I feel quite good.

Attendant: Would you like a _____ in the sauna bar?

Guest: All right. I feel so hungry.

Attendant: This way, please.

Important 特别关注

▲ In order to stop steam evaporation, please close the door as soon as you open it.
为减少热气蒸发，请在进出桑拿室时随手关门。

▲ There is a caution for taking sauna, those who have heart disease or high blood pressure are not allowed to take sauna, for their health's sake.
洗桑拿要注意，考虑到健康原因，不允许有心脏病或高血压的人洗桑拿浴。

Section C

Case and Development 案例与创新

Case 案例

Suppose you are an inexperienced visitor to a sauna center. Ask the attendant some questions to find out what a Finnish sauna is and why sauna is good to people's health.

Development 创新

- Do you know different saunas have different effects on people?
- How to bathe in a Finnish sauna? Describe it in your own words.
- What is a sauna and who cannot take a sauna?

技能实训 25 娱乐服务 Entertainment Service

Section A

Basic Knowledge for Position 岗位基础知识

Ⅰ. Word Stock 语料库

brass band	管乐队
string orchestra	弦乐队
light music	轻音乐
pop music	流行音乐
country music	乡村音乐
jazz music	爵士音乐
rock music	摇滚音乐
hot music	热门音乐
classic music	古典音乐
modern music	现代音乐
lyric song	抒情歌曲
folk song	民歌，山歌
ballad	民谣，小调
love song	情歌
ballet	芭蕾舞
social dancing	交谊舞
waltz	华尔兹舞
foxtrot	狐步舞
tango	探戈舞
rumba	伦巴舞
breaking	霹雳舞
hula-hula	草裙舞
Yangko dance	秧歌舞
discotheque	迪斯科舞厅
karaoke	卡拉 OK
KTV	包间

实训模块五 康乐中心 Recreation Center

voice	声音，嗓音
title (of a song)	歌名
stereo system	立体音响
microphone	麦克风
catalogue/list	歌单，目录
remote control	遥控器
volume	音量
English songs	英文歌
net bar	网吧

Ⅱ. Pronunciation 语音训练

1. Minors are not allowed.
   未成年人不得入内。
2. How many people do you have?
   你们一行一共几个人？
3. There is a minimum charge at the karaoke bar.
   卡拉 OK 吧设有最低消费。
4. If you are not a registered guest, you will be charged at least 100 yuan, excluding drinks.
   如果您不是住店客人，至少要收 100 元，不包括酒水。
5. There is a fashion show in the night club.
   夜总会有时装表演。
6. There is no entrance fee for registered guest.
   住店客人不收入场费。
7. Would you please show me your room cards?
   能够出示你们的房卡吗？
8. Would you like something to drink?
   要不要喝点什么？
9. We have a live floor show featuring a band called Four And One.
   我们有特约的"四加一"乐队的现场表演。
10. Do you use video cassettes or laser discs?
    你们用录像带还是激光唱片？
11. I'd like to have a computer in the Net Bar looming for something.
    我想在你们的网吧上网查点资料。
12. The price is more expensive than the net bars outside the hotel.
    这比外面的网吧贵多了。

13. This is your computer, is it all right? I'll switch on the power; you can use the net by pressing this key.

您使用这台电脑行吗？我帮您接通电源，开启电脑，您只要按这个键，便可直接上网。

Section B

Service Procedure 服务流程

1. Greetings.
   问候。
2. Introduce service items and facilities.
   介绍服务项目和设施。
3. Introduce the charge.
   介绍费用。
4. Lead the guest to the place.
   带客人到指定位置。
5. Settle account.
   结账。
6. Bid farewell to the guest.
   道别。

Ⅰ. Service Performance 服务演练

R＝Receptionist（服务员）　　A＝Andy　　C＝Christine

A：It's a nice day, isn't it?
　　今天天气真好，对吧？
C：Absolutely. How about going to a karaoke bar and relax?
　　绝对是的。去卡拉OK吧唱歌放松一下怎么样？
A：Good idea. Are there any karaoke bars nearby?
　　好主意。这附近有卡拉OK吧吗？
C：Yeah. I know there is an excellent karaoke bar in Holiday Inn.
　　有的。我知道假日酒店有一个很不错的卡拉OK吧。
A：It sounds great.
　　好的。
（They arrive at the hotel.）（抵达酒店。）

A: Where is the karaoke bar?
卡拉 OK 吧在哪儿?

C: Maybe it is on the third floor! Oh, I'm not sure. Let me ask the receptionist. Just a minute. Excuse me, could you tell me the way to the karaoke bar?
可能在三楼。我不是很确定。我去问问前台服务员,稍等。对不起,你能告诉我卡拉 OK 吧在哪儿?

R: Certainly. Go straight to the elevator from here and go down to the second floor. Turn left when you get out of the lift and you'll find it.
当然。从这里直接走到电梯下到二楼,出了电梯后然后向左转就可以看到了。

A: Is it open now?
现在营业吗?

R: Yes, it opens at 9:00 p.m. and closes at 3:00 a.m..
是的。晚上 9 点开到凌晨 3 点。

C: Is there anything we should take care of?
我们有需要注意的事项吗?

R: Actually, no.
没有。

C: I think we'd better get a private room. We don't want to be disturbed.
我想我们最好要一个包间。我们不想别人打扰我们。

R: It's no problem. We have a very nice private room.
没问题。我们有一个很好的包间。

A: How about the drinks here?
有饮料吗?

R: There are 30 kinds of drinks for you to choose from, so you can choose any one you like.
我们提供 30 种饮料供您选择。您可以选择任何一种。

C: I heard you also provide different kinds of cocktails made by good bartenders.
我听说你们还提供由非常优秀的酒吧调酒员调制的各种各样的鸡尾酒。

R: Yes. That's right. What's more, you can enjoy beautiful music from the band.
是的,没错。另外,您还可以欣赏乐队演出的非常动听的音乐。

A: Wonderful! I cannot wait to see their performance. By the way, what's the charge?
太好了!我已经等不及了想看他们的表演。顺便问一下,价格多少?

R: Are you staying at our hotel?
你们是住在我们酒店吗?

A: No.
不是。

R：According to our rules, if you are registered guests, we charge you for the drinks. If you are not, we charge 100 RMB for each private room excluding drinks.

根据我们的规定，如果你们是登记入住的客人，我们只收酒水费。如果你们不是我们的住店客人，除了收酒水费用外，每个包间我们还要收 100 元。

A&C：Thank you so much, we have to go now.

非常感谢。我们现在就去。

R：See you! Have a good time.

再见！希望你们玩得愉快。

Ⅱ. Position Practice 岗位实训

★ Karaoke Bar.（卡拉 OK 吧）

1. How many people do you have?

    你们一行一共几个人？

2. There is a minimum charge at the karaoke bar.

    卡拉 OK 吧设有最低消费。

3. If you are not a registered guest, you will be charged at least 100 yuan, excluding drinks.

    如果您不是住店客人，至少要收 100 元，不包括酒水。

★ Night Club.（夜总会）

1. People under 18 are not allowed in the night club.

    不满 18 岁不允许进入夜总会。

2. There is a fashion show in the night club.

    夜总会有时装表演。

★ At the ball room.（舞厅）

1. There is no entrance fee for registered guest.

    住店客人不收入场费。

2. Would you please show me your room cards?

    能够出示你们的房卡吗？

3. Would you like something to drink?

    要不要喝点什么？

4. Will you honor me with a dance?

    请赏光跳个舞，好吗？

5. I'm engaged with this Tango.

    已经有人约我跳探戈舞了。

★ Mahjong's room.（麻将室）

1. Mahjong is a traditional Chinese recreational activity.

    麻将是中国传统的娱乐活动。

2. It is somewhat like playing cards.
   玩麻将有点像打扑克牌。
3. Playing Mahjong is very time-consuming.
   玩麻将很浪费时间。

Ⅲ. Listening Practice 听力实训

★ A. Listen to the following passage about entertainment and complete the missing information.

Most hotels and resorts have outstanding _____ and entertainment, guests may find plenty options for the _____ . Some guests can dance and _____ after a busy day of sightseeing. Others may listen to the _____ or enjoy a good _____ . If hotels don't have the _____ entertainment facilities, when the sun goes down and the guests may head out for the night, exploring _____ or just watching the sunset with an icy _____, these places are probably within _____ or quick drive. Dazzling and gentle lighting brings the guests into _____, making the guests too delighted to leave in the nightlife.

★ B. Complete the following conversation.

Attendant: Good evening, sir. _____ .

Guest: Good evening. A table in the corner, please.

Attendant: Yes. This way, please... Please take your seat. _____?

Guest: Lemon Juice, please.

Attendant: All right. Just a minute... _____ .

Guest: What beautiful music! Would you care to have a dance with me, Miss?

Attendant: I'd be glad to, _____ .

Guest: All right. To tell the truth, you are the prettiest girl I've ever met.

Attendant: Thank you for saying so.

Guest: Can we be friends?

Attendant: Yes, _____ . But I don't know your name.

Guest: Fox. And yours?

Attendant: Lisa Wang.

(Mr. Fox is about to leave.)

Guest: Lisa. This is for you. Your service is excellent.

Attendant: Thank you, Mr. Fox. _____ .

Guest: Goodbye.

Important 特别关注

▲ Please use the equipments carefully according to the regulation. Any artificially imposed damages caused by wrong use will be compensate.
请按照操作规范使用网吧设备,凡因人为使用不当所造成的损坏均须按酒店规定予以赔偿。

▲ If you meet any problems when you are running the computer, please ask our staff for help. Don't change or delete data of the computer by yourselves.
上网时,若遇到疑难问题,请咨询服务人员帮忙解决。不得改变或删除电脑数据。

▲ Please don't listen, watch and copy unhealthy contents which are obscene, superstitious or reactionary. It's not allowed to do anything that has nothing to do with the service contents.
不得在网吧收听、收看、拷贝淫秽、迷信、反动等不健康的内容。不得在网吧从事与服务内容无关的其他任何活动。

Section C

Case and Development 案例与创新

Case 案例

A group of young people come into a KTV room to celebrate a birthday party. The waitress is receiving them.

Development 创新

• If there is a minimum charge at the karaoke bar, shall you inform the guests in advance?

• What shall you explain to the children under 18 when they want to enter the night club?

• Are drinks free of charge for the registered guest at the ball room?

实训模块六
购物服务
Shopping Service

  Shopping arcade is an important composition of a hotel, most of the hotels offer shopping arcade to meet the need of the hotel guests and gain economic benefits as well. As an attendant in a shopping arcade, he has to equip himself with not only a fairly good command of foreign language, friendliness and politeness, but also the knowledge of the goods he sells, to provide the guests with a proper introduction, giving them a pleasant shopping experience during the tour.

  商场是酒店经营的一个重要组成部分,涉外酒店多设有自己的商场以在满足住店客人的需要的同时,赢得经济效益。作为商场服务员,在具有较好的外语交际能力的基础上,不仅要友好礼貌地对待客人,还需要对自己所销售的商品有足够的了解,向客人进行恰到好处的介绍,以方便游客在游玩的闲暇中享受购物的乐趣。

技能实训 26　旅游纪念品 Souvenir

Section A

Basic Knowledge for Position 岗位基础知识

I. Word Stock 语料库

antique shop	古玩店
antique	古玩
bracelet	镯子
brooch	胸针
calligraphy	书法
chain bracelet	手链
change	零钱
cosmetics	化妆用品
electric razor	电剃刀
crystal	水晶
ear ring	耳环
free of charge	不收费
genuine	真的
gold jewelry	金饰
imitation	仿制品
jewelry, jewels	首饰，珠宝
necklace	项链
pearl	珍珠
porcelain	瓷器
price tag	标价签
ring, finger ring	戒指
shop assistant, salesman	售货员
show window	橱窗
silk fan	绢扇
silk flower	绢花
silk painting	绢画

silver jewelry	银饰
souvenir	纪念品
deliver	送
keep the bill	留发票
wrap up	包装

Ⅱ. Pronunciation 语音训练

1. China is the homeland of giant pandas so it could be an ideal gift for your relatives or friends.
   中国是大熊猫的故乡，所以它应该是给您亲戚或朋友理想的礼物。

2. The artists can produce various kinds of paper cutting like human figures, landscapes, flowers, birds, etc.
   艺术家可以剪不同形状的纸，如人物、风景、花朵、鸟类等。

3. Paper cutting of Yangzhou has created a unique artistic style and strong local features.
   扬州剪纸创造了独特的艺术风格和鲜明的地方特色。

4. You have an excellent shape. Cheongsam is so popular with young ladies nowadays in China.
   你的身材非常好。如今旗袍在中国很受年轻女士的欢迎。

5. It might be a little expensive, but the material is of the best quality, and our workmanship is the best in the city. It's worth every penny of it.
   这件衣服也许有点贵，但用料上乘，而且我们的工艺在这个城市是最好的，非常值。

6. What color do you think is the most suitable for me?
   你认为哪种颜色适合我？

7. Will you please let me have a close look at the silk fabrics?
   能让我仔细看看这块真丝面料吗？

8. The suit looks terrific on you. Would you like to take it?
   这套西装穿在你身上很棒。你要买它吗？

9. I'd like to buy some cutting seals. Would you please show me some for selection?
   我想买几块石章。你能拿一些让我挑选吗？

10. This is the right Yixing Earthen teapot that he has dreamed of for years.
    这正是他多年来梦寐以求的宜兴紫砂壶。

Section B

Service Procedure 服务流程

1. Greetings.
   问候。
2. Find out what the guest wants.
   获得关于客人所需的信息。
3. Recommend or introduce products to the guest.
   向客人介绍产品。
4. Praise the products that the guest chooses.
   称赞客人挑选的产品。
5. Tell the guest where and how to pay.
   告诉客人去哪里及怎么样付款。
6. Bid farewell to the guest.
   道别。

Ⅰ. Service Performance 服务演练

A＝Shop Assistant（商场服务员）　　　G＝Guest（客人）

A：Can I help you?
　　需要帮助吗?

G：I want to find something typically Chinese to decorate my room.
　　我想买代表典型中国特色的东西装饰我的房间。

A：How about this artistic tapestry and this cloisonné vase?
　　这个艺术挂毯和这个景泰蓝花瓶怎么样?

G：Well，I am looking for something a little different. These teapots are beautiful. The color is similar to that of my sitting room. Are they made of porcelain?
　　我想买一些特别的东西。这些茶具很漂亮，颜色和我的客厅的颜色很相近。它们是瓷制的吗?

A：No，they are made of clay. They are Yixing purple clay teapots. This kind of tea ware is very famous in China.
　　不是的。它们是由黏土做成的，是宜兴紫砂壶。这种茶具在中国很有名。

G：Ah，I see. How can I make tea with this teapot?
　　哦，知道了。用这个茶具怎么泡茶?

A：That depends on what kind of tea you want to make, the Chinese tea is classified into green tea, white tea, oolong tea, black tea, Pu'er tea, scented tea and etc. What kind of tea do you like?
这取决于你要泡什么茶。中国茶分为绿茶、白茶、乌龙茶、红茶、普洱茶和花茶等。你想喝什么茶？

G：Well, I am a little familiar with black tea. Can you show me how to make the tea?
哦，我比较熟悉红茶。你能泡给我看吗？

A：I am sorry to say we do not have any tea in this shop, but I can tell you the steeping method. First, put the tea leaves into the pot, then our hot water into it, the amount of tea in proportion to water is 1 to 9. The temperature of the water is 100℃. After 10 seconds, the tea is ready.
对不起，我们店里现在没有茶叶。但我可以教您浸泡方法。首先，把茶叶放入茶壶中，然后加上开水，茶叶和水的比例是1∶9。水的温度是100℃。10秒钟后，茶水就泡好了。

G：Thanks. What is the price of this tea set?
多谢，这套茶具价格是多少？

A：It is 600 yuan.
价格要600元。

G：That's too much, I will take it if you give me a 40% discount.
太贵了。如果你给我打6折，我就买一些。

A：Well, I can just take 100 yuan off the price.
哦。我只能给您减掉100元。

G：All right, I will take this set.
好的。我买了。

A：Anything else for you?
您还需要其他的吗？

G：Yes, what is the design of this paper cut?
是的。这个剪纸是什么？

A：They are lotus flowers.
是荷花。

G：Ah, how beautiful! How much is it?
哦，真漂亮！多少钱？

A：It is 20 yuan.
20元。

G：I will take it as well. Can I have it framed? I want to hang it up in the bedroom.
这个我也买了。能帮我镶个镜框吗？我想把它挂在卧式里。

A：Yes, but you will have to pay for the frame. It is 30 yuan.
好的。但你得付镜框的钱，30元。

G：All right. Here is the money. It is 550 yuan altogether.
好的。给你钱。一共是550元。

A：Thank you.
谢谢。

G：Would you give me a shopping bag?
你能给我一个购物袋吗？

A：Yes, here you are.
当然，给您。

Ⅱ. Position Practice 岗位实训

★ Introduce different tea to the guest.（向客人介绍不同的茶）

1. The top grade Longjing Tea is manually baked. It is fresh green with a strong aroma.
极品龙井茶是手工焙制的。它色泽碧绿，香味特别浓郁。

2. Anhui Tieguanyin is fine both in appearance and in quality, and it has a weight-reducing / adiposia-reducing effect.
安徽铁观音无论外形还是质量均属上乘，而且它具有减肥效果。

3. It's a high quality green tea mixed with dried jasmine flowers.
这种绿茶质量高，里面有晒干的茉莉花。

★ Introduce "Four Treasures of Study" to the guest.（向客人介绍文房四宝）

"Four Treasures of Study" are the four stationery items indispensable to any traditional Chinese scholar. Which include a brush pen, an ink stick, paper, and an ink stone.
"文房四宝"指的是古代中国学者不可缺少的书房用具：笔、墨、纸、砚。

★ Introduce different paintings.（介绍不同的画）

Briefly speaking, Western oil paintings are created by colors and brush touches while traditional Chinese paintings are by lines and strokes.
简单地说，西方油画是由颜色和油画笔画出来的，而传统中国画是由线条勾勒一笔一笔画出来的。

Ⅲ. Listening Practice 听力实训

★ A. Listen to the following passage about souvenirs and find out the missing information.

Millions of foreigners, _____ Chinese visit mainland of China every year _____, _____, or exchanges in different fields. Many of them return home loaded with _____ . Souvenirs are precious _____ for most tourists. Some guests will buy T-shirts, key chains, _____ or any candies that are native to a place. Others may buy some _____ from a native city or some souvenirs with the name of the city on it. _____ are also a good choice as souvenirs. It is a way to remember the _____ places. Guests can _____ souvenirs for themselves or their family and friends.

★ B. Complete the following conversation.

▲ If the guest says: "I'm just looking." This means they want to choose the articles they prefer in no hurry without being interfered.
如果客人说:"我只是看看。"说明他们不想被关注,希望自己慢慢挑选合意的商品。

▲ If the articles which the guest has bought are antiques and valuables, the shop assistant still needs to remind him to keep the receipt or invoice well in case it is inspected by the customs.
如果客人购买的是古玩或特别贵重的物品,还需要提醒客人保存好收据或发票,以备海关查验。

Section C

Case and Development 案例与创新

Case 案例

A guest comes into your shopping arcade to look for a carpet for his friend. You are the shop assistant there. Try your best to give the guest a detailed introduction to your products. The guest shows great interest in a certain carpet. However, he begins to bargain for it.

Development 创新

• What kind of souvenirs are most attractive to visitors in China?

• Your guest finally decides that she's not going to buy any of the souvenirs which you have shown her. How do you help her to withdraw gracefully?

• Under what circumstances cannot the guests refund what he has bought in shopping arcade?

技能实训 27 当地特产 Local Specialty

Section A

Basic Knowledge for Position 岗位基础知识

 I. Word Stock 语料库

local specialty	当地特产
silk	蚕丝
satin	绸缎
brocade	织锦
silk product	丝绸产品
silk scarf	丝绸围巾
dry cleaning	干洗
press	熨
bed spread	床罩
quilt cover	被套
folding fan	折叠扇
silk umbrella	丝绸伞
bamboo products	竹制品
candied fruit	果脯
handicrafts	手工艺品
carvings	雕刻
scissors	剪刀
embroidery	刺绣
carpet	地毯
Beijing Crisp Candy	北京酥糖
wood-block prints	木版画
compared with	与……比较
cultural atmosphere	文化氛围
delicate appearance	精致的外观
exquisite workmanship	工艺精巧

Ⅱ. Pronunciation 语音训练

1. Silk products are very popular among tourists.
   丝绸产品非常受游客的欢迎。
2. What size would you like to have?
   您要多大的尺寸？
3. Please wash it by hand with special detergent for silk washing and rinse it well.
   手洗时请放一定量的真丝洗涤剂，然后用清水漂洗。
4. I wonder if the color will fade in washing.
   我想知道这种颜色在洗涤中会不会褪色。
5. Do you have T-shirts with Beijing Olympic printed on them?
   你有没有印有"北京奥运会"字样的T恤衫？
6. As a matter of fact, all the T-shirts here are both colorfast and shrink-proof.
   事实上，这里所有的T恤衫都不褪色，并且防缩水。
7. I'd like to buy a dress closely related to Chinese culture as a token for my trip in China.
   我想买一件具有中国文化特色的衣服，作为我中国之行的留念。
8. By the way, the silk shouldn't be hung out in the sunshine.
   顺便提醒您，真丝不能放在阳光下曝晒。

Section B

Service Procedure 服务流程

1. Greetings.
   问候。
2. Find out what the guest wants.
   获得客人需要什么的信息。
3. Recommend specialty to the guest.
   向客人介绍特产。
4. Praise the products that the guest chooses.
   称赞客人挑选的产品。
5. Tell the guest where and how to pay.
   告诉客人去哪里及怎么样付款。
6. Bid farewell to the guest.
   道别。

Ⅰ. Service Performance 服务演练

A= Shop Assistant（商场服务员）　　G= Guest（客人）

A：Good afternoon, madam. Can I help you?
女士，下午好。有什么需要帮忙的吗？

G：Yes. I'm looking for a silk shirt for my husband. Would you show me some, please?
是的。我想给我丈夫买一件真丝衬衣。能拿一件给我看看吗？

A：Certainly. We have a wide selection of silk shirts here. But what size, please?
当然。我们这里有很多真丝衬衣供您挑选。您要什么型号的？

G：Large.
大号。

A：How do you like these?
这几件怎么样？

G：How nice! They all look beautiful. But the problem is that I'm not good at choosing. I wonder if you could help me.
很好啊！看起来都很漂亮。但问题是我不太会挑选。你能帮我挑吗？

A：Yes, with pleasure. By feeling them, I can assure you that these shirts are of fine quality. They are made of silk with super texture. I would recommend the purple one. It is the fashionable color this year. I'm positive that your husband would be grateful to you for such an excellent gift.
好的，很高兴为您服务。用手摸摸，我可以向您保证这些衬衣的质量很好。它们是上好的真丝面料制成的。我向您推荐紫色的这件。今年很流行紫色，我敢保证您丈夫将非常高兴收到这份礼物。

G：Thank you very much. Incidentally, is the color fast?
非常感谢。随便问一下，不褪色吧？

A：Yes, it is and it is washable. But I would suggest that you wash by hand. Please don't rub. Just use soapy water and rinse well.
不褪色，可以水洗的。但我建议您手洗。不要用手搓，仅用肥皂水漂洗就可以了。

G：Right then, I would like to buy it. How much is it?
好的，那我买了。这件多少钱？

A：The price tag says two hundred and eighty yuan.
标签上是280元。

G：That is more than I expected to pay. Shall I see a cheaper one of the same quality?
太贵了。能给我看一件同等质量的便宜一点的吗？

A：I'm afraid not. In my opinion, it is worthwhile for its quality, though a bit expensive. It makes a good gift for your husband. But anyway, you have all the right to make your own decision.

可能没有了。我认为虽然这件贵点，但质量很好，是一件给您丈夫的很好的礼物。但不管怎么说，您可以再考虑考虑。

G：In that case, I might as well take it. Thank you very much for your help.
那好，我买一件。感谢你的帮助。

Ⅱ. Position Practice 岗位实训

★ Introduce Hangzhou silk to the guest. （向客人介绍杭州丝绸）

Silk is the symbol of the oriental culture and it represents the specialty and tradition of Hangzhou. Businesses here are covering silk clothes, artworks, tourist souvenirs, neckties, scarves and various raw silk materials. These products are sharing the consumer markets at home and abroad.

丝绸是东方文化的象征，它代表了杭州的特色和传统。杭州的丝绸产品包括真丝服装、艺术品、旅游纪念品、领带、丝巾和各种各样的真丝面料。这些产品不仅有本国的消费群体，还有海外的消费群体。

★ Make sure what kind of style the guest would like to have. （确认客人喜欢的款式）

1. How do you like the style? / What do you think of the style?
   您觉得这个款式怎么样？

2. This style is in fashion this year.
   这款今年很流行。

3. The style is popular with foreign guests.
   外国人很喜欢这个款式。

4. The style is out of fashion/date now.
   这款现在过时了。

★ Make sure what color the guest would like to have. （确认客人喜欢的颜色）

1. What color do you like?
   您喜欢什么颜色？

2. What's your favorite color?
   您最喜欢什么颜色？

3. Which color do you prefer, pink or orange?
   您喜欢哪种颜色，粉红的还是橙色的？

4. This color is quite in fashion this year.
   今年这种颜色很流行。

5. The color goes well with the skirt.
   这种颜色跟裙子很匹配。

★ Different ways to greet the guest. （招呼客人的不同方式）

1. Excuse me. Can I help you? / What can I do for you?
   能够为您服务吗？

2. Hello. Are you being attended to? Can I be of some assistance for you?
您好，有人招呼您吗？能够帮您什么？

3. Could I be of service to you?
能够为您效劳吗？

★ Make recommendations to the guest. （向客人介绍产品）

1. What about/ How about this one?
这件怎么样？

2. What style do you prefer?
您喜欢什么款？

3. Do you like this design?
这款您喜欢吗？

4. What color and size do you want?
您要怎样的颜色和尺寸？

★ Seeing a guest off. （送别客人）

You are welcome. / Please come again. / Have a good day.
不客气/欢迎再次光临/祝您过得愉快。

Ⅲ. Listening Practice 听力实训

★ A. Listen to five short conversations in shopping arcade and mark "√" where appropriate.

	Food Stuff	Garments	Medicine	Jewelry	Arts &Crafts
Dialogue 1					
Dialogue 2					
Dialogue 3					
Dialogue 4					
Dialogue 5					

★ B. Complete the following conversation.

Assistant：Good afternoon, sir. _____ . May I help you?

Guest：Good afternoon. The shop is well decorated.

Assistant：Thank you. _____?

Guest：Yes，I hear that porcelain in China is fascinating，isn't it?

Assistant：That's right. You _____ .

Guest：Thank you. This set tableware is of perfect traditional Chinese design，do you think so?

　　Assistant：Yes，indeed. ＿＿＿＿＿＿＿＿＿＿. It's made in Jingdezhen，"the capital of porcelain".

　　Guest：How much is it?

　　Assistant：$260. ＿＿＿＿＿＿＿＿＿＿＿＿＿＿＿＿＿＿＿＿＿＿＿＿＿＿＿＿＿＿＿.

　　Guest：Great! I'll take this set.

Important 特别关注

▲ When the guest enters a shop，what we should do is just to introduce the items，but cannot persuade him to buy anything.
进入商店后，我们应该做的是向客人介绍商品，不能劝客人购物。

▲ When guests do the shopping，we should keep the principle of good faith.
客人进商场购物时，我们应本着诚信的原则。

Section C

Case and Development 案例与创新

Case 案例

　　Mr. and Mrs. Ashmore come to your store to buy some silk products. But they don't know how to choose. Show them what you have in the store and give them some advice as to what and how to choose.

Development 创新

　　• An British woman is looking for a baby's dress. A shop-assistant shows her the samples and explains the quality，size and styles.

　　• You are a shop-assistant. You are now discussing with a guest about her preference of light color. How can you give her some suggestions?

　　• Why would most guests like to buy some local specialty?

实训模块七
会展服务
Convention and Exhibition

This module focuses on the function of Banqueting and Convention Department, especially on the working skills of hotel staff required on the occasions such as convention reservation, convention registration and exhibition arrangement.

本模块介绍宴会部中会展服务的功能,尤其关注酒店工作人员在会务预订、会议代表签到及展览安排中涉及的工作技能。

技能实训 28　会议服务 Convention Service

Section A

Basic Knowledge for Position 岗位基础知识

I. Word Stock 语料库

convention	会议（总称）
conference	会议
plenary session	全体会议
seminar	研讨会
workshop	专业讨论会议
product launch	产品发布会
board meeting	董事会
forum	论坛
panel	专门小组讨论
training session	培训会议
boardroom	小会议室
function room	多功能厅
multimedia	多媒体
prospectus	会议简介
attendee	与会者
venue	会场
side curtain	边幕
drop curtain	幕布
laptop computer	手提电脑
keynoter	主演讲者
lectern	演讲台
projector	投影
video conferencing	视频会议
lapel microphone	领夹式话筒
sponsor	主办
convention service manager	会议服务经理

Ⅱ. Pronunciation 语音训练

1. How many participants will be in the conference?
   一共有多少人参加会议?
2. What kind of function room would you like for the conference?
   你们需要哪种类型的会议室?
3. Do you have any special demands for the conference facilities?
   你们对会议设施有何特殊要求?
4. Do you have any special demands for the conference service?
   你们对会议服务有何特殊要求?
5. Shall we confirm the details for the services and facilities?
   我们确认一下服务和设施的细节好吗?
6. How would you like to make payment, sir?
   先生,请问你们用何种方式付款?
7. Besides the service guidance and the price list of the services in our hotel, I'll send you a plan of the actual conference center.
   除了本酒店的服务指南和服务价目单以外,我还给您传一张会议中心的平面图。
8. Could you tell me your requirements for arranging catering for the conference?
   请问您对会议的餐饮安排有什么要求?
9. The suppers on the first day and last day of the conference are banquets. Buffets are for other meals.
   会议的第一天和最后一天的晚餐为宴会。其他时间采用自助餐。
10. Here is your meeting badge and meeting packet.
    这是您的会议证章和会议塑料袋。

Section B

Service Procedure 服务流程

1. Booking the meeting.
   预订会议。
2. Discuss the service details for the meeting.
   讨论会议服务细节。
3. Show facilities and the decoration of the meeting hall.
   向预订会议者展示会议设施和会议厅装饰。

4. Register for the conference.
   登记会议。

5. Routine service.
   日常服务。

6. Check the rental equipments.
   检查租用的设备。

7. Payment.
   付账。

Ⅰ. Service Performance 服务演练

S＝Susan（苏珊）　　H＝Hilton（希尔顿）

S：Shanghai Convention Center. How may I assist you?
　　这里是上海会议中心，我能为您服务吗?

H：I'm calling from New York Export Company. I wonder if I'd enquire about holding a conference in your place.
　　我是美国纽约出口公司。我想了解是否能在你们酒店举办会议。

S：I'd glad to help you. For how many people, sir?
　　很高兴为您服务。先生，会议有多少人参加?

H：A party of 300.
　　一共300人。

S：When will the event be held?
　　会议什么时候召开?

H：October the 16th, the 17th and the 18th.
　　从10月16—18日。

S：Let me have a check, please. Sorry to have kept you waiting, sir. We do have vacant suites and conference hall during the period you desire for.
　　我帮您查一下……先生，对不起，让您久等了。在这个时间段里我们有空的套房和会议室。

H：That's good. Our attendees are all famous people. Is it possible that they each have a suite?
　　好。与会代表都是些名人。每人一间套房可以吗?

S：Don't worry, sir. Since ours is an all-suite convention center, every attendee is offered a suite and therefore receives VIP treatment.
　　先生，别担心。因为我们的酒店是全套房的会议中心，因此，我们会给每个客人提供一间套房，客人享受的是贵宾级待遇。

H：I like that very much. Then what is the rate?
　　太好了。价格如何?

S：We offer rates competitive with standard hotel rooms, 1230 RMB per person per day, an equivalent to 150 US dollars. Besides, we also offer complimentary "perks", including breakfast and afternoon tea.

我们的价格和普通酒店的价格差不多,每人每天人民币 1230 元,也就是 150 美元。另外,我们还提供免费的优惠待遇,包括早餐和下午茶。

H：Great. Sounds reasonable. We can enjoy suite service. Everybody's dream!

很好。听起来很合理。我们可以享受套间待遇。这是每个人的梦想!

S：Exactly, sir. Our homely atmosphere will bring your dream to come true. If you are really interested in our center, I'll send you a reservation form and a prospectus about our meeting facilities.

是的,先生。我们营造的家一样的氛围将使你梦想成真。如果你们有意入住我们酒店,我将发一个预订单和一份关于我们会议中心设施的说明书给您。

H：That's very kind of you. Can you send them by fax?

好的。能传真给我吗?

S：Yes, sir. May I have your name and your fax number?

好的,先生。能告诉我您的名字和传真号吗?

H：John Hilton. John, H-I-L-T-O-N. My fax number is 708682-3352.

John Hilton, H-I-L-T-O-N。我的传真号是 708682-3352。

S：Mr. Hilton. Your fax number is 708682-3352. Yes, I'll make it right away, Mr. Hilton.

希尔顿先生,您的传真号是 708682-3352。我马上就给您发传真。

H：Thank you very much. Goodbye.

非常感谢。再见。

S：Goodbye, Mr. Hilton. Thanks for calling.

再见,希尔顿先生。感谢您的来电。

Ⅱ. Position Practice 岗位实训

★ Obtain the information in reservation.（预订会议时要了解下列信息）

1. What size of the conference or how many participants.
   会议规模或参加会议的人数。
2. What kind of conference or what kind of function room.
   会议类型或所需具有何种功能的会议室。
3. The special demands for the meeting facilities.
   对会议设施的特殊要求。
4. The special demands for the meeting service.
   对会议服务的特殊要求。

5. The time of the conference.
   会议的时间。
6. The number of the rooms needed.
   房间数。
7. Discussing the service details for the meeting.
   讨论会议服务细节。

★ Confirm the following details with the meeting planner.（与会议策划人确认以下细节）

1. The number of the participants.
   与会人数。
2. The number and the size of the conference rooms.
   所需的不同大小的会议室的间数。
3. The facilities for the meeting.
   所需的会议设施。
4. The arrangements and demands for catering for the meeting.
   会议餐饮安排和要求。
5. The demands in detail for the meeting services and meeting facilities.
   会议服务的细节要求以及会议设施的要求。
6. The number of the rooms and the room rates.
   房间数和房价。
7. The food and beverage rates.
   餐饮费用。
8. Ways of payment.
   付款方式。

Ⅲ. Listening Practice 听力实训

★ A. Listen to the following passage about convention and complete the missing information.

A convention center or conference center is a _____ that is designed to _____ a convention, where individuals and groups _____ to promote and _____ common interests. Convention centers typically _____ sufficient floor area to accommodate _____ attendees. Very large venues, suitable for major _____, are sometimes known as _____. Convention centers typically have at least one auditorium and may also contain concert halls, _____, meeting rooms, and _____. Some large resort area hotels _____ a convention center.

★ B. Complete the following conversation.

Manager: Hello. _____.

Guest: Me too. I'm here to discuss with you about holding a meeting at your hotel.

Manager: _____. What meeting is it?

Guest: An annual convention of the Writers Association.

Manager: _____?

Guest: Certainly. Here it is.

Manager: Oh, I see. There are 50 attendees. I think our functioning room _____.

Guest: Do you have enough brainstorming rooms? We have several seminars after the lecture.

Manager: Don't worry. We'll reorganize some rooms _____.

Guest: Shall we discuss some details about meeting facilities?

Manager: Here are the convention brochures _____ about meeting facilities.

Guest: Thank you. We'll let you know as soon as we've decided.

Important 特别关注

▲ Since the customer is the most important asset of a company, any conference that is arranged should be well organised. Among all aspects, the setting location of the conference is of utmost importance.
客户是公司最重要的资产，任何会议都应该有序组织。在组织会议中，会议位置的选择是最为重要的。

▲ The conference venue should be selected based on its location, services and reputation. It is important that it should be organised in a well-known and centralised location.
会议场所的选择应考虑它的地理位置、服务及信誉，重要的是它应该选在一个著名并集中的地方。

▲ Entertaining and hosting the guests with good food, and drink is also important. Customers feel valued if they are given a hospitable experience.
娱乐客人和用美食招待客人同样也很重要。如果你热情招待了客人，他们会觉得自己很受重视。

Section C

Case and Development 案例与创新

Case 案例

Suppose you are the planner for the World Tourism Seminar lasting 3 days which will be held next year. There will be 300 attendees and the venue will be in the Shangri-La Hotel. You go to the hotel to make a site inspection about its facilities. A sales clerk receives you and introduces all the facilities you need.

Development 创新

- What is included in a conference packet?
- What is the duty of a convention service manager?
- Why is the convention business very profitable for the hotel industry?

技能实训 29　展览服务 Exhibition Service

Section A

Basic Knowledge for Position 岗位基础知识

I. Word Stock 语料库

auditorium	礼堂，会堂
high-tech	高科技
presenter	演讲人，发言人
sight line	视线
laptop computer	手提电脑
heating	供暖
air conditioning	空调
slide presentation	幻灯演示
recreational amenities	娱乐设施
parking lot	停车场
conference table	会议桌
set-up and breakdown	布置和撤台
function room charge	会议室费用
advance set-up	提前布置
late tear-down	拖后撤台
labor cost	人工费用
function book	会议活动簿
procedure manual	工作程序手册
folding equipment	可折叠设备
round table	圆桌
function name	会议名称，活动名称
room name	会议室名称
number of people	出席人数
setup	布局
facility name	设施名称
sample facility	设施样板
display table	展示桌
buffet table	自助餐桌

Ⅱ. Pronunciation 语音训练

1. May I know what kind of the exhibition it is?
   能告诉我这是哪种类型的展览吗?
2. How many participants will there be in the exhibition?
   会有多少人来参加展览?
3. Do you have any special requirements for the exhibition?
   您对展览有什么特殊的要求吗?
4. We need some writing surface or area for handout materials.
   我们需要一个供书写的桌面或摆放资料的地方。
5. This may mean that the speaker or panel needs to be elevated on a platform.
   也就是说,发言人或发言小组应该位于一个高些的平台上。
6. Chairs are lined up in rows, facing the speaker or focal point in the room.
   椅子成行排列,面对发言人或会议室中心。
7. This format can take several shapes, which include closed classroom with no center aisle, open classroom which has rows with aisles to provide easy access to seats.
   这种布局有好几种形式,包括没有中间走道的封闭式布局和有走道便于寻找座位的开放式布局。
8. We have modern facilities and first class service for the exhibition.
   我们有现代化的展览设施和一流的服务。

Section B

Service Procedure 服务流程

1. Book an exhibition.
   预订展览。
2. Discuss about the exhibition.
   讨论展览事宜。
3. Set up the booths.
   搭建展台。
4. Serve during the exhibition.
   展览期间服务。
5. Tear down the booths.
   拆展台。

6. Make the payment.
付款。

Ⅰ. Service Performance 服务演练

G= Guest（客人）　　C=Clerk（服务生）

C：Glad to see you, Mr. Brown.
布朗先生，很高兴见到您。

G：Glad to see you, too. Miss Wang, Have you begun the work?
王小姐，见到你我也很高兴。你们开始工作了吗？

C：Yes, we've made the preparation. Let's go to the exhibition halls. This is the North Exhibition Hall and that's the South Exhibition Hall. How can we arrange the exhibition halls?
开始了，我们已做好准备。我们到展厅去吧。这是北展厅，那是南展厅。我们怎么安排展厅？

G：The gate of the North Exhibition Hall is decorated as the entrance of the International Exhibition for silk. The North Exhibition Hall is arranged as the exhibition hall for the silk materials, and the silk products are shown in the South Exhibition Hall.
北展厅大门入口处布置成此次国际丝绸展的入口。北展厅用作丝绸面料展厅，南展厅展出丝绸制品。

C：We have the same idea. It's convenient for us to carry those big stools to the exhibition hall from the storehouse. How can we deal with the two rooms?
我们的想法也一样。从仓库搬那些大型的工具也方便。这两间房间怎么布置？

G：The east room is used as our exhibition office, and the west one is for the negotiation. The trade negotiation and reaching contracts can be carried out here.
东边的房间用作我们的展览办公室，西边的房间用作洽谈室，贸易洽谈、签合同都在这里进行。

C：How about setting up the stands? The exhibitors of silk materials are more than those of silk products.
怎样布置展台？丝绸面料参展商要比丝绸制品参展商多。

G：The material booths are arranged in a peninsula, while the product booths are fixed up in the shape of an island.
材料展台布置成半岛形，成品展台布置成岛形。

C：Would you like some flowers and plants to decorate the booths and the halls?
展台和大厅需要用鲜花和绿色植物来装饰吗？

G：Certainly.
当然需要。

C：Will you provide some snack and refreshment for the visitors?
为参观者提供小吃和饮料吗？

G：Yes, we plan to provide some free snack and mineral water for the visitors.
是的，我们计划提供一些免费的小吃和矿泉水。

C：Food and beverage service is at the corridor connecting the two halls.
餐饮服务就设在两个大厅的过道上。

G：It's a good idea.
好主意。

C：Are there any other suggestions and demands for our work?
对我们的工作还有什么建议或要求吗？

G：No.
没有了。

C：Could you come to exam our work at 10 o'clock in the morning of October 26?
10月26日上午10点您能过来检查我们的工作吗？

G：Yes, I will. See you two days later.
能，我会来的。两天以后见。

C：See you.
再见。

Ⅱ. Position Practice 岗位实训

★ Get the following information in reservation. （预订展览时获取下列信息）

1. The size of the exhibition hall.
   所需展厅的大小。
2. The number of the participants.
   参展商数。
3. The number of the visitors.
   看展的人数。
4. What kind of exhibits and special demands for the exhibition hall.
   展品的类型及展品对展厅的要求。
5. Whether a storehouse is needed or not and what size.
   是否需要仓库，要多大的仓库。
6. The demands for the exhibition.
   对展览服务的要求。
7. The special demands for the clerks who will take part in setting up the exhibition service.
   对布展员工的特殊要求。

8. The time of the conference.
展出的时间。

★ Introduce the facilities and services of the hotel. （介绍酒店的会议设施和服务）
We have modern facilities and first class service for conference.
我们拥有现代化的会议设施及一流的会议服务。

★ Get the name of the exhibition planner and his telephone number. （获得布展商的姓名、电话号码）
May I have your name and telephone number, sir?
先生，请告诉我您的名字和电话号码好吗？

Ⅲ. Listening Practice 听力实训

★ A. Listen to the following passage about convention and complete the missing information.

There are many different kinds of _____ . Some exhibitions are displayed for _____ of time such as _____ or art galleries. In some cases, like traveling exhibitions or _____ , space may be rented for this _____ in similar buildings or in a more commercial setting. Exhibition of this kind can be divided into _____ . They are cultural exhibitions, commercial cultural exhibitions and _____ displays. The most _____ one in an exhibition center is company display. Company displays can be found in _____ , _____ or display cases. These are commercial exhibitions.

★ B. Complete the following conversation.

Manager: Good morning. _____!

Guest: Good morning. I'd like to confirm the details of the coming exhibition in person.

Manager: Sure. The exhibition is to be held _____, for two days. Is that right?

Guest: Yes, that's right. And how many people can you hold in your exhibition hall? We have about 500 attendees.

Manager: _____ . Our exhibition hall can hold 1000 people.

Guest: Oh, that's good.

Manager: Do you have any _____ about the exhibition hall?

Guest: Yes. As for the light, I think the hall should be _____ .

Manager: Sure, no problem.

Guest: We also need some flowers and green plants.

Manager: Yes. The flowers and plants can help to _____ atmosphere.

Guest: Thank you. You are always helpful.

 Important 特别关注

▲ Determine the goals and problems, the stand type and its location of your exhibition.
确定展览的目标和问题以及展览的类型及展位。

▲ Do not forget to clarify with the exhibition manager the schedule of exhibits delivery and taking-out before hand, because the installation and setting-up of the large-scale equipment takes more time.
一定要和展览经理确认展品交货卸货的时间,因为安装大型设备往往需要很多时间。

▲ It is necessary to organize stand cleaning. The dust and fingerprints will not decorate your stand. As usual, the organizers clean the passage, but you have to take care about the stand yourself.
非常有必要组织展位清洁工作。展位上的灰尘和指纹会让你的展位大打折扣。通常,主办单位要清理通道,但你必须要对自己的展台负责。

Section C

Case and Development 案例与创新

Case 案例

The exhibition was planned to open at 9 o'clock on the morning of October 26. At 8:10, everything was ready. But at that time, the exhibition planner Mr. Harry Brown came to the manager's office in a hurry with two exhibitors. They complained the presentation table you arranged for them was too small.

Development 创新

• If the facilities and services you supply don't meet the need of the exhibition, how can you solve the problem?

• Will you get in touch with the guests after the exhibition comes to an end, why or why not?

• What will you do if you want to make potential customers become the regular customers?

实训模块八
其他服务
Other Services

This modular focus on Lost and Found, deposit service and tourism information introduction as well. The room attendant should check the room thoroughly after the guest checks out. Should the guest leave his belongings in the room, the room attendant should inform the Front Desk immediately and record the information in the lost and found log with details including the room number, the guest's name, time, item name and the finder's name. The term for keeping the belongings is one year.

这个模块重点学习失物招领、寄存服务及旅游信息介绍。客人离店后，服务员要仔细检查客房。若发现有客人遗留物品，应立即通知总台。若此时客人已离去，则将客人的遗留物品记录于《失物招领登记表》上并注明房号、客人的姓名、时间、物品名称、拾物者的姓名。失物一般保存一年。

技能实训 30　失物招领服务 Lost and Found

Section A
Basic Knowledge for Position 岗位基础知识

Ⅰ. Word Stock 语料库

Lost and Found	失物招领处
problem	麻烦，问题
purse	钱包（女用）
wallet	钱包（男用）
check	检查
unusual	不寻常的
common	正常的
ordinary	普通的
directions	方向
visible	看得见的
worried	着急的
concerned	关心的
anxious	焦虑的
electronic dictionary	电子词典
description	描述
portable	手提的
contact	联系
make appointment	预约
in advance	提前
lost property	失物

Ⅱ. Pronunciation 语音训练

1. Today is a terrible day. I have just lost my mobile phone. All my contacts are in it. It is really important to me.
   今天真不走运。我刚刚丢了手机。所有的通讯录都在里面，它对我太重要了。
2. What is the make and model of your phone? And what's the color?
   您的手机是什么牌子的？什么颜色？

3. Can you give us a detailed description of your lost watch?
   您能够详细给我们描述一下您丢失的手表吗?
4. When did you last use your laptop computer?
   您最后一次使用您的手提电脑是在什么时候?
5. Would you please fill in lost property form?
   请您填写一下失物表格好吗?
6. Would you please show us your passport?
   请出示您的护照好吗?
7. We will send the room attendant for the cost now. We will see you at the Lost and Found.
   我们会让客房服务员立刻查看。我们在失物招领处等您。
8. You are really lucky, our staff found one in the hallway yesterday. I think it belongs to your daughter.
   您真幸运。昨天我们的工作人员在走廊捡到一条。我想是您女儿的。
9. You may find your handbag at the Lost and Found.
   您也许可以在失物招领处找到您的手袋。
10. They decided to send it to the hotel's Lost and Found.
    他们决定把它送到本城的失物招领处去。

Section B

Service Procedure 服务流程

1. Put numbered tags on the items found.
   对拾到的物品进行编号。
2. Ask the guest to fill in the lost report.
   请客人填写报失单。
3. Keep the record of the lost and found.
   保存好丢失物品记录。
4. Ask the guest to fill in the request slip.
   请客人填写取物单。
5. Ask the guest to show his identity.
   请客人出示身份证明。
6. Check and return the lost property to the guest.
   核对并归还失物。

Ⅰ. Service Performance 服务演练

A=Mrs. Brown（布朗太太）　　B=Mr. Brown（布朗先生）　　S=Security Department（保安部）

A：Operator, put me through to the Security Department, please.
　　接线员，请帮我接通保安部。

S：Security Department. How can I help you?
　　我是保安部。我能为您做什么？

A：My husband's gold watch is missing and I need your help.
　　我丈夫的金表不见了，我需要你的帮助。

S：Just take it easy. I'll be in your room in a minute. What's your name and room number, please?
　　别着急。我马上去您的房间。您能告诉我您的姓名和房号吗？

A：Mrs. Brown, Room 802.
　　我是802房间的布朗太太。

（A few minutes later, there is a knock at the door. Mr. Brown opens the door.）
（一会儿，敲门声响起。布朗先生打开了门。）

S：How do you do, Mr. And Mrs. Brown?
　　布朗先生，布朗太太，你们好。

B：How do you do, officer. Please come in and take a seat.
　　你好，先生。请进，请坐。

S：Are you sure that your watch isn't still somewhere in your room?
　　您确信您的手表不在房间里吗？

B：Yes. I've looked everywhere in my room and I can't find it.
　　是的。我找遍的整个房间，但找不到。

S：When and where did you last see it?
　　您最后一次看到它是什么时候？在哪里看见的？

B：Let me see … Last night on the dresser. I took it off before I went for a shower and forgot to put it back this morning.
　　让我想想……是昨晚在梳妆台上。我洗澡前把它摘下来的，今天早上忘了戴上它。

S：Are you sure you didn't wear it this morning?
　　您确定您今天早上没戴吗？

B：Yes, I'm positive.
　　是的，我肯定。

S：Did you remember to lock your door before you left then?
　　您记得在你们离开房间的时候把门锁好了吗？

B：Yes, I think I did.
　　是的，我想是的。

S: Has anyone been to your room since then?
之前有人来过你们的房间吗？

B: Er ... the room attendant came with two bottles of water and newspaper.
嗯……客房服务员来过，拿了两瓶水和一份报纸。

A: And the laundryman came to collect our laundry.
洗衣房服务员来拿我们要洗的衣服。

B: (Writing all the details down) Don't worry about that, Mr. And Mrs. Brown. We will try our best to get back for you.
（写下所有的细节）别担心，布朗先生和布朗太太。我们将尽力为您找到。
(There is a knock at the door. Mr. Brown opens the door and a laundryman（L）comes in with a gold watch in his hand.)
（敲门声响起。布朗先生打开了门，洗衣房服务员手中拿着金表进来了。）

L: Is this yours, Mr. Brown? I found it in the laundry.
布朗先生，这是您的吗？我在您要洗的衣服里找到的。

B: Yes, it is mine.
是的，是我的。

M: You are always so careless.
你总是不小心。

B: I am sorry for that. I'll be careful next time.
不好意思。我下次一定小心。

S: It's all right.
没关系。

A: (To the laundryman) Thank you very much.
（对洗衣房服务员）非常感谢你。

L: You are welcome.
别客气。

Ⅱ. Position Practice 岗位实训

★ Show sympathy for the guest. （对客人表示同情）

1. Don't worry, sir/madam, we'll see to it immediately.
请您不要担心，我们会立刻为您查询。

2. I am really sorry to hear this, but we will try to help you with it.
很抱歉听到这个消息，但我们会尽力帮助您。

★ Ask for the details of the item. （询问丢失物品的信息）

1. What is the make of your watch/phone/wallet?
您的手表/手机/钱包是什么牌子的？

2. What color is it?
那是什么颜色的？

3. Is it brand new?

是崭新的吗?

★ Respond to the guests' request. (回复客人的请求)

1. We will see to it immediately.

我们立刻处理此事。

2. I am sorry, it has not been found yet.

很抱歉，还没有找到。

★ Ask for the guest's personal information. (询问客人的个人信息)

1. May I have your name/room number/address?

能留下您的姓名/房号/地址吗?

2. Could you show me your ID card?

能否出示您的身份证?

3. Would you mind leaving your name/address here?

可否留下您的姓名/住址?

★ Ask the guest to fill out the relevant forms. (要求客人填写相关表格)

1. Could you fill in the lost report?

您能填写报失单吗?

2. Would you mind finishing this request slip?

请您填写领物单。

Ⅲ. Listening Practice 听力实训

★ A. Listen to the following passage about Lost and Found and complete the missing information.

What's the most commonly _____ from guests in hotel rooms? It's not the _____ peanuts from the _____ . Hotel guests are walking away from some of their most private possessions when they _____ of hotels, but just how personal are the items? _____ a check of its 31 UK hotels' lost property departments, you may _____ about the _____ objects left behind in hotel rooms by its guests. Because of the amount of items housekeeping has picked up in hotel rooms, _____ chargers and underwear top the list of most commonly left behind items, amongst the more unusual items guests forgot to take with them when they checked out were a _____ , wigs, musical instruments and _____ . We want to know: What items have you left behind in hotel rooms? Did you get them back?

★ B. Complete the following conversation.

Attendant: You look worried, sir. _____?

Guest: I've lost my key.

Attendant: Oh, perhaps _____ .
Guest: Thanks. It must be here somewhere.
Attendant: _____ ?
Guest: Yes. It's not there.
Attendant: Have you checked in your bag?
Guest: Hold on, let me see... No, it's not in there.
Attendant: Well, _____ ?
Guest: It wouldn't be in there, would it? I'll check anyway? Nope!
Attendant: _____ ?
Guest: Under my desk?
Attendant: Did you look on the floor?
Guest: On the floor? Wait a moment... Ah ha! I've got it. Thanks.
Attendant: You're welcome.

Important: 特别关注

▲ When reporting lost property, please provide a detailed description. Due to the high volume of enquiries, please include any unique characteristics rather than giving a generic description.
报告失物时请提供一份详细的描述。因为有大量的失物查询，所以要提供有特征的描述而不是通用的描述。

▲ If you are picking property up for another person, their written authorisation will be required. Personal Identification will be required in all cases of property collection.
如果您为他人领取财物，必须要有那人的书面授权。在领取财物时也必须提供个人的身份证明。

Section C

Case and Development 案例与创新

Case 案例

Suppose the receptionist at the Lost and Found Office gets a phone call from Mr. Brown in the morning. He has checked out, but he has left his laptop computer in the room. The room attendant will take the laptop computer to the Lost and Found Office.

Mr. Brown will come to claim it.

Development 创新

• What information should be filled in the lost and found form?

• If the guest made a mistake about what he lost, what will you do if you are a hotel attendant?

• What are the most important points you should make sure when the guest comes to claim the lost property?

技能实训 31 寄存服务 Deposit Service

Section A

Basic Knowledge for Position 岗位基础知识

Ⅰ. Word Stock 语料库

switch	开关
master key	万能钥匙
wardrobe	衣柜，衣橱
slot	插槽
nightstand	床头柜
socket	插座
activation pin	激活销
indicate	显示，暗示
cipher code	密码
arbitrarily	任意地
decode	解密

Ⅱ. Pronunciation 语音训练

1. Excuse me. I will check out later at noon. I wonder whether I could leave my luggage here after I check out.
   您好，我中午要退房。我想问一下退房后能否在这里寄存行李？

2. We do provide deposit service. When will you collect them?
   我们有寄存服务。您想什么时候提行李？

3. We will collect your luggage at 11 a.m.. Would you then come to the service desk to get your storage receipt?
   我们会在 11 点钟为您提取行李。然后请您来服务台领行李单好吗？

4. I would like to use a safety deposit box. Will it fit into this size of the box?
   我想使用一个保险箱。这个东西放得下吗？

5. Could you fill out this form and sign at the bottom, please?
   请您填写这份表格并在下面签字。

6. Please put your items in this bag, and we will seal it.

请您把东西放在这个袋子里，我们会密封它。

7. If you would like to use the items during the period of storage, please come here in person with the tag. After confirming your signature, we will open the box.
   如果在寄存期间您要领取物品，请您亲自过来，出示取物牌。我们核对签字后会为您打开保险箱。

Section B

Service Procedure 服务流程

1. Greeting.
   问候。
2. Ask the guest to fill in deposit form.
   请客人客人填写物品寄存单。
3. Explain the cost of the service and charge the guest.
   解释收费标准并收费。
4. Give the guest a tag for withdrawing.
   给客人取物牌。
5. Extend good wishes to the guest.
   向客人表达良好的祝愿。

Ⅰ. Service Performance 服务演练

A = Attendant（服务生）　　G = Guest（客人）

A: Good morning, sir. What can I do for you?
　　先生，早上好。我能为您做什么？

G: Yes. Can you show me how to use the safe in my room? I'll go to Beijing on business for two days and I want to keep some documents in it while I'm away.
　　是的。你能告诉我我房间的保险箱怎么使用吗？我将去北京出差两天。我想在离开的时候把文件保存在保险箱里。

A: Certainly, sir. If you want to use the safe, please go to the service center first and fill out a signature card, then the clerk there will give you an activation pin.
　　当然可以，先生。如果您想使用保险箱，请先到服务中心填一张签名卡，然后那里的服务员会给您一根激活销。

G：Activation pin? What's the use of it?

激活销？它有什么用处？

A：Once you get the pin, please plug in and open the door of the safe, insert the pin, then "OPEN" will be indicated on the door.

您拿到激活销后，请接通电源拉开箱门，插入激活销，这时门上会显示"开锁"。

G：How do I lock the safe?

那我怎么锁保险箱呢？

A：After "OPEN" is shown, you must input a six-digit cipher code and the safe will be locked when closed. And "LOCK" will be indicated, then you can set the code arbitrarily.

当门上显示"开锁"时，你必须输入一个六位数的密码。当门关上时，保险箱就会锁上了。而且保险箱上就会显示"锁"字样，然后您任意调乱密码即可。

G：How do I open it when I come back?

当我回来后，我如何打开保险箱呢？

A：Just put in the cipher code and open the safe after it is decoded. If you keep the code unchanged, the safe will be locked automatically when the door is closed.

需要开门时，只要输入设置的密码，待解锁后，再拉开柜门。如不改变密码，则关上门便会自动锁上。

G：Can other people open it?

其他人能打开它吗？

A：Unless they know the code. The safe will not unlock if you put in the wrong code, and it will show "ERROR".

除非他们知道密码。如果您输入错误的密码，保险箱是打不开的，门上将会显示"错误"字眼。

G：Well, it's very safe.

哦，非常安全。

A：I think so. But be sure not to forget the code you set. Otherwise, you have to contact the Service Center and ask the clerk to open it for you.

是的。但是记住别忘了您设置的密码，否则的话，您就必须联系服务中心，请工作人员帮您开保险箱了。

G：Oh, I see. Thank you very much indeed.

哦，我明白了。非常感谢。

A：It's my pleasure. One more thing, if you stop using the safe, please remove the activation pin and return it to the service center.

很高兴为您服务。还有一件事，如果您不用保险箱了，请拿走激活销并还给服务中心。

G：Sure. Thank you again. Good-bye.

当然。再次谢谢。再见。

A：Good-bye, sir. Wish you a pleasant journey.

再见，先生。希望您旅途愉快。

Ⅱ. Position Practice 岗位实训

★ When the guest comes to the desk, you can greet him/her by saying.（当客人来到服务台时，你可以用如下表达问候客人）

1. May I help you?

   能为您效劳吗？

2. Good morning/afternoon, would you like to deposit or withdraw something?

   早上好/下午好，您要存取什么吗？

★ If the guest needs a safety deposit box to store valuables, remind the guest.（如果客人需要保险箱寄存贵重物品，提醒客人）

1. Keep the key carefully.

   小心保存钥匙。

2. Fill out the application form.

   填写申请表。

3. Sign his/her name.

   签名。

4. Keep the tag in a safe place.

   保存好取物牌。

★ Inform the guest of the price with the following expressions.（用下列表达告知客人收费标准）

1. The service costs you ×× yuan per bag per day.

   行李寄存需要支付每件每天××元。

2. The safety deposit box service is free.

   保险箱寄存服务是免费的。

Ⅲ. Listening Practice 听力实训

★ A. Listen to the following passage about deposit service and complete the missing information.

Small hotels don't usually have luggage _____ although they will usually _____ for people _____ whose room isn't _____ or for people _____ who need to leave bags until a _____. Most hotel luggage storage spaces are just _____ to hold bags for a few hours as people _____. So, if the answer is "we don't have enough room", that's probably _____. If you just want to _____ your bags and _____ them when you return and move on _____ additional nights stay, they may not be so accommodating as storage for _____, not guests who've left and won't be returning. Again, due to space available.

★ B. Complete the following conversation.

Receptionist: Here is your bill, madam. _____ Yuan. Please _____.

Guest: Sure. My flight is 11p.m. _____?

Receptionist: Certainly, madam. Is there anything _____ in your bag?

Guest: No, there isn't.

Receptionist: We'll keep it for you. _____.

Guest: Thank you. When does the cloakroom close?

Receptionist: This cloakroom is _____.

Guest: Oh, dear! I won't be back until about 8:30 tonight. Where can I pick up my bag?

Receptionist: We will transfer your bag to _____. You may collect it there, ma'am.

Guest: I see. Thanks a lot.

Receptionist: You're welcome.

Important 特别关注

▲ When a guest wants to deposit some valuables, confirm his identification. If he is a staying guest, the service can be provided.
存物品时，确定客人身份。如是住店客人，可以提供此项服务。

▲ Asking the guest to show his room card and confirm his room number. Finally verifying the registered name in the computer.
请客人出示房卡，确认房号，核对电脑系统中客人的登记姓名。

▲ When the guest wants to take out his belongs, check his identification.
取寄存物时,验证客人的身份。

Section C

Case and Development 案例与创新

Case 案例

A guest wants to store his luggage in the hotel after checking out, for he will be taking several days' trip. He will be checking out at 11:30 this morning, and will claim his luggage a week later. The charge for the service is 5 yuan per bag per day.

Development 创新

- Who should be responsible for the valuables guests lost in his room?
- If the guest forgets his cipher code of the safety box in his room, what can you do to help him?
- How can you help the guest if he has lost the claim tag?

技能实训 32　介绍旅游信息 Tourist Information

Section A
Basic Knowledge for Position 岗位基础知识

Ⅰ. Word Stock 语料库

city tour	城市观光
sightseeing	观光
scenic spots	景点
tourist attraction	旅游景点
public transport	公共交通
art gallery	艺术馆
historical museum	历史博物馆
theme park	主题公园
castle	城堡
monument	纪念碑
fascinating	引人入胜的
enjoyable	有趣的
unusual	不寻常的
charming	迷人的
impressive	留下深刻印象的
unforgettable	难忘的
exhausting	累人的
rewarding	值得做的
Palace Museum	故宫博物院
Summer Palace	颐和园
The Great Wall	长城
The West Lake	西湖
The Olympic Nest Building	奥运鸟巢

Ⅱ. Pronunciation 语音训练

1. I have just arrived here. I know little about Hangzhou. Could you tell me some places to visit?

我今天刚到，还不熟悉杭州这座城市。你能给我介绍一些值得游览的地方吗？

2. I suggest you first visit the West Lake where there are many famous and fantastic places to see such as Melting Snow at Broken Bridge and Three Pools Mirroring the Moon.

   我建议您先去西湖游览，那里有很多著名的和非常迷人的景点，比如断桥残雪和三潭印月。

3. If you are interested in the modern side of the city, you could have a look at the Central Business Districts and do some pleasant shopping.

   如果您对这座城市现代化的一面感兴趣，可以看看中央商务区一带，体验购物乐趣。

4. Why don't you take a free traveling brochure here? It can give you a lot of useful information, including restaurant lists.

   您从这里取一份免费的旅游指南吧，里面有很多有用的信息，还有餐馆名录。

5. I was told that there is a famous temple in the city center. Could you tell me where it is?

   别人告诉我在市区有一座非常著名的寺庙，您能告诉我在哪吗？

Section B

Service Procedure 服务流程

1. Greetings.
   问候。
2. Ask whether a guest needs help.
   询问客人是否需要帮助。
3. Introduce some famous scenic spots.
   介绍著名旅游景点。
4. Arrange tour or introduce means of transportation.
   安排旅游或介绍交通方式。
5. Extend good wishes to the guest.
   表达良好祝愿。

Ⅰ. Service Performance 服务演练

R＝Reservationist（预订人员）　　A＝Mr. Brown（布朗先生）　　B＝ Mrs. Brown（布朗太太）

R: Good morning!
早上好!

B: Good morning! Today we can afford a whole day for sightseeing, could you tell us some outstanding scenic spots in Hangzhou?
早上好!我们今天有一整天的时间可以游览一下,你能给我们推荐一些杭州著名的景点吗?

R: Is this your first time to Hangzhou?
这是您第一次来杭州吗?

B: No, it's my second time here but last time I was on business, so I didn't go to any places.
不,这是我第二次来了。但上一次我是来出差的,所以哪里都没有去。

R: I'm very pleased to suggest that you go to visit the West Lake and Lingyin Temple. They are the most famous places in Hangzhou.
我非常高兴为您推荐西湖和灵隐寺。它们是杭州最著名的景点。

A: Why are they so famous?
为什么它们如此著名?

R: Because the West Lake is the symbol of Hangzhou and those who came to Hangzhou but didn't go to the West Lake were considered not having been here. The lotuses in the West Lake are very beautiful too.
因为西湖是杭州的象征。来了杭州而没有游览西湖的人被认为是没有来过杭州。西湖的荷花也非常漂亮。

A: Great, I'll go there and take some photos. What about the temple?
很好。我会去转转然后拍些照片。那灵隐寺呢?

R: Lingyin Buddhist Temple is the oldest, the biggest and the most famous Buddhist temple in southeast China. It has two halls: the Front Hall and the Great Buddha Hall.
灵隐寺是中国东南部最古老的、最大的和最著名的佛教寺院。它有两个主要大厅:天王殿和大雄宝殿。

B: Both places sound worth visiting. By the way, can you show us the way to both places?
听起来两个地方都值得一游。随便问一下,你能告诉我怎样去这两个地方吗?

R: Sure, walk out of the hotel gate, turn right until the first traffic light, then take the No. 315 bus, it'll directly take you to the West Lake, you won't miss it. Then you can take No. 7 bus to Lingyin Temple.
当然可以。从酒店大门出去向右转,一直向前走到第一个红绿灯,在那里乘坐315路公交车,它会载你们直达西湖,你不会找不到的。然后你们可以乘坐7路公交车到灵隐寺。

A and B：That's so kind of you.
你真好。

R：My pleasure，have fun.
很高兴为你们服务。希望你们玩得愉快！

Ⅱ. Position Practice 岗位实训

★ Show the directions to the guest. （向客人指路）

1. You can take bus No. 5，and then change to bus No. 7 at…
您先坐 5 路公交车，然后在……站换乘 7 路公交车。

2. Cross the road, go down three blocks and you will see the gallery.
穿过这条路，向前走三个街区就能看到美术馆了。

3. Please go straight and then turn right at the traffic light.
直走，在红绿灯处向右拐。

★ Give some advice about sightseeing. （给予旅游建议）

1. I suggest you go to the West Lake.
我建议您去西湖。

2. If I were you，I would go to the Palace Museum.
如果是我，我会去故宫博物院。

3. Why not go to the Great Wall? It's a must for foreigners.
您为什么不去长城呢？长城对外国游客来说是个必去的地方。

★ The reason why you suggest the scenic spots. （建议为何去该景点）

1. It used to be very unspoiled，there are a lot of parks to walk in.
它未曾受到破坏，有很多公园可以散步。

2. The weather is hot and sunny，you can get everywhere easily by public transport.
天气很好，阳光灿烂，公共交通随处都可以抵达。

3. The beach was beautiful with white sand，it's a great place for a relaxing holiday.
白色的沙滩太美妙了，真是一个度假休闲的好地方。

Ⅲ. Listening Practice 听力实训

★ A. Listen to the following passage about tourist information and complete the missing information.

Most hotels offer _____, including visitor attractions, _____, sightseeing, tourist tips and _____ . They will provide you with _____ to know about the city. You'll find a wealth of information about _____ and _____ . Whether you are looking for

_____ out, food festival or _____, tourist information center will give you some advice. With listings of the top events and offers, you can _____ in the place knowing you are getting _____ for your money. If necessary, buy a _____ about the city, discounts in main tourist attractions and free transportation all round the city will be a _____. Everything is easier with a Tourist Card, and it's the best way to _____ the city highlights.

★ B. Complete the following conversation.

Clerk: Beijing _____, may I help you?

Guest: Yes. This is Mr Harris from Australia. I'd like to have a city tour in Beijing. Could you give me some suggestions?

Clerk: Sure. _____ and how long you plan to sightsee in Beijing?

Guest: I'm staying at the Beijing Hotel. I'll be in the city for 2 days.

Clerk: Mr. Harris, your hotel is near Tian'anmen Square. So it _____ if you visit Tian'anmen Square first. Then, in the north of the square is the Palace Museum.

Guest: Palace Museum? Is it a new museum?

Clerk: No, it _____ the Forbidden City.

Guest: I see. Then how long do you think I need to see the two places?

Clerk: Well, you need _____ to see both Tian'anmen Square and the Palace Museum.

Guest: I see. Then what about tomorrow?

Clerk: I'd like to recommend the Summer Palace and Yuanmingyuan.

Guest: What's interesting there?

Clerk: The Summer Palace is famous for its _____, large lake, and green hills dotted with colorful pavilions. Yuanmingyuan has plenty of historic rains. They _____, not to be missed.

Guest: I see, you are so helpful.

Important 特别关注

▲ When returning to your hotel or motel late in the evening, use the main entrance of the hotel. Be observant and look around before entering parking lots.
晚上迟归回到酒店的时候，要走酒店的大门。进入停车场前要保持警觉并四下环顾。

▲ Don't draw attention to yourself by displaying large amount of cash or expensive jewelry.
不要携带大量现金或贵重珠宝而引起别人的关注。

▲ Don't invite strangers to your room.
不要邀请陌生人到你的房间来。

Section C

Case and Development 案例与创新

Case 案例

Because of your professional knowledge and because you know about your own region, the guest often asks you for your advice. Join in a partner and take it in turns to play the roles of a Guest and a Receptionist talking about what the guest could do this weekend in different weather.

Development 创新

• What are the most important reasons people go for travelling?

• Why are visitors sometimes disappointed when they visit your region? what might discourage them from coming again?

• What is your own idea of an ideal holiday destination?

技能实训 33　托婴服务 Baby-Sitting Service

Section A
Basic Knowledge for Position 岗位基础知识

I. Word Stock 语料库

childcare	照看孩子
regulation	规定
babysitter	临时照看儿童者
nanny	保姆
daycare	白天
experienced	有经验的
professional	专业的
qualified	合格的
attitude	态度
reliability	可靠性
minimum	最少的，最低的
confirmation	确认
emergency	紧急情况，突发事件
newborn	新出生的
entertain	娱乐
outgoing	外向的
contact	联系
feedback	反馈

II. Pronunciation 语音训练

1. I'd like to go out this evening. How can I find someone to look after my baby?
   我晚上要出去，我如何才能找到人来照看我的孩子？
2. We need someone to look after our baby. Is such service available here?
   我们需要有人照看小孩。这里有这项服务吗？
3. Yes. We have qualified babysitter.
   是的。我们有合格的临时照看儿童者。

4. They are all well-educated and reliable.
   她们接受过良好教育，非常可靠。
5. The babysitter are experienced and professional.
   临时照看儿童者都很有经验也很专业。
6. If you need the service, here is a confirmation form for you to fill in.
   如果您需要此服务，这里有一份确认表需要您填写。
7. You have to fill in the time of the service, basic information of the baby and your signature in the form.
   您得在表格上写上服务时间、孩子的基本情况，还有您的签名。
8. We will arrange the service for you soon. Just have a good time.
   我们马上给您安排托婴服务。祝您玩得愉快！

Section B

Service Procedure 服务流程

1. Greetings.
   问候。
2. Ask whether the guest needs help.
   询问客人是否需要帮助。
3. Introduce babysitting service.
   介绍照看儿童服务。
4. Arrange babysitting service.
   安排照看儿童服务。
5. Good wishes.
   良好祝愿。

Ⅰ. Service Performance 服务演练

G=Guest（客人）　　A=Room Attendant（客房服务员）

G：Will you please do me a favor?
　　你能帮我个忙吗?
A：Certainly, if I can do it.
　　如果我能做到，当然可以。
G：My husband and I want to go out this evening. So, can you look after the baby for us? It's till midnight.

我和我丈夫今晚要出去。你能帮我们照看孩子吗？要照看到午夜。

A：I see. But I am afraid that's not possible. It is against our hotel regulations for me to do this service, as attendants cannot do their jobs and look after children properly at the same time.

我明白了。我想我可能不行。这违反了酒店的规定，因为酒店服务员不可能在工作时同时照看好孩子。

G：What shall I do, then?

那我该怎么办？

A：Don't worry, madam. Our Housekeeping Department has a very good baby-sitting service. There are some spare time babysitters under the Room Center.

别担心，女士。我们客房部可以提供很好的托婴服务。在房务中心我们有一些兼职保姆。

G：Are they ... eh... experienced?

她们……很有经验吗？

A：Yes, madam. They are all well-educated and reliable.

是的，女士。他们都是受过良好教育的值得信赖的人。

G：It's great. Now, could you tell me about the terms of this service?

太好了！现在你能告诉我这项服务的条款吗？

RA：It is 50 yuan an hour, for a minimum of 4 hours.

每小时 50 元人民币，4 小时起步。

G：That's very reasonable.

价格合理。

A：If you ask the Housekeeping, they will give you more details and send a confirmation form for you to sign.

如果您问一下客房部，他们会给您更详细的解释。然后他们会给您一份确认函，您要在上面签字。

G：All right. I'll phone them right away. Thank you.

好的。我现在就打电话。谢谢。

(The guest returns 10 minutes later.)（十分钟后，她回来了。）

A：Excuse me, madam. May I ask you to sign this confirmation form? Thank you. I hope I haven't disturbed you.

对不起，女士。您可以在确认函上签名吗？谢谢。希望我没有打扰您。

G：Not at all.

没有打扰。

(Signing the form.)（在表上签字。）

Here you are.
　　给你。
A：Thank you, madam. Good night and have a pleasant evening.
　　谢谢，女士。晚安，希望您度过一个愉快的夜晚。

Ⅱ. Position Practice 岗位实训

★ Inform the guest of the service charge.（告知客人收费标准）
　　There is a minimum charge for the baby-sitting service, you need to pay 50 yuan per hour and the minimum time is two hour.
　　托婴服务有最低消费，您一个小时需付 50 元，最少服务时间为 2 小时。

★ Ask about the baby's information.（询问幼儿的具体情况）
　　1. Can I have the baby's name?
　　　　孩子叫什么名字？
　　2. How old is the baby?
　　　　孩子几岁了？
　　3. Is she in good condition?
　　　　她的健康状况怎么样？
　　4. Does he have any healthy problems?
　　　　他有什么健康问题吗？

★ Ask the guest's telephone number.（询问客人的联系电话）
　　1. May I have your telephone number?
　　　　请告诉我您的电话号码好吗？
　　2. How can I contact you in emergency?
　　　　紧急情况下如何联系您？

★ Confirm details of the baby-sitting service.（确认托婴服务细节）
　　1. So you need the baby sitting service from 8 p.m. to 12 p.m.. Is that right?
　　　　您需要托婴服务，从晚上 8 点到晚上 12 点，对吗？
　　2. You would like to have an active baby-sitter who is well-educated, is that right?
　　　　您需要一个活泼点的受过良好教育的保姆，是吗？

Ⅲ. Listening Practice 听力实训

★ A. Listen to the following passage about baby-sitting and complete the missing information.

　　When traveling with children of ＿＿＿＿＿＿＿, it's impossible to relax and enjoy ＿＿＿＿＿＿＿ (which you're certainly entitled to!) ＿＿＿＿＿＿ getting a sitter. If you want to enjoy the spa or a ＿＿＿＿＿＿＿ in a hotel, you can ask baby-sitting service in the hotel. Quality hotels are very ＿＿＿＿＿＿ about the babysitters they recommend, because of the obvious liability issues. Here is how _____ works: the hotels contract out to a babysitting service, which interviews and screens the babysitters. The concierge _____ the babysitting service with a guest's needs, and the service then finds an _____ sitter. Sitters are paid _____, and a portion of the bill goes back to the service. You should _____ instructions about whether or not the kids are allowed to leave the hotel room.

★ B. Complete the following conversation.

Guest: Excuse me, madam. Could you do me a favor?

Concierge: Yes, _____. What's the matter?

Guest: I've made an appointment with my business partner tonight. I need someone to look after my baby. Is baby-sitting service available here?

Concierge: Yes, we have _____ babysitters.

Guest: That's good. Could you tell me how much baby-sitting service is charged?

Concierge: It is 60 yuan per hour, _____.

Guest: That's OK.

Concierge: Do you have _____?

Guest: Yes, my baby is not allowed to leave the hotel room.

Concierge: Sure. The babysitter _____.

Guest: Thank you.

Concierge: If you need the service, please _____.

Guest: OK, I will finish it right away.

Concierge: _____ here, madam?

Guest: Sure. Here you are.

Concierge: Thank you, madam. We will arrange the service soon. Have a good night.

Important 特别关注

▲ Pay special attention to the baby's safety.
密切关注婴儿的安全问题。

▲ Babysitters should be carefully selected, qualified, professional who are experienced in caring from newborn to school age children.
要精挑细选合格专业的临时照看儿童者,能够照看从刚出生到学龄段的孩子。

▲ If the babysitter is not friendly, not enough confident, looks untidy, or if you have any doubts, it would be better not to leave the baby to that person.
如何保姆不友好,不够自信,看起来不太整洁,或者您有任何怀疑,最好就不要把孩子交给她。

Section C

Case and Development 案例与创新

Case 案例

A guest is complaining that her baby was not taken good care by a babysitter. Make the dialogue.

Development 创新

- If the baby you take care of is not feeling very well, what should you do?
- If the guest doesn't come back on time to bring her baby, what should you do?
- Who shall you inform first when there is an emergency for a baby?

实训模块九

投诉 Complaints

Some complaints may be reasonable or justified, or they may not be your fault. But it's usually best to apologize and offer to take action. In a service industry, the customer is always right (even if he or she is wrong). An apology costs nothing and can help the client to feel better. Remember that complaints can help you to improve your service in future.

有些投诉可能是合理公平的,有些投诉根本就不是你的错。但是最好还是向客人表示道歉并采取措施。在服务行业中,客人永远是对的(即使他/她是错的)。道歉不用你付出任何代价但能够让客人感觉舒服一点。记住:投诉有助于你改善今后的服务。

技能实训 34　处理投诉 Dealing with Complaints

Section A

Basic Knowledge for Position 岗位基础知识

Ⅰ. Word Stock 语料库

complaint	投诉
criticism	批评
justified	公平的，公正的
constructive	建设性的
rude	粗鲁的
abusive	侮辱的
sympathy	同情
reasonable	合理的
patient	耐心的
explanation	解释
satisfied	满意的
dissatisfied	不满意
receptionist	接待员
waitress	女服务员
housekeeper	客房主管
general manager	总经理
restaurant manager	餐厅经理
hotel regulation	饭店规定
misunderstanding	误解
lost and found form	失物表
promise	答应，承诺
request	请求，要求
account	账目
free of charge	免费
overcharge	过度收费，多收费
solve the problem	解决问题

make compensation for	补偿，赔偿
responsible	负责任
deposit	寄存，存放
describe	描述，描写

Ⅱ. Pronunciation 语音训练

1. My steak is overcooked.
   我的牛排太老了。
2. The heating in my room isn't working. It's as hot as hell up there.
   房间的空调好象出了问题，房间里热得像地狱一样。
3. The wine waiter was very rude to me.
   酒水服务员对我很无礼。
4. You forgot to wake me at 6 a.m.. Now I've missed my train.
   你忘了在6点钟叫醒我，我误了火车。
5. There's no hot water in my room.
   我的房间没有热水。
6. Did you have this room checked before we moved in? There's not a scrap of lavatory paper and the toilet doesn't flush properly.
   我住进来之前你们检查过房间吗？卫生间里没有卫生纸，马桶无法正常冲水。
7. Could you speed up your switchboard a bit, please? I booked a call to Tokyo 20 minutes ago and I haven't had a reply yet.
   你们能不能让总机速度快一点？我20分钟前就预订了打往东京的电话，但现在还没有回应。
8. The service is too slow. When can we have our soup?
   服务太慢了，你们什么时候才能上我们点的汤？
9. I'm terribly sorry about that, sir.
   很抱歉，先生。
10. I'm really very sorry about this, madam.
    女士，我真的很抱歉。
11. I'll do it right away, sir.
    先生，我现在马上做。
12. I'll see to it right away, madam.
    女士，我马上处理这件事。
13. I'll send a repairman to your room immediately, Mr. Brown.
    布朗先生，我马上派一个维修人员到您的房间。
14. I'll make sure it doesn't happen again.
    我保证这样的事情不会再发生。

Section B
Service Procedure 服务流程

1. Greeting the guest.
   向客人打招呼。
2. Ask what the matter.
   询问出了什么问题。
3. Listen patiently.
   耐心倾听。
4. Make an apology.
   表达歉意。
5. Ensure the guest to solve the problem.
   向客人保证解决问题。
6. Make good wishes to the guest.
   表达良好祝愿。

Ⅰ. Service Performance 服务演练

M = Manager（经理）　　G= Guest（客人）

M：Good afternoon, madam. Did you want to see me?
　　下午好，女士。您要见我吗？

G：Yes, I did. I'm not all happy.
　　是的。我很不满意。

M：What's wrong? Perhaps you'd like to tell me what the problem is.
　　发生什么事了？也许您愿意告诉我发生了什么事情。

G：It's my fish. Look, there is a hair in it. But when I told your waiter about it, he didn't take any notice.
　　是我点的鱼。你看，我的这盘鱼里有根头发。但当我告诉服务员的时候，他根本就不当回事。

M：I'm very sorry about it, madam. I'm sure the waiter didn't mean to be rude. Perhaps he didn't understand you correctly. In addition, some of our staff are still going through the training. I know he should change it for you, but ...

对此我表示非常抱歉，女士。我可以肯定服务员不是故意表现得很粗鲁，也许他没理解您的意思。另外，我们的一些服务员还在接受培训。我知道他是想帮您换一盘的，但是……

G：Well, why didn't he?

哦，那为什么他没那么做呢？

M：There must be some misunderstanding, madam. I do apologize for it. I'll change your fish right away.

肯定是误会了，女士。我对此表示道歉。我马上就给您换。

G：Good. That's better. And another thing is this wine. I think it is corked.

好的。这还差不多。还有一件事就是这瓶酒，我认为它有一股怪味。

M：Are you sure, madam? The Claret has been very nice.

真的吗？女士。这瓶红葡萄酒味道非常好的。

G：Here, taste it yourself.

那你自己尝尝吧。

（Having tasted a bit.）（尝了一点点。）

M：No, there doesn't seem to be anything wrong with it. Maybe it is a little dry for you. I'd recommend you to try the old Tom Gin next time, madam.

没有啊，酒一点怪味都没有。也许对您来说会有点苦。女士，我推荐您下次可以尝试一下老汤姆金酒。

G：Ok, perhaps I will. Aha, here comes the fish. Shall I pay for that one?

好的，也许吧。哦，鱼来了。这盘鱼我需要付钱吗？

M：Of course not. It's all free of charge. Please take your time and enjoy your meal.

当然不需要，是免费的。请慢慢品尝。

G：Thank you.

谢谢。

M：It's my pleasure. And I'm always at your service.

别客气。愿意随时为您服务。

Ⅱ. Position Practice 岗位实训

★ Practice following ten steps when dealing with complaints.（处理客人投诉时，请注意以下十大步骤）

1. Listen attentively.

专心听。

2. Keep calm.

保持冷静。

3. Sympathize the guest.
   同情客人。
4. Protect guest's self-esteem.
   保护客人的自尊。
5. Value the guest.
   重视客人。
6. Take notes.
   记下客人要求。
7. Keep the guest informed of the measure or actions you intend to take.
   告知客人酒店的措施或你的打算。
8. Make sure when they will be carried out.
   确认这些措施何时实施。
9. Supervise the remedies and corrections.
   监督补救或改正措施的实施。
10. Feedback the information.
    反馈信息。

★ Express your willingness to help the guest. （表达你乐意帮助客人）
1. Thank you for telling us about it, sir. I'll look into the matter at once.
   感谢您为我们提供这些情况，我立即去了解。
2. I'll speak to the person in charge and ask him to take care of the problem.
   我会对负责人员讲，让他来处理这件事。
3. Please calm down, sir. I'll try to help you.
   先生，请您冷静。我会尽力帮助您。
4. Please relax, madam. I will take care of it according to your request.
   请放心，女士。我将按您的要求办。

Ⅲ. Listening Practice 听力实训

★ A. Listen to the following passage about complaints and complete the missing information.

Hotel guest complaints frequently _____ the cleanliness of the bed or bathroom, but there may be complaints about any aspect of the guest's _____ . To deal with a guest complaint in a hotel, the first step is to _____ the guest's full complaint. When expressing a complaint, the guest may be _____ . They need to be fully _____ even if all the relevant details are made known right away. Then ask questions to _____ what actions will be sufficient to fix the

_____ . If a problem cannot be solved, front office staff should admit this to the guest _____ . _____ is the best policy when dealing with guest complaints.

★ B. Complete the following conversation.

Guest: Waitress!
Waitress: Yes? _____?
Guest: Not exactly. _____ . I asked for it well done! And it's rather cold.
Waitress: I do apologize, sir. Would you _____?
Guest: Please.
Waitress: Would you like something else _____?
Guest: Yes, some French fries please. But tell them to hurry.
Waitress: Sure. But the restaurant is very busy today. _____ .

Important 特别关注

▲ In answer to complaints from the guest, it is very important to keep the following four things in your mind: listening, sympathizing, apologizing, and telling the guests what has been done to solve their problems.
在应对客人投诉时，要牢记四点：倾听，同情，道歉，告诉客人你们已经做了哪些努力。

▲ Quickly and properly solving guest complaints can help your business grow and prosper. Ignoring complaints or dealing with them in a dishonest manner can result in loss of business or even lawsuits.
快速合理地处理投诉有助于生意的繁荣，忽视或者用不诚实的手段处理投诉会带来生意上的损失甚至被起诉。

Section C

Case and Development 案例与创新

Case 案例

The guest complained to you:
The chambermaid burst into his room and woke him up this morning.
She didn't come back to make up his room till the afternoon.
She didn't clean the bathroom properly.

Development 创新

• Is it possible and necessary for a department head to fulfill all the requests by guests? If not, what is to be done?

• When you or your staff members are wronged by an unhappy guest, what should you do?

• Shall we encourage guests' complaints? Why or why not?

技能实训 35　刁钻客人 Difficult Guests

Section A

Basic Knowledge for Position 岗位基础知识

Ⅰ. Word Stock 语料库

critical	挑剔的
awkward	固执的，难以应付的
abusive	骂人的，滥用的
compliment	称赞，恭维
commendation	赞扬，推荐
criticism	批评
justified	公正的
constructive	积极的，肯定的
reasonable	合理的
argument	争吵
perspective	角度
fastidious	难以取悦的，吹毛求疵的
undesirable	不受欢迎的，令人不快的
understanding	理解，谅解，领悟
sympathy	同情

Ⅱ. Pronunciation 语音训练

1. There seems to be something strange in my soup.
   我的汤有怪味。
2. I've been waiting a very long time for someone to bring me my bill.
   我等我的账单已经等了很长时间了。
3. I left my Walkman in my room while I was out. When I got back it was lying on the floor, broken.
   我出去的时候把我的随身听放在房间里，回来的时候随身听在地板上，而且摔坏了。
4. Someone came to my room this morning and tried to sell me something.
   今天早上有人来我的房间推销产品。

5. You recommended the sightseeing tour to me but it was a waste of time.
   你给我介绍的城市观光简直是浪费时间。
6. I'm sure the waiter didn't mean to be rude. Perhaps he didn't understand you correctly.
   我确信服务员不想无礼的,他可能没有准确理解您的意思。
7. I'm sorry, sir. There must be some misunderstanding.
   很抱歉,先生,一定有误会。
8. Please relax, madam. I'll take care of it according to your request.
   请放松,夫人,我们会根据您的要求照办的。
9. I'll speak to the person in charge and ask him to take care of the problem.
   我会跟负责的人说,叫他来处理这个问题。
10. Just a moment, sir. I'll get the manager.
    请稍等,先生,我去叫经理。
11. Excuse me, but I should say it's against our hotel regulation.
    请原谅,但我得说这违反我们酒店的规定。
12. Please, sir. If you calm yourself, I'll try to help you.
    先生,请冷静,我将尽量帮您。
13. We'll try our best. But I cannot guarantee anything.
    我们将尽力而为,但我无法保证什么。

Section B

Service Procedure 服务流程

1. Greetings.
   问候。
2. Ask what's the matter.
   询问出了什么问题。
3. Listen patiently.
   耐心倾听。
4. Make an apology.
   表达歉意。
5. Deal with the complaints.
   处理投诉。
6. Make good wishes to the guest.
   表达良好祝愿。

Ⅰ. Service Performance 服务演练

H＝Housekeeper（客房部主管）　　G＝Guest（客人）

H：Housekeeping. May I help?
这里是客房部，需要我帮忙吗？

G：Yes, I'm afraid the room attendant did not properly clean my room.
是的。我想服务员没有把我房间打扫干净。

H：I'm awfully sorry, madam.
对不起，女士。

G：There is dust on the chest of drawers.
衣柜上都是灰。

H：Please let me apologize for this. I will send a room attendant to dust it right away.
对此我表示道歉。我会立刻派一个客房服务员来把它擦干净。

G：And there's another problem. The window of my bedroom will not close properly.
还有一个问题。我卧室的窗户关不好。

H：I will send a repairman to fix it right away. Are there any other problems, madam?
我马上叫一个维修工来修理。女士，还有其他问题吗？

G：Yes, I have been woken up by the noise from the top floor at 7：30 this morning. What's matter?
是的，今天早上7：30我就被顶层的噪音吵醒了。这是怎么回事？

H：I will look into this matter myself. We will make sure that this won't happen again.
我会亲自去调查这件事。我们会确保此类事情不会再发生。

G：That's very kind of you.
谢谢。

H：Please, madam, don't hesitate to contact us again if you have any further problems.
女士，如果还有什么问题，请直接提出来。

G：Well, I think I've complaint enough today.
哦，我想我今天说得挺多了。

H：You're right to complain, madam. We want to make your stay as comfortable as possible. By the way, both the repairman and the room attendant will be right up.
女士，这是应该的。我们希望您在这里住得舒服。顺便告诉您，修理工和客房服务员马上就到。

G：Very well. Thank you very much.
好的。非常感谢。

H: Thank you for calling, madam.
感谢您给我们打电话,女士。

Ⅱ. Position Practice 岗位实训

★ Guests can be difficult in three ways. (三种类型的刁钻客人)

1. The Distracted Guest brings all his problems with him.
   分心的客人带来所有的问题。
2. The Disappointed Guest arrives with certain expectations.
   失望的客人带着某种期待。
3. The Disruptive Guest calls for emergency action.
   破坏性的客人需要采取紧急措施。

★ Suggestions for dealing with difficult guests. (与刁钻客人打交道的一些建议)

1. If the guest's problem is a result of an error on hotel's side, it's best to admit it and apologize.
   如果客人的问题是酒店的失误造成的,最好承认并道歉。
2. Please make a concerned effort to solve the problem and let the guest have as much feedback as possible.
   要做出相关的努力来解决问题,并给客人尽可能多的反馈。
3. Remember to deal with the guest's feelings. Avoid saying things like: "I understand how you feel…?" It's better to say: "This must be frustrating."
   记得照顾客人的感受,避免说类似的话:"我理解你的感受……"最好说:"这一定很恼人。"
4. Everybody wants to make a contribution. So involve the guest in the solution whenever possible. Ask question like: "What would you suggest?"
   每个人都有贡献欲。所以,一旦有可能,就请你的客人参与问题的解决,问他类似的问题:"您有什么建议?"
5. Show your guest some genuine care.
   向客人表达你真诚的关心。

Ⅲ. Listening Practice 听力实训

★ A. Listen to the following passage about difficult guests and complete the missing information.

As a new hotel manager, you have to _____ the unexpected. And among the many challenges faced by all hotel managers is the overly _____. Sometimes, it's a _____ with very specific and unusual demands. There are also the party hearty musicians who leave your _____ a total mess. When you encounter your difficult guest, keep in mind that such guests may have had a _____ while traveling. They may have missed a _____, had their luggage damaged or misplaced, or simply had a bad day or _____. They may have arrived at your hotel with all this negative baggage already in their heads and just need someone or something to vent their frustrations upon. On the other hand, their problem may stem from _____ in your hotel. Either way, here are some _____ to help you deal: hear and understand; don't go on defensive; keep a _____ tone and don't over promise.

★ B. Complete the following conversation.

Receptionist: Good afternoon, madam. May I help you?

Guest: Yes. I settled my account this morning, but _____.

Receptionist: May I have your room number please?

Guest: 1316.

Receptionist: 1316. And _____?

Guest: The laundry charge is too high. I only used the laundry service once. It can't be 300 yuan. It's impossible.

Receptionist: Just a minute, madam. _____. Thank you for your waiting. According to our records you used the laundry service three times. I have our copies of your laundry bills here. _____?

Guest: Yes. I think there must be a mistake. I only used the laundry service once.

Receptionist: Here are your laundry slips, madam. _____?

Guest: No, only one slip is mine.

Receptionist: _____.

Guest: Oh, my god, it's my husband's signature.

Receptionist: I see.

Guest: I'm sorry for trouble.

Receptionist: It doesn't matter. Have a good day.

Important 特别关注

▲ If you promised the guest that you would do something about his problem, do what you promise. Otherwise it will lead your hotel to loads of damage.
如果你答应了客人你将做点什么来解决问题,你就要遵守诺言。言而无信会给酒店带来巨大的损失。

▲ Guests don't start out wanting to be difficult. If they are identified early on and properly handled from the beginning, chances are that you can turn things around.

客人并非一开始就是难缠的。如果他们能够早点被关注或者问题一开始就得到恰当的处理，你就可以扭转局面。

Section C

Case and Development 案例与创新

Case 案例

You are hard to please. You are dissatisfied because:

You ordered breakfast in your room and they brought you coffee instead of tea.

The coffee was cold.

And you ordered it for 8 am but they brought it at 7:30.

Last night the fire alarm rang at midnight. It was a false alarm.

The fire escape route was locked.

You had to stand outside the hotel in your pajamas for half an hour till you were allowed back in.

Nobody apologized for this at the time.

Development 创新

• Have you had any similar experiences of difficult clients? Tell each other what happened and how you dealt with them.

• What kinds of guests do you find most difficult to deal with?

• How do you understand the saying: " Customers are always right?"

附录一

饭店日常英语100句

1. Good morning, sir.
   早上好,先生。
2. Good afternoon, madam.
   下午好,女士。
3. Good evening, ladies and gentlemen.
   晚上好,先生们女士们。
4. Hello. Glad/Nice to meet you.
   您好,很高兴见到您。
5. How are you?
   您好吗?
6. Fine, Thanks. And you?
   很好,谢谢。您好吗?
7. Welcome to our hotel.
   欢迎到我们饭店!
8. Welcome to our restaurant.
   欢迎光临我的餐厅!
9. Welcome to our shop.
   欢迎到我们商店来。
10. Thank you for your coming.
    谢谢您的光临。
11. Have a good time!
    祝您过得愉快!
12. Happy New Year!
    新年快乐!
13. Happy Birthday!
    生日快乐!

14. Happy weekend!
    周末愉快!

15. Merry Christmas!
    圣诞快乐!

16. Have a nice holiday!
    假日快乐!

17. Wish you every success!
    祝您成功!

18. Wish you good luck!
    祝您好运!

19. Wish you a pleasant journey.
    祝您旅途愉快!

20. Wish you a most pleasant stay in our hotel.
    愿您在我们宾馆过得愉快。

21. Wish you have a good sleep.
    祝您休息得好!

22. Thank you (very much).
    谢谢您（非常感谢）。

23. Thank you for your advice /help.
    感谢您的忠告/帮助。

24. It's very kind of you.
    谢谢，您真客气。

25. You are welcome.
    不用谢。

26. Not at all.
    不用谢。

27. Don't mention it.
    不用谢。

28. It's my pleasure. /With pleasure. / My pleasure.
    非常高兴为您服务。

29. I am at your service.
    乐意为您效劳。

30. Thank you for your staying in our hotel.
    感谢您在我们酒店下榻。

31. I'm sorry.
    很抱歉。

32. Excuse me.
    对不起。

33. I'm sorry. It's my fault.
    很抱歉。那是我的过错。

34. Sorry to have kept you waiting.
    对不起,让您久等了。

35. Sorry to interrupt you.
    对不起,打扰您了。

36. I'm sorry about this.
    对此表示抱歉。

37. I apologize for this.
    我为此道歉。

38. That's all right.
    没关系。

39. Can/May I help you?
    我能帮您什么吗?

40. Is there anything else I can do for you?
    还有什么能为您效劳的吗?

41. Just a moment, please.
    请稍等一下。

42. May I know your name, please?
    请问尊姓大名?

43. Have a good rest, sir.
    先生,请好好休息。

44. Please sign here, sir.
    先生,请在这签上您的名字。

45. May I see your passport, madam?
    女士,请出示您的护照好吗?

46. What kind of room would you like?
    您要怎么样的房型?

47. When for? / For which date?
    什么时候要房间?

48. For how many people?
    一共几个人?

49. How long will you be staying?
    您打算住多久?

50. Could you please spell your name?
请拼一下您的名字。

51. May I have your telephone number?
我可以知道您的电话号码吗?

52. May I introduce myself?
请允许我自我介绍一下。

53. I'm the receptionist here, welcome to our hotel.
我是这儿的接待员,欢迎来到我们酒店。

54. That's no problem at all.
没问题。

55. Housekeeping. May I come in?
客房服务员,我可以进来吗?

56. Leave your laundry in the laundry bag, please.
请把要洗的东西放在洗衣袋中。

57. I hope I'm not disturbing you.
我希望没有打扰您。

58. One moment, madam. I'll bring them to you right away.
等一会儿,夫人。我马上送来。

59. I'll send a repairman immediately.
我将马上给您派一个维修工。

60. Will there be anything else, sir?
还有什么事吗,先生?

61. If you need anything else, please call us.
如果您有什么事,请叫我们。

62. It's very kind of you to do so.
您这样做使我很感激。

63. What's your room number, please?
请问您的房间号码是多少?

64. May I have a look at your room card?
我可以看一下您的房卡吗?

65. How do you like this room?
您觉得这个房间怎么样?

66. When would you like me to do your room, sir?
您要我什么时间来给你打扫房间呢,先生?

67. May I do the turn-down service for you now?
我现在可以给您做夜床吗?

68. What time will be convenient for you?
    什么时候对您方便？

69. How do you like Chinese food?
    您喜欢中国菜吗？

70. What do you think of our service?
    您对我们的服务有什么意见？

71. Thank you for your suggestions.
    谢谢您给我们提的建议。

72. Sit down, please. Here is the menu.
    请坐，给您菜单，先生。

73. May I take your order, sir?
    您要点菜吗？

74. What would you like to have, coffee or tea?
    您要喝咖啡还是茶？

75. Here is the bill. Please sign it.
    这是您的账单，请签字。

76. I'm afraid it's against the hotel's regulations.
    这是违反饭店规章制度的。

77. In our hotel we don't accept tips.
    我们饭店是不收小费的。

78. Thank you all the same.
    然而，还是要谢谢您。

79. I'm afraid you'll have to pay for the damage.
    恐怕您得赔偿损失。

80. I'll look into the matter right away.
    我马上去处理这件事情。

81. I assure you it won't happen again.
    我保证此类事情不会再发生。

82. Please don't worry, madam.
    夫人，请不必担心。

83. Reservations, may I help you?
    预订部，我能帮你吗？

84. Room service, may I come in?
    送餐服务，我可以进来吗？

85. I'm afraid that's not a good idea.
    恐怕，那个主意不好。

86. Enjoy you breakfast/ lunch/dinner, sir.
    请享用你的早餐/午餐/晚餐,先生。

87. You are through, please go ahead.
    接通了,请讲。

88. A table for four?
    四人的一张台吗?

89. Did you make a reservation?
    您预订房间了吗?

90. I'll show you to your room. This way, please.
    我会领您去您的房间的,这边请。

91. What kind of currency do you have?
    您有什么货币?

92. Please hold the line. I'll put you through in a minute.
    请拿好电话,马上就可以为您接通。

93. I'm sorry the extension is busy just now.
    对不起,电话分机刚才占线。

94. How about this table over there?
    那边那张餐桌可以吗?

95. I'm sorry. We're rather full tonight.
    对不起,今晚我们这儿客满。

96. You look very nice in that dress.
    您穿上那件衣服显得很漂亮。

97. I'm sorry they're sold out.
    对不起,它们都卖完了。

98. Do you have any special suggestions?
    您有什么特殊建议吗?

99. Hope to see you again.
    希望再次见到您。

100. I'm looking forward to seeing you soon.
     希望很快就能见到您。

附录二 饭店常用词汇

1. à la carte 照单点菜
2. air-conditioner 空调
3. American breakfast/ full breakfast 美式早餐
4. American Express Card 美国运通卡
5. aperitif 餐前酒
6. appetizer 头盘
7. area code 区号
8. arrival list 预期抵店客人名单
9. ashtray 烟灰缸
10. baggage/ luggage 行李
11. barmaid 酒吧女招待
12. barman 酒吧男招待
13. bartender 调酒员
14. base 基酒
15. bathing towel 浴巾
16. bathrobe 浴袍
17. beauty parlor 美容室
18. bed cover 床罩
19. bedside control panel 床头控制板
20. bedside light 床头灯
21. bellman 行李员
22. bill 账单
23. black list 黑名单
24. blanket 毯子
25. brandy 白兰地

26. breakfast knob 早餐牌
27. breakfast vouchers 早餐券
28. business center 商务中心
29. buffet breakfast 自助式早餐
30. buffet 自助餐
31. cancel（动）取消
32. cash 现金
33. cashier 收银员
34. change 零钱
35. charge（动）收费
36. check in 登记入住
37. check/cheque 支票
38. check-out room 走客房
39. claim tag 取物牌
40. cloakroom 寄存处
41. cocktail 鸡尾酒
42. coffee shop 咖啡馆
43. concierge 礼宾部
44. country code 国家代码
45. credit card 信用卡
46. currency 货币
47. curtain 窗帘
48. departure list 离店客人名单
49. deposit 押金
50. dessert 甜点
51. dial 拨电话
52. doorman 门童
53. drawer 抽屉
54. elevator 电梯
55. emergency call 急救电话
56. EMS 邮政特快专递
57. Euro 欧元
58. exchange 兑换
59. express service 快洗服务
60. express 快件
61. extension 分机

62. fast food 快餐
63. fax 传真
64. fill in the form 填表
65. first name 名字
66. flight number 航班号
67. group rate 团队价
68. hanger 衣架
69. ID card 身份证
70. information 问讯处
71. reception office 接待室
72. hotel register 旅客登记簿
73. registration form 登记表
74. postal service 邮局服务处
75. shop 小卖部
76. bar 酒吧间
77. lounge 休息厅
78. roof garden 屋顶花园
79. billiard-room 球房
80. dining-room，dining hall 餐厅
81. men's room 男盥洗室
82. ladies' room 女盥洗室
83. cloak-room 存衣处
84. basement 地下室
85. cellar 地窖
86. broom closet 杂物室
87. room number 房间号码
88. room key 房间钥匙
89. suite 一套房间
90. single room 单人房间
91. double room 双人房间
92. sitting-room/living-room 起居室
93. sofa，settee 长沙发
94. easy chair 安乐椅
95. armchair 扶手椅
96. rocking chair 摇椅
97. stool 凳子

98. bench 条凳

99. tea table 茶几

100. desk 书桌

101. bookshelf 书架

102. wardrobe 衣柜

103. rug 小地毯

104. carpet 大地毯

105. single bed 单人床

106. double bed 双人床

107. twin beds 两张床

108. mattress 褥子

109. quilt 被

110. blanket 毯子

111. sheet 床单

112. bedspread 床罩

113. pillow 枕头

114. pillow case 枕套

115. cushion 垫子

116. bathroom 浴室

117. bath tub 浴盆

118. shower bath, shower 淋浴

119. cold and hot water taps 冷热自来水龙头

120. sprinkle-nozzle/（shower）nozzle 喷头

121. dressing table 梳妆台

122. mirror 镜子

123. washbasin 洗脸盆

124. towel 毛巾

125. toilet, lavatory, washroom 卫生间

126. water closet/W.C. 厕所

127. toilet roll, toilet paper 卫生纸

128. bath towel 浴巾

129. bathrobe 浴衣

130. towel rail, towel rack 毛巾架

131. sponge 海绵

132. waste-paper basket 废纸篓

133. thermometer 温度计

134. balcony 阳台
135. central heating 暖气
136. ashtray 烟灰碟
137. desk lamp 台灯
138. bedside lamp 床头灯
139. floor lamp 落地灯
140. wall lamp 壁灯
141. switch 开关
142. socket 插座
143. plug 插头
144. telephone 电话
145. electric iron 电熨斗
146. clothes-hanger 衣架
147. manager 经理
148. attendant 服务员
149. desk clerk 值班服务员
150. waiter（餐厅）服务员
151. waitress（餐厅）女服务员
152. rent 租金
153. bill 账单
154. invoice 发票
155. key card 钥匙牌，房卡
156. laundry bag 洗衣袋
157. laundry form 洗衣单
158. lobby 大堂
159. luggage cart 行李车
160. medium 五分熟
161. menu 菜单
162. mini bar 小酒吧
163. mini-jar 烧水壶
164. minimum charge 最低收费
165. mirror 镜子
166. morning call/wake-up call 叫早电话/叫醒电话
167. name tag 标有姓名的标签
168. nationality 国籍
169. operator 话务员

170. original 原件
171. package rate 包价
172. parking 停车场
173. passport 护照
174. pillow 枕头
175. postcard 明信片
176. price list 价目表
177. pudding 布丁
178. quilt 被子
179. rare 一分熟
180. refunds 退款
181. registration 登记，注册
182. reservation desk 预订处
183. reservation record 预订记录
184. room attendant 客房服务员
185. room availability 客房预订情况
186. room charge 房价
187. room rate 房价
188. reservation 预订
189. registration 登记
190. safety box 保险柜
191. salad 色拉
192. service charge 服务费
193. sheet 床单
194. shower cap 浴帽
195. signature 签名
196. slippers 拖鞋
197. soap 香皂
198. specialty 招牌菜
199. spirits 烈酒
200. steak house 牛排馆
201. sweater 毛衣
202. table d'hôte 套餐
203. tap 水龙头
204. tip 小费
205. toilet paper 卫生纸

206. tooth paste 牙膏
207. toothbrush 牙刷
208. towel 毛巾
209. transfer 转账
210. traveler's check 旅行支票
211. traveller's cheque 旅行支票
212. trousers 裤子
213. twin room 标间
214. valet 洗衣工
215. valuables 贵重物品
216. Visa Card 维萨卡

附录三 饭店常用告示语

1. Caution! Automatic Door.
   注意！自动门。
2. Caution! Don't Enter.
   注意！切勿进入。
3. Caution! Hot.
   注意！小心高温。
4. Caution! Wet Floor.
   注意！地面潮湿。
5. Caution! Wet Paint.
   注意！油漆未干。
6. Caution! Wet Floor.
   注意！小心地滑。
7. Daily Special.
   今日特价。
8. Disposable Product.
   一次性产品。
9. Dry Cleaning.
   干洗。
10. Emergency Door Release.
    应急门开启。
11. Emergency exit.
    紧急通道。
12. Enter.
    入口。

13. Exit.
    出口。
14. Fire Exit.
    消防通道。
15. Flush After Use.
    便后请冲水。
16. Fragile.
    小心轻放。
17. In Business.
    营业中。
18. Keep Clear.
    保持通畅。
19. Keep Out.
    请离开。
20. Mind Your Head. / Watch Your Head.
    小心碰头。
21. No Admittance Except on Business.
    非公莫入。
22. No Cigarette Disposal.
    禁止乱扔烟头。
23. No Cycling. /No Bicycles.
    禁止驶入。
24. No Littering.
    请勿乱扔废弃物。
25. No Parking.
    不得停车。
26. No Personal Checks.
    不接收个人支票。
27. No Photography.
    严禁拍照。
28. No Spitting.
    禁止随地吐痰。
29. Occupied.
    （厕所）有人。
30. Out of Use.
    停用。

31. Please Be Careful.
    请小心。
32. Please Mind the Step.
    请小心台阶。
33. Please Only Use in An Emergency.
    请仅在紧急情况下使用。
34. Private Parking.
    专用车位。
35. Reserved.
    座位（保留）。
36. Ring Bell for Service.
    需要服务，请按铃。
37. Room in Use.
    请勿打扰。
38. Room Ready for Service.
    可以整理房间。
39. Safety Exit.
    安全通道。
40. Staff Only.
    闲人免进。
41. Toilet for the Disabled.
    残障人士专用厕所。
42. Don't Litter.
    禁止随便丢弃垃圾。
43. Out of use. Please use other doors.
    此门停用。请走旁门。
44. To avoid congestion, please do not stand near the stairs.
    楼梯附近，请勿停留，以防堵塞。
45. Tender grass needs your care.
    柔弱的小草需要你的呵护。
46. Hotel not responsible for articles lost or stolen.
    遗失物品，酒店概不负责。
47. Please do not panic if the hotel is on fire.
    如果饭店发生火灾，请不要惊慌。
48. Don't smoke in bed or the ashes fallen to the ground may be yourself.
    请勿在床上吸烟，否则落地的灰烬可能就是你自己。

49. Distinguished guest：Please sing songs in your heart as our walls are not as thick as you may imagine.

尊敬的客人，请把您的歌藏在心里，因为我们的墙壁并不如您想象的那么厚实。

50. Please remember to：Put towels you want washed on the floor. Leave towels you will use again on the towel racks. This simple gesture helps protect the environment. Thank you.

请牢记：将您需要清洗的毛巾放在地板上，将您准备继续使用的毛巾挂在毛巾架上。您的举手之劳将有助环保。谢谢！

附录四 中餐特色菜肴

1. Braised Pork with Abalone 鲍鱼红烧肉
2. Shredded Pork with Vegetables，Sichuan Style 川味小炒
3. Braised Pork with Preserved Vegetables 冬菜扣肉
4. Braised Pork with Bamboo Shoots 方竹笋炖肉
5. Griddle Cooked Spare Ribs and Chicken 干锅排骨鸡
6. Gulaorou (Sweet and Sour Pork with Fat) 咕噜肉
7. Stewed Pork Ball in Brown Sauce 红烧狮子头
8. Sautéed Sliced Pork with Pepper and Chili 回锅肉片
9. Yu-Shiang Shredded Pork (Sautéed with Spicy Garlic Sauce) 鱼香肉丝
10. Four-Joy Meatballs (Meat Balls Braised with Brown Sauce) 四喜丸子
11. Braised Pork with Vermicelli 猪肉炖粉条
12. Sautéed Beef Filet with Bell Peppers 彩椒牛柳
13. Sizzling Beef Steak 铁板牛肉
14. Spicy Ox Tripe 麻辣牛肚
15. Braised Beef with Potatoes 牛肉炖土豆
16. Roast Lamb Leg 烤羊腿
17. Roast Whole Lamb 烤全羊
18. Braised Chicken with Chestnuts 板栗焖仔鸡
19. Crispy Chicken 脆皮鸡
20. Kung Pao Chicken 宫保鸡丁
21. Curry Chicken 咖喱鸡
22. Stewed Duck in Beer 啤酒鸭
23. Sautéed Diced Chicken with Chili and Pepper，Sichuan Style 四川辣子鸡
24. Steamed Spring Chicken 清蒸童子鸡
25. Chicken Wings and Legs with Brown Sauce 贵妃鸡

26. Beggars Chicken (Baked Chicken) 叫花子鸡
27. Quanjude Roast Duck 全聚德烤鸭
28. Beijing Roast Duck 北京烤鸭
29. Stewed Duck with Ham and Bamboo Shoots 火腿春笋老鸭煲
30. Braised Goose Feet with Sea Cucumber 辽参扣鹅掌
31. Braised Dried Goose and Lettuce in Spicy Sauce 菜头烧板鹅
32. Grilled Goose Liver with Matsutake 松茸扒鹅肝
33. Pan-Fried Goose Liver 香煎鹅肝
34. Roast Goose, Chaozhou Style 潮州烧雁鹅
35. Fried Eggs with Chopped Chinese Toon Leaves 香椿煎蛋
36. Sautéed Eel with Duck Blood Curd 山城血旺
37. Griddle Cooked Tea Tree Mushrooms 干锅茶树菇
38. Braised Tofu with Mushrooms 野菌烧豆腐
39. Braised Abalone 红烧鲍鱼
40. Steamed Scallops with Tofu 白玉蒸扇贝
41. Steamed Mandarin Fish 清蒸桂鱼
42. Sweet and Sour Mandarin Fish 松鼠桂鱼
43. Assorted Seafood with Vermicelli en Casserole 海鲜粉丝煲
44. Steamed Turtle 清蒸甲鱼
45. Sautéed Crab in Hot Spicy Sauce 香辣蟹
46. Steamed Fish Head with Diced Hot Red Peppers 剁椒鱼头
47. Boiled Fish with Pickled Cabbage and Chili 酸菜鱼
48. West Lake Fish in Vinegar Gravy 西湖醋鱼
49. Fotiaoqiang——Steamed Abalone with Shark's Fin and Fish Maw in Broth 佛跳墙
50. Steamed Abalone with Chopped Garlic 蒜蓉蒸九孔
51. Shelled Shrimps with Longjing Tea Leaves 龙井虾仁
52. Steamed River Crab 清蒸闸蟹
53. Fish Filets in Hot Chili Oil 水煮鱼
54. Shark's Fin with Papaya 木瓜鱼翅
55. Sautéed Pumpkin with Lily Bulbs 百合炒南瓜
56. Sautéed Chinese Broccoli 炒芥蓝
57. Sautéed Lettuce 炒生菜
58. Sautéed Seasonal Vegetable 炒时蔬
59. Sautéed Sweet Corn with Salted Egg Yolk 黄金玉米
60. Stewed Baby Cabbage in Broth 浓汤娃娃菜
61. Sautéed Broccoli without Garlic 蒜茸西兰花

62. Sautéed French Beans 四季豆

63. Sautéed Spinach 清炒菠菜

64. Pickles，Sichuan Style 四川泡菜

65. Sautéed Mushroom and Bamboo Shoots 炒二冬

66. Braised Eggplant with Soy Bean Paste 酱爆茄子

67. Dongpo Pork 东坡肉

68. Fried Tofu，Home Style 家常豆腐

69. Mapo Tofu (Stir-Fried Tofu in Hot Sauce) 麻婆豆腐

70. Pork Ribs and Turnip Soup 萝卜煲排骨汤

71. Tomato and Egg Soup 西红柿鸡蛋汤

72. Sister Song's Fish Broth 宋嫂鱼羹

附录五

技能实训听力文本

技能实训 4　Ⅲ. Listening Practice 听力文本

★ A. Listen to the conversation and fill in the reservation form.

Reservations: Good morning. Zhejiang Narada Grand Hotel. Reservations, May I help you?

Caller: Good morning, I'd like to reserve a room next Wednesday. That's November 12th.

Reservations: Certainly, madam. How many nights will you need the room?

Caller: Three nights.

Reservations: I see. What type of room do you need?

Caller: A twin.

Reservations: Is that a superior twin or a deluxe twin?

Caller: May I know the difference in price?

Reservations: The superior twin is 780 yuan a night and the deluxe one is 980 yuan a night. Both include buffet breakfast.

Caller: I think I'll take the deluxe twin, please.

Reservations: May I have your name, please?

Caller: Mm, It's Elizabeth Beaulieu——that's B-E-A-U-L-I-E-U, Beaulieu.

Reservations: Thank you, madam. May I know your phone number, please?

Caller: Sure. It's 1357788××××.

Reservations: Thank you. Let me confirm your reservation, madam. You have booked a deluxe twin at 980 yuan per night for three nights from November 12th in the name of Ms Elizabeth Beaulieu. Is that right?

Caller: Yes, that's right.

Reservations: Thank you for your reservation, Ms Beaulieu.

Caller: Thank you, goodbye.

Reservations: Goodbye, Ms Beaulieu.

★ B. Make confirmation about the details of the reservation.

Miss Yang, can I repeat the details of your reservation? You are reserving a room for Mr. Jacob. Smith, who will be arriving on flight CX 837 at 8 p. m. on April 7th and staying until 21st April. Mr. Smith requires a deluxe suite for four people. The room rate is ＄150 per night. Your address in Singapore is 237 East Street, and your telephone number is 678-4526, is that right?

技能实训 5　Ⅲ. Listening Practice 听力文本

★ A. Listen to the conversation and fill in the registration form.

Receptionist: Is there anything I can do for you, sir?

Guest: Yes, I have rather poor eyesight. Would you fill in the registration form for me?

Receptionist: Certainly, sir. Can I have your name, please?

Guest: Henry Michel. That's M-I-C-H-E-L.

Receptionist: And your nationality is...

Guest: Australian.

Receptionist: and your address?

Guest: 25 Oakwood Street, Sydney.

Receptionists: Right. Are you here for a visit or on business, sir?

Guest: Just for sightseeing.

Receptionist: Ok, now, can you give me your passport number?

Guest: It's 02140768.

Receptionist: Thank you. May I know your next destination?

Guest: I'm going to Hong Kong after this.

Receptionist: How would you like to pay, sir?

Guest: Er... by credit card... American Express.

Receptionist: Now... er... today is December 10th. When are you leaving, sir?

Guest: The 13rd.

Receptionist: Very good. Mr. Michel. Now, I've put you in Room 1106. That's single room at 800 per night on 11st floor. Have a good stay with us.

Guest: Thank you. You are so helpful.

Receptionist: It's my pleasure.

★ B. Complete the following dialogue.

Guest: Good evening, my name is Mrs. John. I've just arrived from New York. I had a reservation.

Receptionist: Welcome to Marriot Hotel, Mrs. John.

Guest: Thank you.

Receptionist: Just a minute, please. I'll check the reservation record for you. Just a minute, please. Are you traveling with your family?

Guest: No, I'm here on business.

Receptionist: I see. So you don't require a family suite, do you?

Guest: No, of course. My secretary booked a deluxe single.

Receptionist: I see. Well, I'm afraid we have made a mistake about the reservation. I do apologize for it. Do you have a faxed confirmation of your reservation?

Guest: Yes, just one moment. Here it is——, "one deluxe single" for five nights. That's until 15th.

Receptionist: Mm. Yes, I see. Well, could you please fill out the registration form while I find out if there are any deluxe singles still available?

Guest: Very well, but I hope this won't happen again.

技能实训6 Ⅲ. Listening Practice 听力文本

★ A. Listen to the conversation and fill in the baggage form.

Concierge: Good afternoon, Concierge. How can I help you?

Guest: Good afternoon. I have to check out and go to deal with an emergency now. I call you because I don't know how to take care of my baggage.

Concierge: Don't worry, madam. Could you tell me your name and your room number please?

Guest: Alicia Forrick, Room 1618.

Concierge: Ms. Forrick, I'll send a bellman to Room 1618 to fetch your baggage immediately. Please make sure to put your name tag on your baggage. Is there anything valuable and breakable in your baggage?

Guest: Yes, there is a bottle of wine in one of the pieces. I'll put a special notice on it.

Concierge: OK. When will you be back to our hotel for the baggage?

Guest: At 1:30 p.m..

Concierge: My name is Lily. We'll take good care of your baggage until you come back for it.

Guest: Thank you so much for your help. Where shall I collect my baggage out then?

Concierge: At the Concierge Desk.

Guest: It's very kind of you. See you.

Concierge: See you.

★ B. Complete the following dialogue.

Guest: Hi, I was told to see you about going sightseeing.

Concierge: It's my pleasure. I'm the hotel's concierge, at your service.

Guest: Concierge? Could you explain that to me?

Concierge: We help direct hotel visitors to popular places to visit, eat, and shop.

Guest: Very good. So where shall I begin my sightseeing?

Concierge: I would suggest the Forbidden City first.

Guest: Gee, I've already seen the Forbidden City. What else would you suggest?

Concierge: Let me see. What do you like to do in your spare time?

Guest: Well, I really like climbing mountains.

Concierge: Well, there you go! Have you ever visited the Great Wall?

Guest: No, but I've been meaning to.

Concierge: Well, the Great Wall is fantastic. It will really impress you.

Guest: That sounds like a great plan. I'll do that.

Concierge: Enjoy your visit!

技能实训 7 Ⅲ. Listening Practice 听力文本

★ A. Listen to the conversation and take the caller's message.

Operator: Blue Beach Hotel. Can I help you?

Caller: Yes, can you put me through to Mrs. Chen in Human Resources Department, please?

Operator: Certainly, sir.

…

Operator: Hello, sir, I'm afraid there's no response. Would you like to leave a message for her?

Caller: Yes, please. Could you ask her to call me back to discuss the schedule of employment?

Operator: Can I have your name, please, sir?

Caller: Yes, It's Mr. Johnson.

Operator: And your telephone number, Mr. Johnson?

Caller: Certainly. My number is 3689686.

Operator: 3689686. Thank you sir, I'll make sure she gets the message.

Caller: Thank you very much, goodbye.

Operator: Goodbye.

★ B. Complete the following dialogue

Operator: White Swan Hotel. Can I help you?

Caller: Yes, my flight is 6:00 a.m. tomorrow morning. I'd like to have a morning call.

Operator: Sure, when would you like your morning call?

Caller: How long will it take to go to the airport?

Operator: About 30 minutes.

Caller: Then 4:30 a.m. will be OK.

Operator: Yes, and may I have your name and room number, sir?

Caller: Certainly. Mr. Spink, room 1215.

Operator: Thank you sir, I'll be sure to give you a morning call at 4:30 a.m..

Caller: Thank you very much, have a good night.

Operator: Have a good night.

技能实训 8　Ⅲ. Listening Practice 听力文本

★ A. Fill the information in the following exchange memo.

Cashier: Good morning, sir. Is there anything I can do for you?

Guest: Yes, I'd like to change some foreign currency, please.

Cashier: What kind of foreign currency have you got, sir?

Guest: US dollars.

Cashier: May I have your name and room number please?

Guest: Mr. Peter Forrick, room 1218. What's rate today?

Cashier: According to today's exchange rate, every 100 US dollars comes to 601 yuan RMB. How much would you like to change, sir?

Guest: 800 dollars and here is the money.

Cashier: Thank you sir. May I see your passport, sir?

Guest: Sure. Here it is.

Cashier: Thank you. The total is 4808 RMB, please keep the exchange memo in case you change the money back.

Guest: I see. Thank you.

★ B. Complete the following dialogue.

Guest: I'd like to change some Euros, please.

Cashier: Are you a guest at the hotel, sir?

Guest: Yes, Here's my room card.

Cashier: How much would you like to change, sir?

Guest: EUR 500, please. What's rate today?

Cashier: It's 8 yuan 30 to the Euro... So that's a total of 4150 yuan.

Guest: Thank you.

Cashier: You are welcome, sir. Goodbye.

技能实训 9　Ⅲ. Listening Practice 听力文本

★ A. Listen to the conversation and fill in the hotel bill with the information you hear.

Guest: Could you explain the bill item by item for me?

Cashier: Certainly. Mr. Black. The first item is room number 3516.

Guest: I see. I thought it might have been the total.

Cashier: No, the total is the last item: 3380 yuan RMB. The second item is the restaurant-meals during the three days. It's 912 yuan in all.

Guest: That's it. And the third item must be the fax to New York. And what's the next item for?

Cashier: That's for one-day tour, a sum of 200 yuan.

Guest: I ordered room service for my breakfast yesterday. Is this 60 yuan here?

Cashier: No, sir. This 60 yuan is for laundry service. The room service is 66 yuan.

Guest: I see. I went to the bar yesterday evening and I signed bill for it.

Cashier: Yes, item five is for the bar. That's 120 yuan.

Guest: I bought something in the shopping center. But I paid cash for them.

Cashier: Of course, Mr. Black. That doesn't appear in the bill. And the eighth item is the room rates for three nights, 1950 yuan altogether, including service charge.

Guest: You're most helpful.

★ B. Complete the following dialogue.

Cashier: Good morning, madam. How may I help you?

Guest: I'd like to check out now.

Cashier: May I have your name and room number, please?

Guest: Klinda Fox in Room 2306, here is my room card.

Cashier: Have you used mini-bar since breakfast, madam?

Guest: Yes, I had a bottle of beer.

Cashier: One moment please. Let me prepare the bill for you.

...

Cashier: Sorry to have kept you waiting. Your bill is total 2800 yuan, including 15% service charge. Please have a check.

Guest: That's OK.

Cashier: You have paid 1000 yuan deposit, haven't you?

Guest: Yes, here's the deposit receipt.

Cashier: Then how would you like to pay the other 1800 yuan?

Guest: In cash, here is the money.

Cashier: Thank you, here is the receipt. I hope you've enjoyed your stay with us.

Guest: Thank you, goodbye.

Cashier: Goodbye, have a nice day.

技能实训 10　Ⅲ. Listening Practice 听力文本

★ A. Listen to the conversation and fill the information in the fax sending and receiving form.

Clerk：Good morning, sir. May I help you?

Guest：Good morning. My name is Carter, Henry Carter. I am expecting a fax from a friend in California, USA.

Clerk：Just a moment, Mr. Carter. Let me have a check. May I know your friend's name?

Guest：Yes. His name is George Smith.

Clerk：Oh, I'm sorry. I am afraid we haven't got it up to now.

Guest：But I was told he would fax it to me this morning.

Clerk：Don't worry, Mr. Carter. Please leave your room number and we will send it up to your room as soon as we get it.

Guest：OK. My room number is 1819.

Clerk：Is there anything else, Mr. Carter?

Guest：Oh, please send this fax to New York.

Clerk：Yes, sir. May I have the fax number?

Guest：Here you are. It's 001－2115678588.

Clerk：Very good.

Guest：How much for the fax?

Clerk：80 yuan. Would you mind sign your name on the bill here? It will be on your account.

Guest：Certainly not. Here you are.

★ B. Complete the following dialogue.

Clerk：Good morning, sir. Is there anything I can do for you?

Guest：Yes. I'd like you to send an express mail for me.

Clerk：What is it?

Guest：It's a company document.

Clerk：What delivery method do you prefer?

Guest：What do you offer?

Clerk：There are two ways, overnight and two-day delivery.

Guest：Overnight delivery. What's the charge?

Clerk：It's 20 yuan for your express mail. Would you please show your room card?

Guest：Here you are.

Clerk：And your telephone number?

Guest：1368871××××.

Clerk：Would you like to pay in cash or charge it to your room?

Guest：Go with room charge please.

Clerk：That's fine. Goodbye.

Guest：Goodbye.

技能实训 11　Ⅲ. Listening Practice 听力文本

★ A. Listen to the tape and complete the conversation.

Room attendant：Housekeeping，May I come in?

Guest：Come in，please.

Room attendant：Good morning，sir. May I clean your room now?

Guest：Not now，I have a bad headache.

Room attendant：I'm sorry to hear that. Shall I get you a doctor?

Guest：Not necessary. Could you give me some aspirin tablets?

Room attendant：Oh，I'm sorry，but I can't offer you any medicine.

Guest：I see. I just need a good rest.

Room attendant：Let me put out the DND sign out. If you remove it，I'll know you want me to clean your room.

Guest：All right.

Room attendant：I hope you feel better soon.

★ B. Listen to the tape and tell what a room attendant should do and should not do while making up the guestroom. Write "√" for what a room attendant should do，write "×" for what a room attendant should not do.

Room attendants in a hotel are responsible for making up rooms for guests who are staying and prepare the rooms for new arrivals. When making up a guest's room, a room attendant is required to vacuum the carpet, change bed linens, replace towels and facecloths and restock toilet tissue, complimentary toiletries and refreshments offered for sale in the rooms' mini bars. She also needs to collect the laundry for the guest and send it to the laundry department. But a room attendant should not do anything beyond her duties. Concierge will deal with baby－sitting service and send for a doctor for the guest when a guest doesn't feel well. Treating guests with courtesy and respect is important for a room attendant.

1.（√）2.（√）3.（√）4.（√）5.（√）6.（×）7.（×）8.（×）

技能实训 12　Ⅲ. Listening Practice 听力文本

★ A. Listen to the tape and complete the conversation.

Guest：I have some clothes to be washed. Do you have laundry service here?

Room Attendant：Yes，sir. We have very good laundry service here.

Guest: How long does it usually take to have laundry done?

Room attendant: Usually it takes one day, but we have express service, it takes only four hours.

Guest: What's the difference in price?

Room attendant: We charge 50% more for it.

Guest: Where can I leave my laundry?

Room attendant: Just leave your laundry in the laundry bag in the bathroom. Be sure not to forget to fill in the laundry form.

Guest: I see. Just one more thing, what if there is any laundry damage?

Room attendant: In such a case, the hotel will pay for it, but the indemnity should not exceed ten times of the laundry charge.

Guest: That's OK. I hope that won't happen.

Room attendant: Don't worry. The valets are experienced in their work.

★ B. Listen to the tape and tell what a laundry attendant should do and should not do while collecting laundry. Write "√" for what a laundry attendant should do, write "×" for what a laundry attendant should not do.

Laundry service is one of the most important products which hotel sells to their guests. A laundry attendant performs tasks such as washing, drying and folding clothing and linens according to the hotel' standards. The flow of laundry starts with collecting guests' laundry and transporting them to the laundry department and transferring laundry to the guests. When collecting laundry for the guests, make sure about the information filled in the laundry form such as washing method, number of the clothes or any special requirements about washing. Besides, the laundry attendant should check whether there is any damage on the clothes or anything left in the pockets. Sometimes, when the guest asks for express service, he may have to pay 50% extra for express. If there is any damage in doing laundry, the hotel will pay for the damage according to the hotel policy. Needless to say, the laundry service always counts.

1. (√) 2. (√) 3. (√) 4. (√) 5. (√) 6. (×) 7. (×) 8. (×)

技能实训 13 Ⅲ. Listening Practice 听力文本

★ A. Listen to the conversation and take room service orders

Room Service: Good evening. Room Service. May I help you?

Guest: Yes, I'd like you to send some food up to room 816, please.

Room Service: Of course, Mr. Williams.

Guest: Can you bring up one tomato and cheese pizza and French fries and a French onion soup?

Room Service: One tomato and cheese pizza and French fries and a French onion soup. Is that right?

Guest: Yes, that's right. And can you bring two beers, please? Carlsberg.

Room service: I'm afraid we don't have Carlsberg. We have Fosters or Heineken.

Guest: Make it two Fosters then.

Room Service: Yes, certainly.

Guest: How long will it be?

Room Service: Your order will be ready in about half an hour.

Guest: Oh, that's fine.

Room Service: Thank you, sir. Goodbye.

★ B. Complete the following dialogue.

Room Service: Room Service.

Guest: Come in please.

Room Service: Thank you, madam. Shall I put it on the table here?

Guest: Yes, sure.

Room Service: Would you care to check the order?

Guest: Yes, that's right. That looks great.

Room service: Would you like to sign the bill please?

Guest: OK! Do you have a pen handy?

Room Service: Here you are, madam.

Guest: Thanks... OK?

Room Service: Yes, madam. Could you please ring Room Service when you have finished? They'll come and collect the tray.

Guest: Thank you. I'll do that.

Room Service: Goodbye, madam. Enjoy your meal.

Guest: Thank you. Goodbye.

技能实训 14 Ⅲ. Listening Practice 听力文本

★ A. Listen to the tape and complete the conversation.

Repairman: (Knocking at the door) Housekeeping. May I come in?

Guest: Yes, come in please.

Repairman: Good afternoon, sir. I've come to repair the room facilities. What's the trouble, sir?

Guest: The air-conditioner doesn't work, it is terribly hot.

Repairman: I'm sorry, sir. Let me have a look. Oh, the remote control is out of order, sir. I'll change one for you.

Guest: Thank you. By the way, there is something wrong with the faucet. I can't turn off the faucet above the washbasin.

Repairman: Thank you for what you have told me.
Guest: How long shall I have to wait?
Repairman: About fifteen minutes.
Guest: OK.
Repairman: Everything is all right, sir. Sorry to have caused you so much trouble.
Guest: That's OK. Thank you very much.

★ B. Listen to the tape and make out what a room attendant should do and what a repairman should do. Write "RA" for room attendant, write "R" for repairman.

Different position may have different job descriptions. Hotel personnel constantly do repair and maintenance work because of wear and tear. Repairmen in hotels are responsible for running the hotel's heating and air-conditioning, for maintaining its refrigeration, plumbing, lighting and hotel's equipment. Duties of a repairman vary from those of a room attendant who should do her best to keep the guest's room in good order and offer warm service to the guest.

1. RA 2. R 3. RA 4. RA 5. R 6. R 7. RA 8. R

技能实训 15 Ⅲ. Listening Practice 听力文本

★ A. Listen to the tape, decide what each short dialogue is about and mark (√) where appropriate.

1. Woman: What do you serve in your restaurant?
   Man: We serve very nice Guangdong cuisine.
2. Woman: Does your bar serve Chinese cocktails?
   Man: Yes, we have a good variety of Chinese and foreign cocktails.
3. Woman: Where would the New Year's Party be held?
   Man: It'll be held in our largest banquet hall.
4. Woman: Oh, I'm so tired; I'd like to have a cup of coffee.
   Man: Let's go to the café.
5. Woman: Where can we have the buffet?
   Man: Please go to the cafeteria on the second floor.

	Bar	Cafe	Restaurant	Cafeteria	Banquet Hall
Dialogue 1			√		
Dialogue 2	√				
Dialogue 3					√
Dialogue 4		√			
Dialogue 5				√	

★ B. Complete the following conversation.

Reservationist: Babylon Hotel. Can I help you?

Caller: Yes. Could I make a booking at the Bay view Restaurant?

Reservationist: Certainly, madam. How many people is it for, and when will you be coming?

Caller: It's for me and my husband on Friday the twenty-third.

Reservationist: So that's two people on Friday the twenty-third? In what name, please?

Caller: Hudson.

Reservationist: Ms. Hudson. Thank you, madam. And what time is it for, Ms. Hudson?

Caller: 7:30.

Reservationist: Let me just confirm. That's a table for two at 7:30 on Friday the twenty-third in the name of Hudson.

Caller: Yes, that's correct.

Reservationist: Thank you very much, Ms. Hudson.

Caller: Thank you. Goodbye.

Reservationist: Goodbye.

技能实训 16 Ⅲ. Listening Practice 听力文本

★ A. Listen to the conversation and tell different features of four main cuisines.

Waiter: Good evening, Madam. Welcome to our restaurant.

Diner: Good evening.

Waiter: Do you have a reservation?

Diner: I booked a table in the name of Mrs. Brown.

Waiter: Just a moment please, I'll check the reservation record for you… Yes, this way please.

Diner: Thank you.

Waiter: Please have a seat. This is the menu, please take your time.

Diner: This is my first time to China. I know nothing about Chinese food. Would you please introduce main typical Chinese food to me?

Waiter: Sure. There are four major cuisines, the Shandong Cuisine, Guangdong Cuisine, Sichuan Cuisine, and Huaiyang Cuisine.

Diner: Oh, What are the main differences?

Waiter: Shandong food has a heavy taste while Guangdong food is light and fresh.

Diner: How about Huaiyang food?

Waiter: Huaiyang food is well known for its cutting technique and original flavor.

Diner: I hear Sichuan food is spicy and hot, isn't it?

Waiter: Yes, most Sichuan dishes are hot and spicy, and they taste different.

Diner: Great! I'd like to have a try.

★ B. Complete the following conversation.

Clerk: Good evening, sir. Welcome to our restaurant.

Diner: Good evening. I'd like a table for five, please.

Clerk: Do you have a reservation?

Diner: No, I'm afraid not.

Clerk: This way, please.

…

Clerk: Will this table be all right?

Diner: Well, I prefer a table by the window.

Clerk: I'm sorry, but all the tables by the window have been booked.

Diner: Oh, I see. We'll have to make up with this one.

Clerk: Thank you for your understanding.

Diner: Can we smoke?

Clerk: Sorry, this is non-smoking area.

Diner: OK.

Clerk: Here is the menu. A waiter will come to take your order soon. Have a good appetite!

Diner: Thank you.

技能实训 17 Ⅲ. Listening Practice 听力文本

★ A. Listen to the short passage about snacks and fill in the missing words.

Snacks can be found in every city and all over the city. Steamed buns, wonton and other "fast food" can be seen everywhere in China. If you are thirsty, you can have a beer from a corner beer shop, and at the same time you may try a small dish of peanuts. If you are in South, it's worth having at least one meal in dim sum restaurant. In the North you would go to a "small snack" restaurant. This is where people meet, from morning until afternoon, to catch up the latest news or even to discuss business. These restaurants are usually large, noisy and friendly but always bring happiness to the guests.

★ B. Complete the following conversation.

Hostess: May I take your order now, sir and madam?

Man: Yes, please. First, a Beijing Roast Duck.

Woman: I overheard that Steamed Mandarin Fish is very nice.

Hostess: Yes, many guests give high comments on it.

Man: What kind of soup can you recommend?

Hostess: I'd like you to try Mushroom soup, it's very fresh and tasty.

Woman: OK. And some Green Beans, please.

Hostess: Is there anything else?

Man: No, that's all.

Hostess: So you have ordered a Beijing Roast Duck, Steamed Mandarin Fish, Mushroom soup and Green Beans, is that right?

Woman: Yes, that's right. How long will it take?

Hostess: About 20 minutes. Would you like some wine with your dinner, sir and madam?

Man: Yes, a bottle of red wine, Dynasty, please.

Hostess: OK. Just a minute.

技能实训 18 Ⅲ. Listening Practice 听力文本

★ A. Listen to the tape, decide what each short dialogue is about and mark "√" where appropriate.

1. Woman: Do you have strawberry ice cream?
   Man: Yes, of course, madam.
2. Man: How would you like the steak to be done?
   Woman: Medium, please.
3. Man: Would you like some wine with your meal?
   Woman: A Red California, please.
4. Man: Anything to follow?
   Woman: A Mushroom Soup.
5. Man: What would you like to begin with?
   Woman: A shrimp cocktail, please.

	Starter	Soup	Main Dish	Dessert	Drink
Dialogue 1				√	
Dialogue 2			√		
Dialogue 3					√
Dialogue 4		√			
Dialogue 5	√				

★ B. Complete the following conversation.

Receptionist: Good evening, madam. Do you have a reservation, please?

Guest: Yes, for two people in the name of Clarkson.

Receptionist: Thank you, madam. This way, please.

...

Waiter: Are you ready to order now, madam?

Guest: Yes, I think so. I will have sole to begin with. Is it good?

Waiter: Oh, Yes, madam. It's very fresh.

Guest: Well, I'm going to have meat, T-bone steak please.

Waiter: How would you like steak, madam?

Guest: Well-done please.

Waiter: And your vegetables?

Guest: Fresh peas with my sole.

Waiter: Would you care for something to drink with your meal?

Guest: Half a bottle of house wine will be all right.

Waiter: Certainly, madam.

技能实训19 Ⅲ. Listening Practice 听力文本

★ A. Listen to the short passage and note the difference of American breakfast and continental breakfast.

American breakfast is also called Full breakfast, it is the standard breakfast offered in most hotels, either individually or (more often) as a buffet. It is a comprehensive meal, usually with eggs, meat, toast, jam, fruit juice, coffee or tea. The quality of the breakfast can vary depending on the establishment. Please note also that in Muslim-owned resorts, no pork is served: 'sausages' and' bacon' will be made with chicken meat. A continental breakfast is a light morning meal, it is served commonly in the continental Europe, North America, and elsewhere, it is simple breakfast. It traditionally includes bread products, fruit juice and hot beverages.

★ B. Complete the following conversation.

Waiter: Good morning, sir.

Guest: Good morning. How are you this morning?

Waiter: I'm fine. Thank you, sir. Did you sleep well last night?

Guest: Yes, I did. Thank you.

Waiter: Would you like coffee or tea this morning?

Guest: Coffee, please. Make it real hot.

Waiter: All right, sir.

Guest: And I'll have some cornflakes, one fried egg and two pieces of toast, please.

Waiter: Cornflakes, one fried egg and two pieces of toast. And how would you like your egg, sir?

Guest: Oh, over easy, please. Thank you.

Waiter: Would you like ham or bacon with your egg?

Guest: Bacon, please. And make it crisp, please.
Waiter: Just a minute, sir.
Guest: Thank you.
Waiter: Sorry to have kept you waiting.
Guest: That's all right, thank you.
Waiter: Would you like some more coffee?
Guest: No. Thank you.

技能实训 20 Ⅲ. Listening Practice 听力文本

★ A. Listen to the tape, decide what each short is about and mark "√" where appropriate.

1. Woman: Could you tell me how to mix cocktail?
   Man: Yes, of course, madam.
2. Man: What about some Vodka?
   Woman: Oh, I'm afraid it's too strong.
3. Man: What would you like to drink?
   Woman: Lemon juice, please.
4. Man: What would you like to drink with seafood?
   Woman: A glass of white wine, please.
5. Man: What about a cup of Longjing?
   Woman: That's good idea.

	Liquor	Cocktail	Soft Drink	Wine	Traditional Drink
Dialogue 1		√			
Dialogue 2	√				
Dialogue 3			√		
Dialogue 4				√	
Dialogue 5					√

★ B. A waiter is introducing some wines to the guest, try to complete the missing information.

1. Bordeau is a dry white wine from south-west France.
2. Rioja is a full-bodied red wine from Spain.
3. Chalish is a very dry white wine from central France.
4. Chianti is quite heavy from Italy.
5. You may like an Australian Chardonnay, which goes well with your lobster.
6. Bourbon whiskey is a type of American whiskey-a distilled spirit made from corn.
7. Burgundy wine is wine made in the Burgundy region in eastern France.

8. Sauternes is a very sweet white wine.

技能实训 21　Ⅱ. Listening Practice 听力文本

★ A. Listen to the following passage about table manners and complete the missing information.

Table manners are the rules of etiquette used while eating. Different cultures observe different rules for table manners. Many people feel out of place when dining simply because they don't know how to follow table manners, especially if they have been invited to a nice place. Talking about table manners, unlike the West, where everyone has their own plate of food, in China the dishes are placed on the table and everybody shares. If you are being treated by a Chinese host, be prepared for a ton of food. And sometimes the host will serve some dishes with his or her own chopsticks to guests to show his or her hospitality. This is a sign of politeness. If you feel uncomfortable with this, you can just say a polite "thank you" and leave the food there. There are some other rules that are suggested you follow to make your stay in China happier, though you will be forgiven if you have no idea of what they are.

★ B. Listen to the statements and put a "DO" or a "DON'T" in front of each statement.

1. Don't eat and drink at the same time.
2. Don't chew with your mouth open.
3. Don't put elbows on the table.
4. Do wipe your mouth with the corners of your napkin.
5. Do sit up straight while eating.
6. Don't eat and talk at the same time.
7. Don't place your silverware on the table after use.
8. Do place your napkin on your lap before eating.
9. Don't make loud eating noises.
10. Don't use a napkin to clean your face.
11. Do excuse yourself if you must leave the table during a meal.
12. Don't stand up to get the salt if it is out of your reach.

技能实训 22　Ⅲ. Listening Practice 听力文本

★ A. Listen to the following passage about gym service and complete the missing information.

Like other travelers, you hope for a stress-free stay at any hotel. With services like gym facilities, visitors in Radison Plaza Hotel find it to be a convenient choice for both business and leisure. The hotel provides a variety of services all designed with your fitness needs in mind. You will also be given instruction on technique and exercise advice during the exercise. Gym service is free to all the guests staying in our hotel. Gym service is included in your room rate. Come to our gym center and make yourself energetic!

★ B. Complete the following conversation.

Attendant: Good afternoon, sir. May I help you?

Guest: Yes, please. Life has been easy and I'm gaining weight.

Attendant: I think the best way to lose weight is to do some exercises.

Guest: What activities do you offer?

Attendant: We offer a variety of activities, running, cycling, muscle building and chest expanding.

Guest: Do you have a coach here to supervise the exercises?

Attendant: Yes, we have a resident coach here. He supervises all the activities.

Guest: And your service hour?

Attendant: We don't close until 10 p.m..

Guest: Good. I'll try cycling first.

技能实训 23　Ⅲ. Listening Practice 听力文本

★ A. Listen to the following passage about beauty salon and complete the missing information.

There are many different kinds of beauty salons. The different types of salon services provide care and beautification for the body from head to toe. Hair salon services are the most common. The style of service varies in different hairdressing salons. Day Spa salons may also serve guests tea as well as a light lunch. Services at a day spa often include massage, facials and skin care treatments. Many different types of salons feature skin care services. Makeup services are available at many kinds of salons. Traditionally, salon cosmetic services were offered to women only, but increasingly, men's makeup options are also available.

★ B. Complete the following conversation.

Beautician: Hi. How can we help you today?

Customer: Yeah. I'd like to get my hair trimmed a little. Nothing fancy. Just a basic trim.

Beautician: Well, can we interest you in today's special?

Customer: Um … Nah, nah …

Beautician: We'll shampoo, cut, and style your hair for one unbelievable low price of＄9.99.

Customer: Well, I don't know. I don't have much time, and …

Beautician: Best service in town!

Customer: Well, okay. I'll have the complete service today, but as I said before, I just want to get my hair trimmed. A little off the top and sides. That's all. I mean, that's all.

Beautician: No problem. Relax. You're in good hands. Okay, here we go.

Customer: Hey, can I see a mirror?

Beautician: Nothing to worry about, sir. Relax. I'm just making some adjustments to the hair trimmer.

Customer: Oh, that really hurt! What are you doing anyway?

Beautician: Relax, sir, relax. I'm almost finished.

Customer: Yeah, just wait till I get finished with you!

Beautician: Okay, now let's dry your hair, if you're not completely satisfied ...

Customer: Satisfied? I'm anything but satisfied. I want to talk to the manager ... now!

Beautician: I'm sorry, but he's on vacation, and he left me in charge, so if you ...

技能实训 24 Ⅲ. Listening Practice 听力文本

★ A. Listen to the following passage about sauna and complete the missing information.

Sauna has a long history. In Finland it has at least a thousand years of history. Sauna is a small room or hut heated to around 80 degrees centigrade. It is used for bathing as well as for mental and physical relaxation. While a hot sauna may seem a cruel punishment to inexperienced bathers, it is actually a very pleasant experience. All you need is a towel and at least half an hour of time. Start with a shower, and then enter the sauna for a few minutes, listening to your senses. When you've had enough, take a refreshing shower, cool off for a while and repeat once or twice. And there is no need to worry, it's entirely safe.

★ B. Complete the following conversation.

Attendant: Good evening, sir. Welcome to the sauna center.

Guest: Good evening. What kind of sauna do you have here?

Attendant: Ours is Finnish dry sauna.

Guest: What's the temperature in the sauna proper?

Attendant: About 212℉. If you feel too hot, please don't stay too long.

Guest: I see.

Attendant: Here's the key to the locker and towel.

Guest: Thank you.

(A few minutes later, the guest rushes out, sweating all over)

Attendant: How are you feeling, sir?

Guest: I feel quite good.

Attendant：Would you like a sauna snack in the sauna bar?

Guest：All right. I feel so hungry.

Attendant：This way, please.

技能实训 25　Ⅲ. Listening Practice 听力文本

★ A. Listen to the following passage about entertainment and complete the missing information.

Most hotels and resorts have outstanding nightlife and entertainment, guests may find plenty options for the evening hours. Some guests can dance and have a cup of coffee after a busy day of sightseeing. Others may listen to the local music or enjoy a good live performance. If hotels don't have the best entertainment facilities, when the sun goes down and the guests may head out for the night, exploring local bars or just watching the sunset with an icy cocktail, these places are probably within a short walk or quick drive. Dazzling and gentle lighting brings the guests into another world, making the guests too delighted to leave in the nightlife.

★ B. Complete the following conversation.

Attendant：Good evening, sir. Welcome to our ballroom.

Guest：Good evening. A table in the corner, please.

Attendant：Yes. This way, please... Please take your seat. What would you like to have?

Guest：Lemon juice, please.

Attendant：All right. Just a minute... Here you are sir.

Guest：What beautiful music! Would you care to have a dance with me, Miss?

Attendant：I'd be glad to, but I'm working now, you see.

Guest：All right. To tell the truth, you are the prettiest girl I've ever met.

Attendant：Thank you for saying so.

Guest：Can we be friends?

Attendant：Yes, you are my friend already. But I don't know your name.

Guest：Fox. And yours?

Attendant：Lisa Wang.

(Mr. Fox is about to leave.)

Guest：Lisa. This is for you. Your service is excellent.

Attendant：Thank you, Mr. Fox. Hope to see you soon.

Guest：Goodbye.

技能实训 26　Ⅲ. Listening Practice 听力文本

★ A. Listen to the following passage about souvenirs and complete the missing information.

Millions of foreigners, overseas Chinese visit mainland of China every year on business, for sightseeing, or exchanges in different fields. Many of them return home loaded with souvenirs and gifts. Souvenirs are precious memories for most tourists. Some guests will buy T-shirts, key chains, sweets, or any candies that are native to a place. Others may buy some famous food from a native city or some souvenirs with the name of the city on it. Postcards are also a good choice as souvenirs. It is a way to remember the unique places. Guests can keep souvenirs for themselves or their family and friends.

★ B. Complete the following conversation.

W: Yes, would you like some for your family?

	Food Stuff	Garments	Medicine	Jewelry	Arts & Crafts
Dialogue 1					√
Dialogue 2				√	
Dialogue 3		√			
Dialogue 4	√				
Dialogue 5			√		

★ B. Complete the following conversation.

Guest: An annual convention of the Writers Association.

Manager: Can I see the name list of the attendees?

Guest: Certainly. Here it is.

Manager: Oh, I see. There are 50 attendees. I think our functioning room can serve the purpose.

Guest: Do you have enough brainstorming rooms? We have several seminars after the lecture.

Manager: Don't worry. We'll reorganize some rooms if necessary.

Guest: Shall we discuss some details about meeting facilities?

Manager: Here are the convention brochures showing the details about meeting facilities.

Guest: Thank you. We'll let you know as soon as we've decided.

技能实训 29 Ⅲ. Listening Practice 听力文本

★ A. Listen to the following passage about convention and complete the missing information.

There are many different kinds of exhibitions. Some exhibitions are displayed for long periods of time such as museums or art galleries. In some cases, like traveling exhibitions or commercial displays, space may be rented for this purpose in similar buildings or in a more commercial setting. Exhibitions of this kind can be divided into three main groups. They are cultural exhibitions, commercial-cultural exhibitions and company displays. The most common one in an exhibition center is company display. Company displays can be found in design centers, trade centers or display cases. These are commercial exhibitions.

★ B. Complete the following conversation.

Manager: Good morning. How nice to see you again!

Guest: Good morning. I'd like to confirm the details of the coming exhibition in person.

Manager: Sure. The exhibition is to be held on 20th and 21st, for two days. Is that right?

Guest: Yes, that's right. And how many people can you hold in your exhibition hall? We have about 500 attendees.

Manager: I don't see any problem. Our exhibition hall can hold 1000 people.

Guest: Oh, that's good.

Manager: Do you have any special requirement about the exhibition hall?

Guest: Yes. As for the light, I think the hall should be bright.

Manager: Sure, no problem.

Guest: We also need some flowers and green plants.

Manager: Yes. The flowers and plants can help to create friendly atmosphere.

Guest: Thank you. You are always helpful.

技能实训 30　Ⅲ. Listening Practice 听力文本

★ A. Listen to the following passage about Lost and Found and complete the missing information.

What's the most commonly left item from guests in hotel rooms? It's not the missing peanuts from the mini-bar. Hotel guests are walking away from some of their most private possessions when they check out of hotels, but just how personal are the items? Following a check of its 31 UK hotels' lost property departments, you may be surprised about the strange objects left behind in hotel rooms by its guests. Because of the amount of items housekeeping has picked up in hotel rooms, mobile phone chargers and underwear top the list of most commonly left behind items, amongst the more unusual items guests forgot to take with them when they checked out were a car keys, wigs, musical instruments and dinner suits. We want to know: What items have you left behind in hotel rooms? Did you get them back?

★ B. Complete the following conversation.

Attendant: You look worried, sir. What's wrong?

Guest: I've lost my key.

Attendant: Oh, perhaps I can help you find it.

Guest: Thanks. It must be here somewhere.

Attendant: Have you looked in your pockets?

Guest: Yes. It's not there.

Attendant: Have you checked in your bag?

Guest: Hold on, let me see... No, it's not in there.

Attendant: Well, how about in your pencil case?

Guest: It wouldn't be in there, would it? I'll check anyway? Nope!

Attendant: Did you look under your desk?

Guest: Under my desk?

Attendant: Did you look on the floor?

Guest: On the floor? Wait a moment... Ah ha! I've got it. Thanks.

Attendant: You're welcome.

技能实训 31　Ⅲ. Listening Practice 听力文本

★ A. Listen to the following passage about deposit service and complete the missing information.

Small hotels don't usually have luggage storage rooms although they will usually hold bags for people checking in whose room isn't ready or for people checking out who need to leave bags until a later flight. Most hotel luggage storage spaces are just large enough to hold bags for a few hours as people check in and check out. So, if the answer is "we don't have enough room", that's probably true. If you just want to leave your bags and collect them when you return and move on without additional nights stay, they may not be so accommodating as storage for overnight guests, not guests who've left and won't be returning. Again, due to space available.

★ B. Complete the following conversation.

Receptionist: Here is your bill, Madam. Totally 1850 yuan. Please sign your name here.

Guest: Sure. my flight is 11p.m. May I store my luggage here?

Receptionist: Certainly, madam. Is there anything valuable or breakable in your bag?

Guest: No, there isn't.

Receptionist: We'll keep it for you. Here is your tag 33.

Guest: Thank you. When does the cloakroom close?

Receptionist: This cloakroom is open until 8:00 p.m..

Guest: Oh, dear! I won't be back until about 8:30 tonight. Where can I pick up my bag?

Receptionist: We will transfer your bag to the luggage center. You may collect it there, ma'am.

Guest: I see. Thanks a lot.

Receptionist: You're welcome.

技能实训 32　Ⅲ. Listening Practice 听力文本

★ A. Listen to the following passage about tourist information and complete the missing information.

Most hotels offer tourist information, including visitor attractions, museums, sightseeing, tourist tips and climate information. They will provide you with all you need to know about the city. You'll find a wealth of information about things to do and places to go. Whether you are looking for a family day out, food festival or live music, tourist information center will give you some advice. With listings of the top events and offers, you can plan your time in the place knowing you are getting the most for your money. If necessary, buy a Tourist Card about the city, discounts in main tourist attractions and free transportation all round the city will be a nice surprise. Everything is easier with a Tourist Card, and it's the best way to travel, taste and enjoy the city highlights.

★ B. Complete the following conversation.

Clerk: Beijing City Tour Information Services, May I help you?

Guest: Yes. This is Mr. Harris from Australia. I'd like to have a city tour in Beijing. Could you give me some suggestions?

Clerk: Sure. Where you are staying and how long you plan to sightsee in Beijing?

Guest: I'm staying at the Beijing Hotel. I'll be in the city for 2 days.

Clerk: Mr. Harris, your hotel is near Tian'anmen Square. So it would be a good idea if you visit Tian'anmen Square first. Then, in the north of the square is the Palace Museum.

Guest: Palace Museum? Is it a new museum?

Clerk: No, it used to be known as the Forbidden City.

Guest: I see. Then how long do you think I need to see the two places?

Clerk: Well, you need at least half a day to see both Tian'anmen Square and the Palace Museum.

Guest: I see. Then what about tomorrow?

Clerk: I'd like to recommend the Summer Palace and Yuanmingyuan.

Guest: What's interesting there?

Clerk: The Summer Palace is famous for its beautiful scenery, large lake, and green hills dotted with colorful pavilions. Yuanmingyuan has plenty of historic rains. They are worth seeing, not to be missed.

Guest: I see, you are so helpful.

技能实训33 Ⅲ. Listening Practice 听力文本

★ A. Listen to the following passage about baby-sitting and complete the missing information.

When traveling with children of small age, it's impossible to relax and enjoy a nice dinner (which you're certainly entitled to!) without getting a sitter. If you want to enjoy the spa or a long quiet meal in a hotel, you can ask baby-sitting service in the hotel. Quality hotels are very careful about the babysitters they recommend, because of the obvious liability issues. Here is how baby-sitting service works: the hotels contract out to a babysitting service, which interviews and screens the babysitters. The concierge calls the babysitting service with a guest's needs, and the service then finds an available sitter. Sitters are paid by the hour, and a portion of the bill goes back to the service. You should leave instructions about whether or not the kids are allowed to leave the hotel room.

★ B. Complete the following conversation.

Guest: Excuse me, madam. Could you do me a favor?

Concierge: Yes, I'm willing to try my best. What's the matter?

Guest: I've made an appointment with my business partner tonight. I need someone to look after my baby. Is baby-sitting service available here?

Concierge: Yes, we have reliable and experienced babysitters.
Guest: That's good. Could you tell me how much baby-sitting service is charged?
Concierge: It is 60 yuan per hour, for a minimum of two hours.
Guest: That's OK.
Concierge: Do you have any special instructions?
Guest: Yes, my baby is not allowed to leave the hotel room.
Concierge: Sure. The babysitter will do as told.
Guest: Thank you.
Concierge: If you need the service, please fill in the confirmation form.
Guest: OK, I will finish it right away.
Concierge: Would you please sign your name here, madam?
Guest: Sure. Here you are.
Concierge: Thank you, madam. We will arrange the service soon. Have a good night.

技能实训 34　Ⅲ. Listening Practice 听力文本

★ A. Listen to the following passage about complaints and complete the missing information.

Hotel guest complaints frequently have to do with the cleanliness of the bed or bathroom, but there may be complaints about any aspect of the guest's experience. To deal with a guest complaint in a hotel, the first step is to listen to the guest's full complaint. When expressing a complaint, the guest may be quite angry. They need to be fully heard even if all the relevant details are made known right away. Then ask questions to figure out what actions will be sufficient to fix the problem. If a problem cannot be solved, front office staff should admit this to the guest early on. Honesty is the best policy when dealing with guest complaints.

★ B. Complete the following conversation.
Guest: Waitress!
Waitress: Yes? Is everything all right, sir?
Guest: Not exactly. This steak is raw. I asked for it well done! And it's rather cold.
Waitress: I do apologize, sir. Would you like it cooked a little more?
Guest: Please.
Waitress: Would you like something else while you're waiting?
Guest: Yes, some French fries please. But tell them to hurry.
Waitress: Sure. But the restaurant is very busy today. I hope you can understand.

技能实训 35　Ⅲ. Listening Practice 听力文本

★ A. Listen to the following passage about difficult guests and complete the missing information.

As a new hotel manager, you have to be prepared for the unexpected. And among the many challenges faced by all hotel managers is the overly demanding guest. Sometimes, it's a VIP with very specific and unusual demands. There are also the party-hearty musicians who leave your best suite a total mess. When you encounter your difficult guest, keep in mind that such guests may have had a difficult day while traveling. They may have missed a flight, had their luggage damaged or misplaced, or simply had a bad day or a poor night's sleep. They may have arrived at your hotel with all this negative baggage already in their heads and just need someone or something to vent their frustrations upon. On the other hand, their problem may stem from something or someone in your hotel. Either way, here are some tips to help you deal: hear and understand; don't go on defensive; keep a friendly tone and don't over promise.

★ B. Complete the following conversation.

Receptionist: Good afternoon, madam. May I help you?

Guest: Yes. I settled my account this morning, but I have a question about my bill.

Receptionist: May I have your room number please?

Guest: 1316.

Receptionist: 1316. And what's your problem?

Guest: The laundry charge is too high. I only used the laundry service once. It can't be 300 yuan. It's impossible.

Receptionist: Just a minute, madam. I'll get your laundry slips. Thank you for your waiting. According to our records you used the laundry service three times. I have our copies of your laundry bills here. Could you please check them?

Guest: Yes. I think there must be a mistake. I only used the laundry service once.

Receptionist: Here are your laundry slips, madam. Is this your signature?

Guest: No, only one slip is mine.

Receptionist: The other two are signed by Mr. White.

Guest: Oh, my god, it's my husband's signature.

Receptionist: I see.

Guest: I'm sorry for trouble.

Receptionist: It doesn't matter. Have a good day.

参 考 文 献

[1] 胡扬政. 酒店英语服务实训[M]. 北京：清华大学出版社，2008.
[2] 肖璇. 现代酒店英语实务教程[M]. 北京：世界图书出版公司，2006.
[3] 雷兵. 酒店英语听说实训教程[M]. 北京：科学出版社，2009.
[4] Grahame T. Billow. 朗文现代酒店业英语[M]. 北京：外语教学与研究出版社，2005.
[5] 郭兆康. 饭店情景英语[M]. 上海：复旦大学出版社，2007.
[6] 程中锐. 饭店工作英语[M]. 北京：中国旅游出版社，2008.
[7] 柯淑萍. 饭店英语听说教程[M]. 杭州：浙江大学出版社，2008.
[8] 张伟. 饭店英语[M]. 天津：南开大学出版社，2008.
[9] 郭兆康. 酒店实用英语[M]. 大连：东北财经大学出版社，2000.
[10] 李佳. 饭店英语[M]. 2版. 北京：化学工业出版社，2014.
[11] 梁文霞. 酒店饭店英语口语[M]. 大连：大连理工出版社，2015.
[12] 许雪敏. 饭店英语视听说[M]. 上海：上海交通大学出版社，2015.